Ms. Brubaker

The NYSTROM

ATLAS of UNITED STATES HISTORY

NYSTROM

HERFF JONES EDUCATION DIVISION

Contents

Page 15

Page 47

African American 59%
White 41%

Page 61

Printed in U.S.A.

10 9 8 7 6 5 4 3 2   15 14 13 12 11 10 09

ISBN 13: 978-0-7825-1361-5   ISBN 10: 0-7825-1361-1

For information about ordering this atlas, 9AUSH-1, call 800-621-8086.

Statistics and estimates are from government sources: for the date given where specified, otherwise for the most recent available date.

CONTENT REVIEWERS

Betty B. Franks, History Teacher and Department Chairperson, Maple Heights High School, Maple Heights, OH

Jacqueline L. Frierson, Principal and former History Teacher, William H. Lemmel Middle School at Woodbourne, Baltimore, MD

Robert Hagopian, History Teacher, Scotts Valley Middle School, Scotts Valley, CA

Francis N. Stites, Professor of History, Department of History, San Diego State University, San Diego, CA

Arthur Zilversmit, Distinguished Service Professor, Emeritus, Department of History, Lake Forest College, Lake Forest, IL

ATLAS OF UNITED STATES HISTORY

Page 67

Reference Materials and Index

Page 93

Page 107

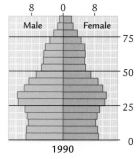

Photo Credits

Credit abbreviations

GI	Getty Images	GC	The Granger Collection, New York
HA	Hulton Archives	LOC	Library of Congress
NW	North Wind Picture Archive	SB	Stock Boston
TLP	Time & Life Pictures	TS	Tony Stone

Front cover *Left*, John Eastcott/YVA Momatiuk/SB, *Right*, Stock Montage **Back cover** *Top*, Frank Driggs Collection/GI, *Bottom*, TLP/GI **2** *Top*, Patrick Curtet/Point de Vue, *Bottom*, GC **3** GC **7D** Claudia Ziegler/Anzenberger Agency/Jupiter Images **8C** Wolfgang Kaehler **9A** Frans Lemmens/GI **10A** GC **11D** Simeone Hunter/TS/GI **12A** Paul Chesley/TS/GI **13D** Don Farrall/GI **15C** Patrick Curtet/Point de Vue **20B** NW **22A** Harald Sund/GI **23E** Kindra Clineff/TS **29E** GC **31D** Stock Montage **32D** GC **33H** NW **35E** NW **36A** HA/GI **38A** GC **39D** Chris Johns/ National Geographic/GI **40B** Stock Montage **41D** GC **42A** Jake Rajs/TS/GI **44B** GC **45D** GC **47C** GC **48A** John Eastcott/YVA Momatiuk/SB **51F** GC **57C** Terry Farmer Photography **58A** Dave Bartruff/SB **59D** Selmar Rush Seibert/TLP/GI **60B** GC **61E** GC **63D** Idaho State Historical Society **64B** Archive Photos **67D** GC **68A** GC **69E** LOC, LC-DIG-ppmsc-01627 **70C** LOC, LC-USZ62-97319 **75C** LOC, LC-USZC4-7934 **75C** GC **76A** LOC, LC-USZC4-3859 **77E** GC **79E** Frank Driggs Collection/GI **79F** GC 88 FPG International LLC **81E** LOC, Lewis Wickes Hine, LC-DIG-nclc-00753 **83C** Culver Picture Inc./Superstock **84C** TLP/GI **86A** HA/GI **87E** LOC, LC-USZ62-133825 **88A** GC **89E** GC **90A** TLP/GI **91E** US Coast Guard/TLP/GI **92A** Central Press/GI **94A** FPG International LLC **96B** Walter Sanders/TLP/GI **98C** AP Photo **100B** Philip J. Griffiths/Magnum Photos **101E** Costa Manos/Magnum Photos **102A** altrendo images/GI **105D** Robert Giroux/GI **106A** Ariel Skelley/GI **109D** Ulf Wallin/TS/GI **110D** David McNew/GI **111G** Michael Newman/PhotoEdit

Using This Atlas

The Nystrom Atlas of United States History is much more than a collection of maps. It uses graphs, photos, charts, and explanatory text to explore the history of our country. To get the most out of *The Nystrom Atlas of United States History*, follow these steps.

Cross-references can tell you if there is a map or graph on the same topic. Use cross-references to track change over time.

1 First look at the **era title** and **dates**. The title states the theme for the section, and the dates give you the time frame.

2 Read the **timeline**, which shows key events from this era.

3 Check the **topic title** to find out what these two pages cover.

4 Next, read the **overview** for more about the topic.

5 Now follow the **A-B-C-D** markers for the clearest path through the pages.

Maps show places, movement, people, and events from specific times.

Call-outs are mini-captions right on the map.

Legends give the title of the map or graph and explain what its colors and other symbols mean.

Quotations provide a glimpse of what people thought about the events of their time.

ERA **6**

Development of the Industrial United States
1865–1900

1869 Union Pacific and Central Pacific link East and West.

1866 Sedalia Trail brings Texas cattle to Missouri railhead.

1865 Civil War ends.

| 1860 | 1865 | 1870 |

Early 1860s Chinese immigrants in California begin work on Central Pacific Railroad.

1867 Alaska purchased from Russia.

Immigration Swells the Work Force

After the Civil War, immigration increased so much that total U.S. population rose despite wartime losses.

★ Immigrants provided a vast new pool of labor for the rapidly industrializing nation. They built railroads, worked in mines and factories, and farmed the Great Plains.

★ By 1890 almost one out of every seven people in the United States was foreign-born.

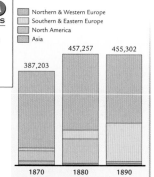

A IMMIGRANT ORIGINS
Most immigrants still came from Northern and Western Europe, but the numbers from Southern and Eastern Europe were increasing. Compare this graph with graph A on page 50.

Northern & Western Europe
Southern & Eastern Europe
North America
Asia

387,203   457,257   455,302

1870   1880   1890

"Give me your tired, your poor, your huddled masses yearning to breathe free . . ."
—INSCRIPTION AT THE BASE OF THE STATUE OF LIBERTY FROM THE POEM, "NEW WORLD COLOSSUS," BY EMMA LAZARUS, 1883

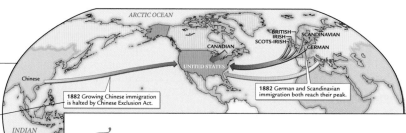

ARCTIC OCEAN

BRITISH
IRISH
SCOTS-IRISH
SCANDINAVIAN
GERMAN
CANADIAN
Italian
UNITED STATES

Chinese

1882 Growing Chinese immigration is halted by Chinese Exclusion Act.

1882 German and Scandinavian immigration both reach their peak.

INDIAN OCEAN

IMMIGRANTS
1861–1895

Largest Groups
← Movement
GERMAN Ethnicity

Other Groups
→ Movement
Chinese Ethnicity

62

The United States Enters World War I

At first the United States resisted involvement in World War I, but eventually U.S. troops helped win the war.

★ Austria-Hungary had declared war on Serbia in 1914. The rest of Europe quickly took sides in the conflict.

★ On one side were the nations known as the Central Powers. On the other side were the Allies.

★ Much of the fighting was done from trenches dug along two battlefronts in Europe: the Western Front and the Eastern Front.

★ The United States joined the Allies in 1917. After another year of brutal trench warfare, the Central Powers surrendered.

"In one instant the entire front, as far as the eye could reach. . . was a sheet of flame."
—AMERICAN CORPORAL EUGENE KENNEDY BATTLE OF ST. MIHIEL, SEPTEMBER 12–16, 1918

I WANT Y
FOR U.S.A
NEAREST RECRUITING

A The familiar character Uncle Sam appe on an Army recruiting poster in 1917.

4

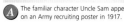

ARCTIC OCEAN

1914 BELGIUM
1914 UNITED KINGDOM
1914 CANADA
1914 GERMANY
1914 AUSTRIA-HUNGARY
1914 RUSSIA

The A-B-C-D **captions** help you understand each map, graph, and picture

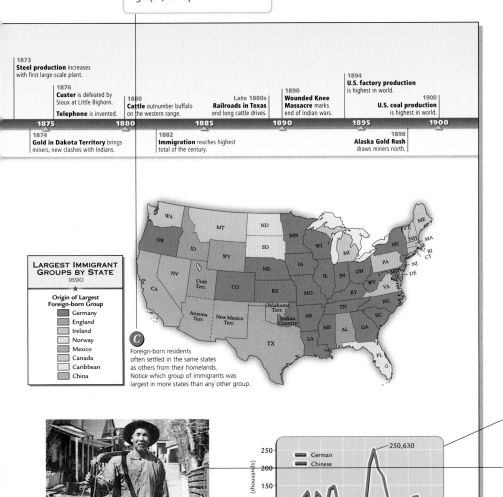

1873
Steel production increases with first large-scale plant.

1876
Custer is defeated by Sioux at Little Bighorn.

Telephone is invented.

1880
Cattle outnumber buffalo on the western range.

Late 1880s
Railroads in Texas end long cattle drives.

1890
Wounded Knee Massacre marks end of Indian wars.

1894
U.S. factory production is highest in world.

1900
U.S. coal production is highest in world.

| 1875 | 1880 | 1885 | 1890 | 1895 | 1900 |

1874
Gold in Dakota Territory brings miners, new clashes with Indians.

1882
Immigration reaches highest total of the century.

1898
Alaska Gold Rush draws miners north.

LARGEST IMMIGRANT GROUPS BY STATE
1890

Origin of Largest Foreign-born Group
- Germany
- England
- Ireland
- Norway
- Mexico
- Canada
- Caribbean
- China

C Foreign-born residents often settled in the same states as others from their homelands. Notice which group of immigrants was largest in more states than any other group.

250,630

— German
— Chinese

250
200
150
100

ants (thousands)

What else can you find in this atlas?

★ **Presidents of the United States** are listed on the inside front cover.

★ **Abbreviations** are explained on the inside front cover too.

★ **References maps** of the United States and the world on pages 112–119 show our country and the world today.

★ The **glossary** on pages 120–121 defines special words and names used in the atlas.

★ **State facts** on pages 122–123 provide important information about each state.

★ The **index** on pages 124–128 lists all the pages where people, places, or events are mentioned.

★ The **thematic index** on the inside back cover lists all the pages related to certain big topics.

Graphs and **charts** organize information visually.

Photos and **pictures** show people and places related to the information told by the maps and graphs.

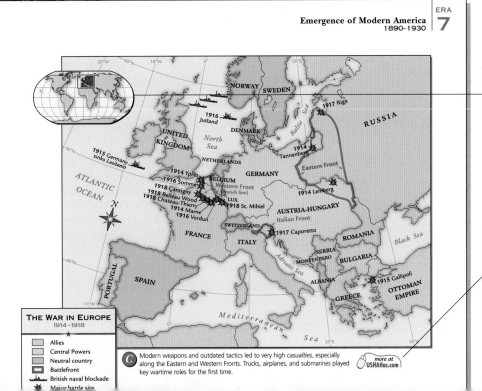

Emergence of Modern America
1890-1930

ERA **7**

Locator maps tell what part of the world is shown.

This symbol lets you know that the website **USHAtlas.com** has more maps, graphs, photos, and/or primary sources on the topic.

THE WAR IN EUROPE
1914–1918

- Allies
- Central Powers
- Neutral country
- Battlefront
- British naval blockade
- Major battle site

C Modern weapons and outdated tactics led to very high *casualties*, especially along the Eastern and Western Fronts. Trucks, airplanes, and submarines played key wartime roles for the first time.

more at USHAtlas.com

Three Worlds Meet

BEGINNINGS TO 1620

800
Maya civilization dominates Central America.

12,000 B.C.
Later migrations from Asia and perhaps Europe begin.

Ghana controls trade between West and North Africa.

| 25,000 B.C. | 12,000 B.C. | 800 | 900 |

25,000 B.C.
Earliest Americans may have migrated from Asia.

850
Hohokam civilization peaks in North America.

The Long Journey to the Americas

The first human inhabitants reached North and South America long after Africa, Europe, Asia, and Australia were populated.

★ During the last *Ice Age*, sea level dropped. People could walk from Asia to what is now Alaska.

★ Some then walked to warmer parts of North America by an ice-free route east of the Rocky Mountains.

★ Most people, however, probably came in boats. They followed the edge of the ice: most of them from Asia, some from Europe.

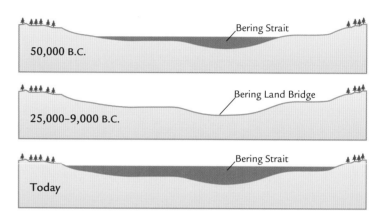

50,000 B.C. — Bering Strait

25,000–9,000 B.C. — Bering Land Bridge

Today — Bering Strait

A **CHANGING SEA LEVEL**

Sea level dropped during the Ice Ages, exposing dry land at the Bering Strait. When the ice later melted, the seas rose. *more at* USHAtlas.com

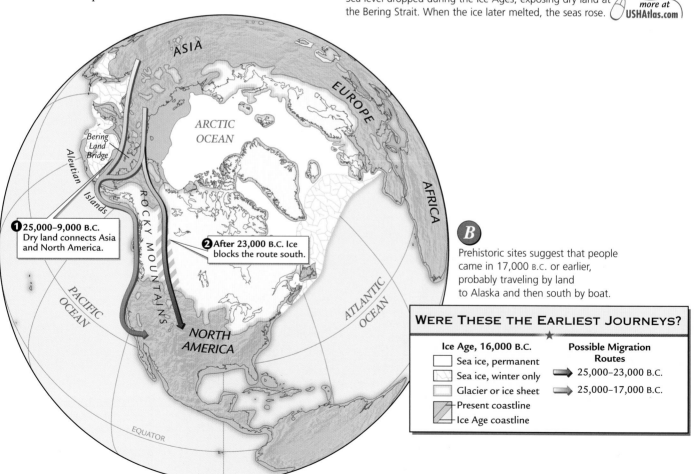

ASIA

EUROPE

ARCTIC OCEAN

Bering Land Bridge

Aleutian Islands

AFRICA

❶ 25,000–9,000 B.C. Dry land connects Asia and North America.

❷ After 23,000 B.C. Ice blocks the route south.

ROCKY MOUNTAINS

PACIFIC OCEAN

NORTH AMERICA

ATLANTIC OCEAN

EQUATOR

B

Prehistoric sites suggest that people came in 17,000 B.C. or earlier, probably traveling by land to Alaska and then south by boat.

WERE THESE THE EARLIEST JOURNEYS?

Ice Age, 16,000 B.C.
- Sea ice, permanent
- Sea ice, winter only
- Glacier or ice sheet
- Present coastline
- Ice Age coastline

Possible Migration Routes
- ➡ 25,000–23,000 B.C.
- ➡ 25,000–17,000 B.C.

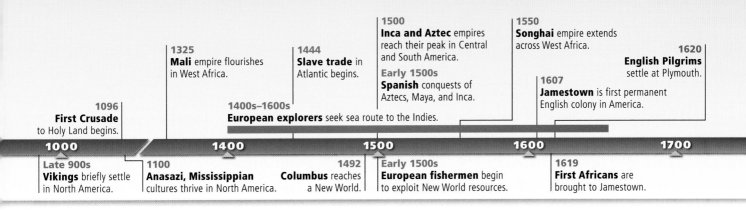

1096
First Crusade
to Holy Land begins.

1325
Mali empire flourishes
in West Africa.

1444
Slave trade in
Atlantic begins.

1400s–1600s
European explorers seek sea route to the Indies.

1500
Inca and Aztec empires
reach their peak in Central
and South America.

Early 1500s
Spanish conquests of
Aztecs, Maya, and Inca.

1550
Songhai empire extends
across West Africa.

1607
Jamestown is first permanent
English colony in America.

1620
English Pilgrims
settle at Plymouth.

1000 · 1400 · 1500 · 1600 · 1700

Late 900s
Vikings briefly settle
in North America.

1100
Anasazi, Mississippian
cultures thrive in North America.

1492
Columbus reaches
a New World.

Early 1500s
European fishermen begin
to exploit New World resources.

1619
First Africans are
brought to Jamestown.

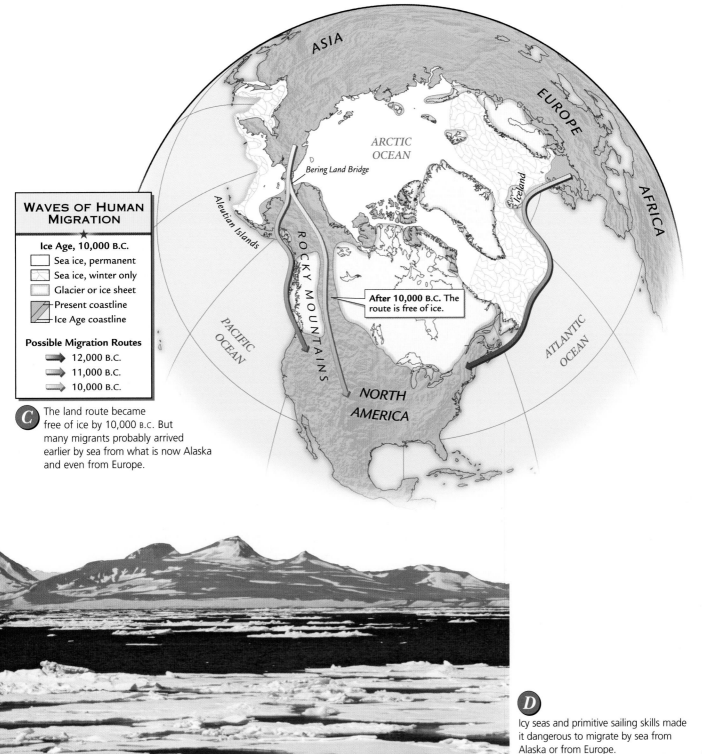

WAVES OF HUMAN MIGRATION

Ice Age, 10,000 B.C.

☐ Sea ice, permanent

☒ Sea ice, winter only

▨ Glacier or ice sheet

▨ Present coastline
◰ Ice Age coastline

Possible Migration Routes
⇒ 12,000 B.C.
⇒ 11,000 B.C.
⇒ 10,000 B.C.

ASIA

ARCTIC OCEAN

Bering Land Bridge

Aleutian Islands

ROCKY MOUNTAINS

PACIFIC OCEAN

EUROPE

AFRICA

Iceland

ATLANTIC OCEAN

After 10,000 B.C. The route is free of ice.

NORTH AMERICA

C The land route became free of ice by 10,000 B.C. But many migrants probably arrived earlier by sea from what is now Alaska and even from Europe.

D Icy seas and primitive sailing skills made it dangerous to migrate by sea from Alaska or from Europe.

7

The World of the First Americans

Thousands of years after *migration* ended, most people in the Americas lived in small hunting or farming villages. But complex *empires* emerged too.

★ The Maya flourished from 250 to about 900. They built pyramids and developed an accurate calendar.

★ The Aztecs ruled their region from the early 1400s to 1521. They built canals, aqueducts, and large cities.

★ The Incas expanded along the Andes Mountains from 1438 to 1532. They devised bookkeeping, a road network, even brain surgery.

ASIA

ARCTIC OCEAN

EUROPE

McKenzie Corridor

By 4000 B.C. Ice sheet has melted.

NORTH AMERICA

ATLANTIC OCEAN

EQUATOR

PACIFIC OCEAN

SOUTH AMERICA

N

MIGRATION THROUGH THE AMERICAS
★

Ice Age, 10,000 B.C.
- Sea ice, permanent
- Sea ice, winter only
- Glacier or ice sheet
- Present coastline
- Ice Age coastline

0   750   1500 miles
0   750   1500 kilometers

Possible Migration Routes
- 12,000 B.C.
- 11,000 B.C.
- 10,000 B.C.
- 7,000 B.C. Athabascan
- 4,000 B.C. Aleut, Inuit
- Internal migration

A After reaching land free of ice, early migrants to North America spread out by land and by sea. The far north was settled last.

NORTH AMERICA

ANASAZI

HOPEWELL

MISSISSIPPIAN

HOHOKAM

Gulf of Mexico

Tenochtitlán

MAYA

Chichén Itzá

AZTEC

Tikal

Caribbean Sea

PACIFIC OCEAN

ATLANTIC OCEAN

SOUTH AMERICA

INCA

Machu Picchu

Cuzco

CIVILIZATIONS OF THE AMERICAS
★

Civilizations
- Hopewell, 200–400
- Maya, 250–900
- Anasazi, 900–1350
- Hohokam, 300 B.C.–1450
- Aztec, 1400–1521
- Inca, 1000–1532
- Mississippian, 700–1600

0   500   1000 miles
0   500   1000 kilometers

B North of the Maya, Aztecs, and Incas were the Anasazi and Mississippian civilizations and the *irrigated* lands of the Hohokam.

C Mayan temples and cities can still be found in southern Mexico, Belize, and Guatemala.

The World of West Africa

Trade with Mediterranean ports linked West Africa to Europe and Asia 1700 years ago.

★ Empires and smaller kingdoms developed along the southern edge of the Sahara, connected to the north by trade routes.

★ The most powerful empires controlled the north bend of the Niger River, gateway to the shortest routes to the Mediterranean Sea.

★ Mali, and then Songhai, dominated this key region along with the richest gold mines.

★ Timbuktu, Mali's main trade center, and Gao, capital of Songhai, were important centers of learning.

A Arab traders carried goods by camel caravan between Mediterranean ports and West African empires. They traded luxury goods from Europe and salt from the Sahara for gold, leather, and *slaves* from West Africa.

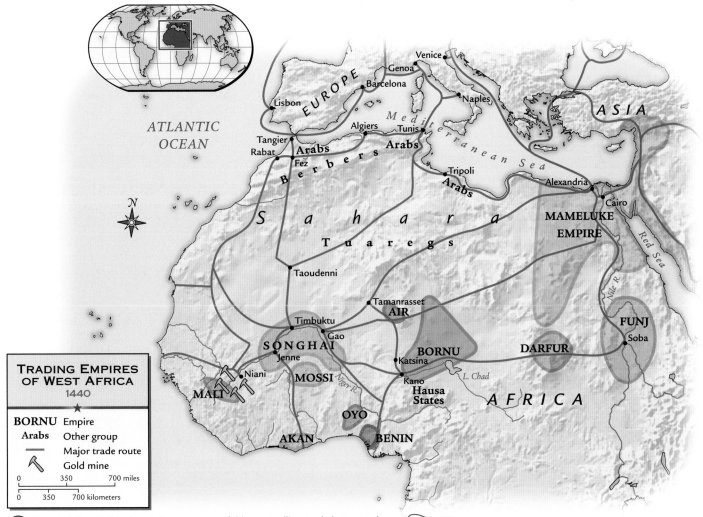

TRADING EMPIRES OF WEST AFRICA
1440

BORNU Empire
Arabs   Other group
——   Major trade route
⚒   Gold mine

0   350   700 miles
0   350   700 kilometers

B Songhai, like Mali before it, became powerful by controlling trade between the Mediterranean and the gold mines upstream along the Niger River.

more at USHAtlas.com

The World of Europe

The period from about 1300 to 1600 in Europe is known as the *Renaissance*.

★ The Renaissance was marked by a revival of learning, as Europeans studied both the ancient world and what was known of their own world.

★ The new printing press, invented in the 1450s, let knowledge spread quickly and inexpensively. Art, science, and exploration flourished.

★ Seafaring nations used newly acquired knowledge to broaden trade, increase wealth, and gain power.

"The world is small and six parts of it are land, the seventh part being entirely covered by water."

—CHRISTOPHER COLUMBUS

A Explorers sailing from Lisbon and other European ports knew that the earth was a sphere. What surprised them was how big it was.

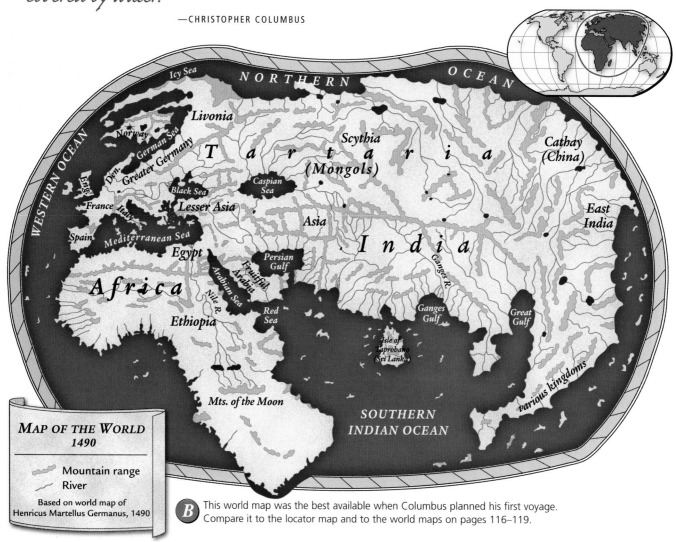

NORTHERN OCEAN

Icy Sea

Livonia

Norway

German Sea

Den.

Greater Germany

Engl.

WESTERN OCEAN

France

Italy

Spain

Mediterranean Sea

Black Sea

Lesser Asia

Caspian Sea

Scythia

Tartaria
(Mongols)

Cathay
(China)

Asia

India

East
India

Egypt

Africa

Arabian Sea

Nile R.

Ethiopia

Fruitful Arabia

Persian Gulf

Red Sea

Ganges R.

Ganges Gulf

Great Gulf

Isle of Taprobano
(Sri Lanka)

Mts. of the Moon

various kingdoms

SOUTHERN
INDIAN OCEAN

MAP OF THE WORLD
1490

Mountain range

River

Based on world map of
Henricus Martellus Germanus, 1490

B This world map was the best available when Columbus planned his first voyage. Compare it to the locator map and to the world maps on pages 116–119.

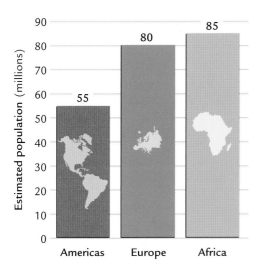

 C **POPULATION SIZES, 1492**

Europe was smaller and more crowded than Africa and the Americas, and far more of its people lived in cities.

more at
USHAtlas.com

D The modern city of Venice is part of Italy, but 500 years ago it was the heart of a powerful seafaring and trading nation of its own.

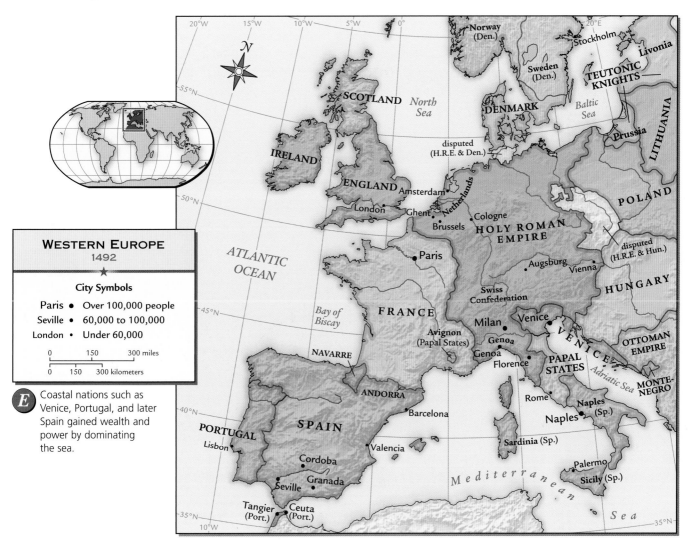

WESTERN EUROPE
1492
★
City Symbols

Paris ● Over 100,000 people
Seville • 60,000 to 100,000
London · Under 60,000

0   150   300 miles
0   150   300 kilometers

E Coastal nations such as Venice, Portugal, and later Spain gained wealth and power by dominating the sea.

Trade With the Indies Spurs Exploration

From the 1000s through the 1200s, European soldiers returned from the *Crusades* in the Middle East carrying treasures from Asia as souvenirs.

★ Soon Europeans were trading for spices, perfume, precious stones, and other goods from the region they knew as the *Indies*.

★ Muslim empires and Italian merchants controlled the routes to the *Indies*. Western Europeans wanted a share of this wealth.

★ Portugal and Spain sought trade routes that they could control. Portugal looked for an eastern route; Spain looked for a western one.

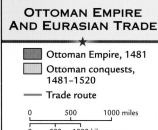

OTTOMAN EMPIRE AND EURASIAN TRADE

★

- �▬ Ottoman Empire, 1481
- ▢ Ottoman conquests, 1481–1520
- ▬▬ Trade route

0   500   1000 miles
0   500   1000 kilometers

A Smooth, colorful, and lightweight, silk has been valued for thousands of years. Its origin in China established the Indies as a source of prized goods even after silk production had spread to western Asia and Europe.

B As the Ottoman Empire gained control of the traditional trade routes, goods from the Indies became even more expensive. These rising prices further encouraged Western Europeans to find new trade routes.

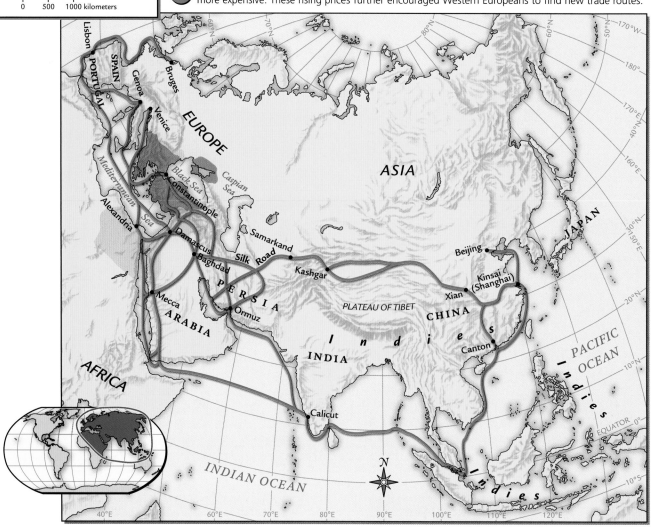

12

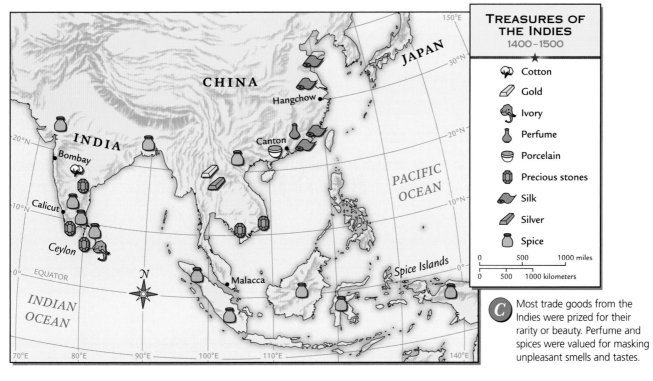

more at
USHAtlas.com

TREASURES OF THE INDIES
1400–1500

	Cotton
	Gold
	Ivory
	Perfume
	Porcelain
	Precious stones
	Silk
	Silver
	Spice

0   500   1000 miles
0   500   1000 kilometers

C Most trade goods from the Indies were prized for their rarity or beauty. Perfume and spices were valued for masking unpleasant smells and tastes.

"Go back and go still further."
—PRINCE HENRY THE NAVIGATOR
ORDERS TO PORTUGUESE EXPLORERS

D Gemstones from the Indies such as diamonds, rubies, emeralds, and amethysts were valued for their beauty. Many Europeans thought the gems had magical powers.

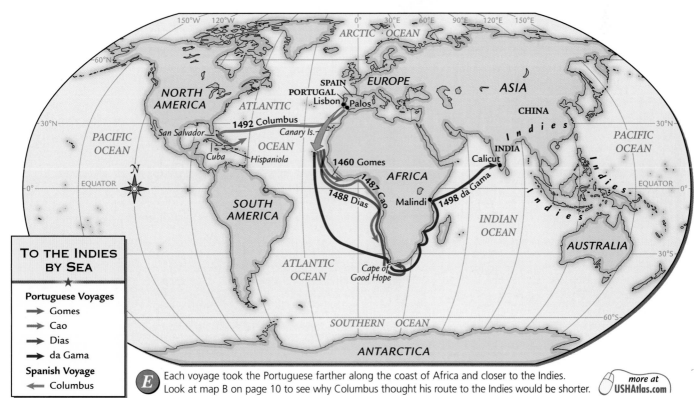

TO THE INDIES BY SEA

Portuguese Voyages
→ Gomes
→ Cao
→ Dias
→ da Gama

Spanish Voyage
← Columbus

E Each voyage took the Portuguese farther along the coast of Africa and closer to the Indies. Look at map B on page 10 to see why Columbus thought his route to the Indies would be shorter.

Europeans Explore the New World

In the 900s Vikings from Scandinavia sailed to North America. But word of this unfamiliar land did not reach the rest of Europe.

★ Five hundred years later, Columbus believed he had reached the islands of the Indies and referred to their inhabitants as *Indians*.

★ After finding no sign of the cities and treasures of the Indies, other European explorers began calling the Americas the *New World*.

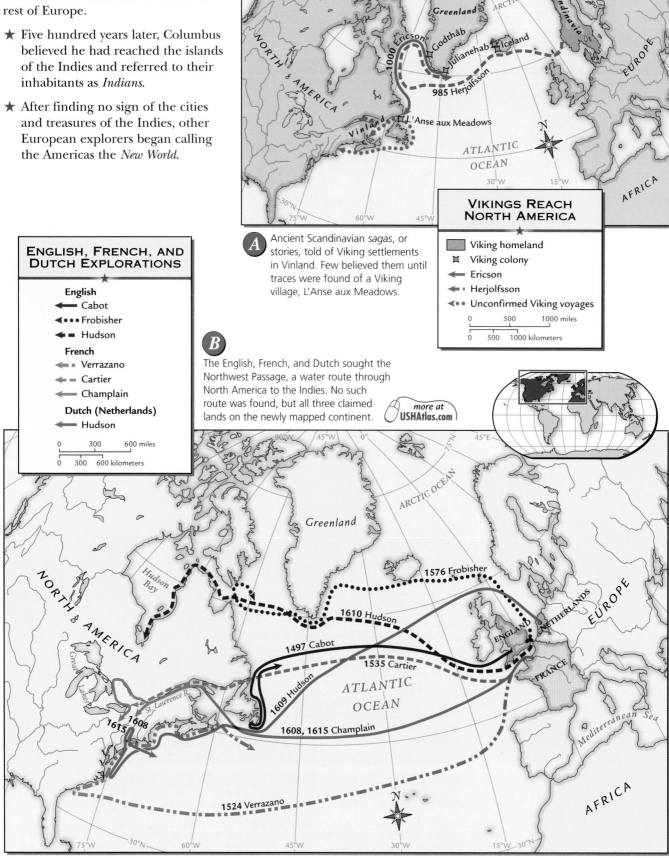

A Ancient Scandinavian *sagas*, or stories, told of Viking settlements in Vinland. Few believed them until traces were found of a Viking village, L'Anse aux Meadows.

VIKINGS REACH NORTH AMERICA
★

- ▨ Viking homeland
- ⚝ Viking colony
- ← Ericson
- ←⊣ Herjolfsson
- ◄••• Unconfirmed Viking voyages

0   500   1000 miles
0   500   1000 kilometers

ENGLISH, FRENCH, AND DUTCH EXPLORATIONS
★

English
- ← Cabot
- ◄••• Frobisher
- ←– Hudson

French
- ← Verrazano
- ←– Cartier
- ← Champlain

Dutch (Netherlands)
- ← Hudson

0   300   600 miles
0   300   600 kilometers

B The English, French, and Dutch sought the Northwest Passage, a water route through North America to the Indies. No such route was found, but all three claimed lands on the newly mapped continent.

more at USHAtlas.com

1576 Frobisher
1610 Hudson
1497 Cabot
1535 Cartier
1609 Hudson
1608, 1615 Champlain
1615
1608
1524 Verrazano

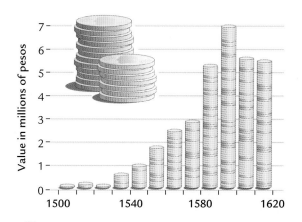

C Treasures of the Incas and the Aztecs fueled Spain's quest for gold.

D GOLD AND SILVER SENT TO SPAIN

Spanish explorers soon stopped looking for the Indies and started looking for gold. They mined silver and seized gold objects made by Aztecs and other Native Americans.

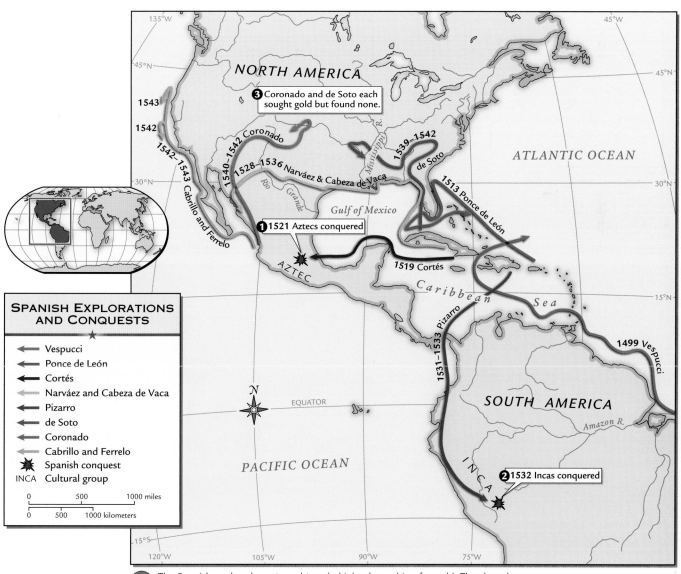

SPANISH EXPLORATIONS
AND CONQUESTS

→ Vespucci
→ Ponce de León
→ Cortés
→ Narváez and Cabeza de Vaca
→ Pizarro
→ de Soto
→ Coronado
→ Cabrillo and Ferrelo
✴ Spanish conquest
INCA Cultural group

0   500   1000 miles
0   500   1000 kilometers

E The Spanish explored coasts and traveled inland searching for gold. They based their land claims on their explorations and their conquests of native empires.

15

Exploitation and Settlement Begin

People of the Americas, West Africa, and Europe came together in the New World.

★ By the mid-1400s, Portuguese ships reached the African homeland of people long prized in Europe as slaves. The Atlantic slave trade was born.

★ In the early 1500s, the Spanish enslaved the Caribbean Indians. When the Indians died, slave ships brought Africans to replace them.

★ Soon European fishing captains and landlords made fortunes in the Americas. Indians and Africans died there of disease and overwork.

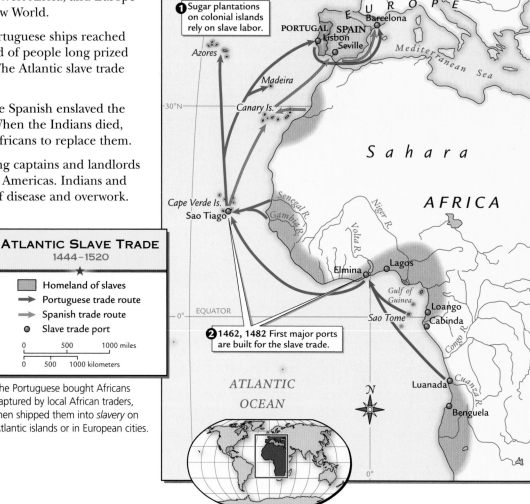

❶ Sugar plantations on colonial islands rely on slave labor.

❷ 1462, 1482 First major ports are built for the slave trade.

ATLANTIC SLAVE TRADE
1444–1520

★

- ▬ Homeland of slaves
- → Portuguese trade route
- → Spanish trade route
- ● Slave trade port

0   500   1000 miles

0   500   1000 kilometers

A The Portuguese bought Africans captured by local African traders, then shipped them into *slavery* on Atlantic islands or in European cities.

B In 1497 John Cabot reported that shallow waters near Newfoundland were filled with codfish. European fishing fleets soon arrived to harvest these waters. Harbors built for repairing ships and drying the catch later became permanent villages.

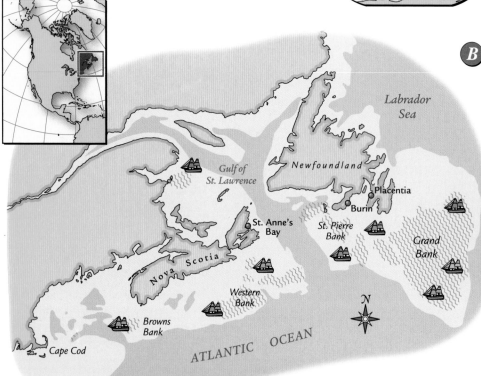

EUROPEANS HARVEST AMERICAN WATERS

★

- ▨ Fishing grounds
- ☐ Shallow water
- ▨ Deep water
- *Bank* Underwater plateau
- ● Fishing harbor

Fishing Fleets of Early 1500s

- 🚢 English
- 🚢 French
- 🚢 Dutch (Netherlands)
- 🚢 Portuguese
- 🚢 Spanish

0   100   200 miles

0   100   200 kilometers

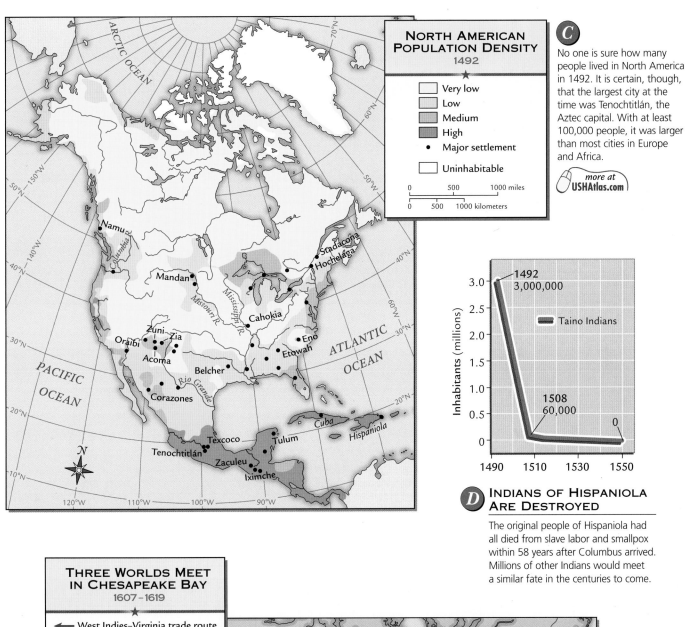

NORTH AMERICAN POPULATION DENSITY
1492

★

- ☐ Very low
- ☐ Low
- ☐ Medium
- ☐ High
- • Major settlement
- ☐ Uninhabitable

0   500   1000 miles
0   500   1000 kilometers

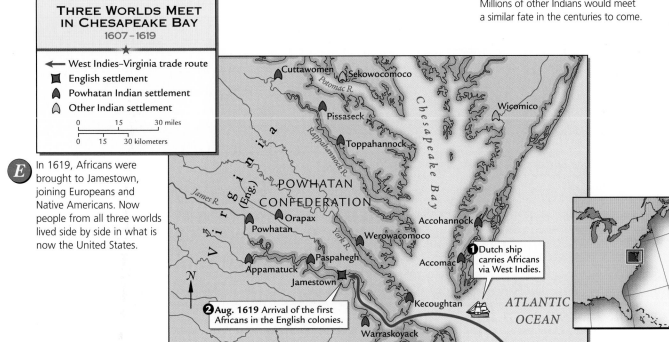

THREE WORLDS MEET IN CHESAPEAKE BAY
1607–1619

★

- ⟵ West Indies–Virginia trade route
- ◆ English settlement
- ◆ Powhatan Indian settlement
- ◆ Other Indian settlement

0   15   30 miles
0   15   30 kilometers

C No one is sure how many people lived in North America in 1492. It is certain, though, that the largest city at the time was Tenochtitlán, the Aztec capital. With at least 100,000 people, it was larger than most cities in Europe and Africa.

more at **USHAtlas.com**

1492
3,000,000

Taino Indians

1508
60,000

0

Inhabitants (millions)

3.0
2.5
2.0
1.5
1.0
0.5
0.0

1490   1510   1530   1550

D **INDIANS OF HISPANIOLA ARE DESTROYED**

The original people of Hispaniola had all died from slave labor and smallpox within 58 years after Columbus arrived. Millions of other Indians would meet a similar fate in the centuries to come.

E In 1619, Africans were brought to Jamestown, joining Europeans and Native Americans. Now people from all three worlds lived side by side in what is now the United States.

① Dutch ship carries Africans via West Indies.

② Aug. 1619 Arrival of the first Africans in the English colonies.

Colonization and Settlement
1585–1763

1607, 1608, 1609
Jamestown, Quebec, Santa Fe settled by the English, French, Spanish.

1585
Roanoke Island settled by the English.

1598
New Spain extends into what is now New Mexico.

1622
Indian Wars begin and continue for nearly three centuries.

1550

1600

1550
African slaves replace last Indians in West Indies.

1565
St. Augustine established by the Spanish.

1600
Horses from Spain first used by Indians.

A New World to the Europeans

Europeans thought the natural resources of the New World—as they called the Americas—were unlimited, to be used as they pleased.

★ Long before Europeans arrived, Native Americans had developed many different *cultures* and ways of life based on the same resources.

★ The meeting of the Old World with the New had a cultural impact that began with Columbus.

★ As explorers crisscrossed the Atlantic, they introduced new plants, animals, and even germs to both areas of the world.

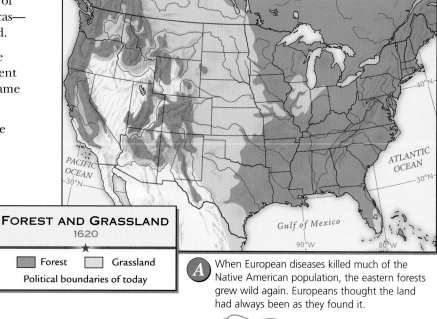

FOREST AND GRASSLAND
1620

■ Forest   □ Grassland

Political boundaries of today

A When European diseases killed much of the Native American population, the eastern forests grew wild again. Europeans thought the land had always been as they found it.

more at USHAtlas.com

NATIVE AMERICANS
1620

Main Source of Food
- Fishing
- Hunting
- Gathering
- Farming
- Balanced hunting and gathering
- Sparsely populated

PIMA Indian nation

Political boundaries of today

B Most hunters and gatherers moved frequently in their search for food. Farmers and fishers had *settlements* that were more permanent.

more at USHAtlas.com

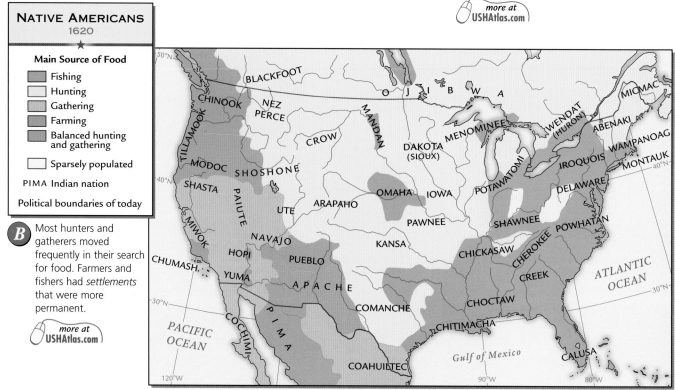

1624		1732	1750
New Amsterdam		**Georgia** established	**Over 1 million people**
settled by		as last of the 13	live in the 13 colonies.
the Dutch.	1661	British colonies.	
	Slavery in	1682	1750
	Virginia	**Mississippi Valley**	**Slavery** exists in
	allowed by law.	claimed by France.	all 13 colonies.

1650   **1700**   **1750**   **1800**

1683	1763
First German immigrants	**French colonial rule** ends
settle in Pennsylvania.	in mainland North America.

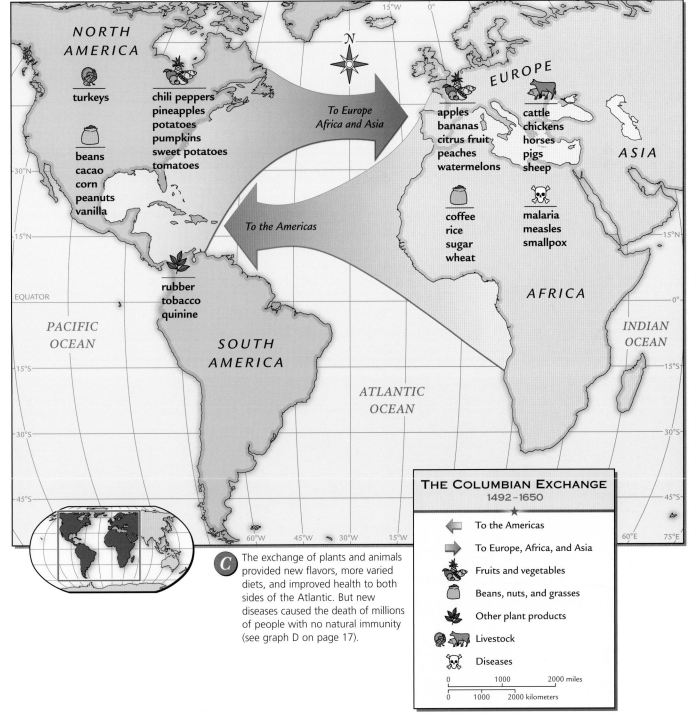

C The exchange of plants and animals provided new flavors, more varied diets, and improved health to both sides of the Atlantic. But new diseases caused the death of millions of people with no natural immunity (see graph D on page 17).

THE COLUMBIAN EXCHANGE
1492–1650

⬅ To the Americas

➡ To Europe, Africa, and Asia

🍍 Fruits and vegetables

🫘 Beans, nuts, and grasses

🌿 Other plant products

🐂 Livestock

☠ Diseases

0   1000   2000 miles
0   1000   2000 kilometers

Early Claims, Early Conflicts

European explorers claimed vast areas of the Americas for the countries that sponsored their expeditions.

★ The largest land claims were made by Spain, France, and England.

★ The European powers were confident of their right to claim the Americas as their own.

★ European claims quickly caused violent conflict with Native Americans throughout the hemisphere.

B The first horses in the Americas were brought by Spanish explorers, such as this one drawn by Frederic Remington (color added). When Plains Indians captured and learned to ride horses, their lives were transformed.

SPAIN'S EMPIRE IN THE NEW WORLD

★

Viceroyalties

New Spain
New Castile
New Granada

Political boundaries of 1625

0   500   1000 miles
0   500   1000 kilometers

NORTH AMERICA

ATLANTIC OCEAN

Santa Fe
St. Augustine
Gulf of Mexico
New Spain
Havana
Hispaniola
Cuba
Puerto Rico
San Juan
Mexico City
Jamaica
WEST INDIES
Santo Domingo
Caribbean Sea
Cartagena
Caracas
New Granada
PACIFIC OCEAN
New Castile
Brazil (Port.)
SOUTH AMERICA
Lima
Cuzco

N

A Spain gained much of its *territory* by conquering the Aztecs in Mexico and the Incas in South America. See map E on page 15.

NEWCOMERS TO THE AMERICAS

In the early 1600s, most Africans in the Americas were slaves in the West Indies and Brazil.

Population in about 1625

Spanish 450,000
African 107,000
Portuguese 45,000
French 360
English 7,600
Dutch 200

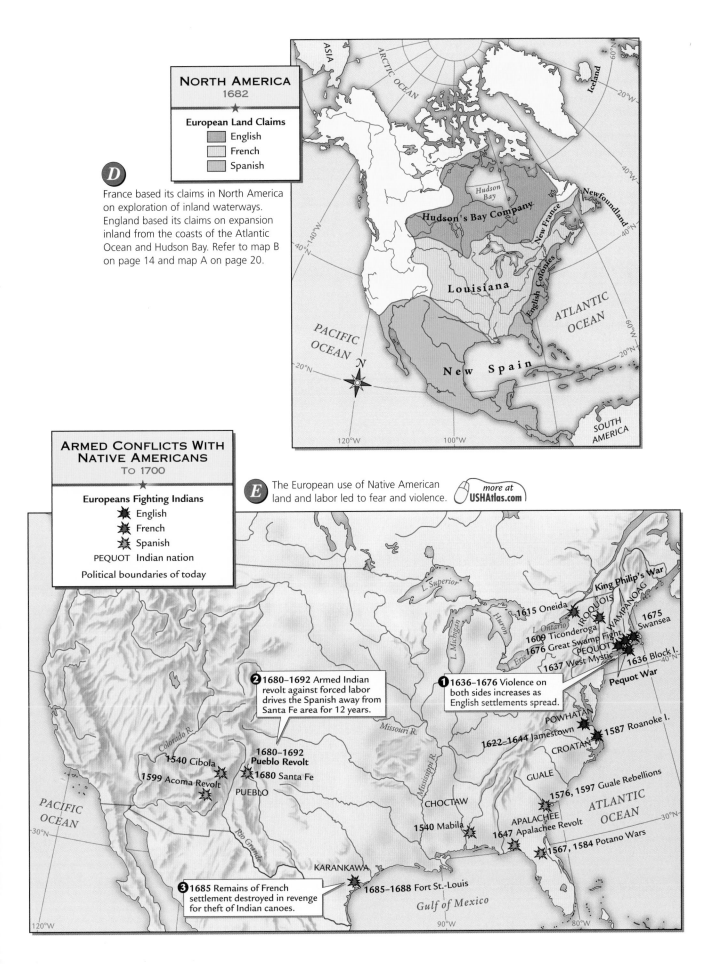

NORTH AMERICA
1682
★
European Land Claims
- English
- French
- Spanish

D France based its claims in North America on exploration of inland waterways. England based its claims on expansion inland from the coasts of the Atlantic Ocean and Hudson Bay. Refer to map B on page 14 and map A on page 20.

ASIA
ARCTIC OCEAN
Iceland
Hudson Bay
Hudson's Bay Company
New France
Newfoundland
Louisiana
English Colonies
ATLANTIC OCEAN
PACIFIC OCEAN
N
New Spain
SOUTH AMERICA
120°W   100°W
20°W   40°W   60°W   20°N   40°N   60°N   140°W

ARMED CONFLICTS WITH NATIVE AMERICANS
To 1700
★
Europeans Fighting Indians
- ✴ English
- ✴ French
- ✴ Spanish
- PEQUOT Indian nation
- Political boundaries of today

E The European use of Native American land and labor led to fear and violence.

more at USHAtlas.com

L. Superior
L. Michigan
L. Huron
L. Ontario
L. Erie

King Philip's War
1615 Oneida
IROQUOIS
WAMPANOAG
1609 Ticonderoga
1676 Great Swamp Fight
1675 Swansea
PEQUOT
1637 West Mystic
1636 Block I.
Pequot War

2 1680–1692 Armed Indian revolt against forced labor drives the Spanish away from Santa Fe area for 12 years.

1 1636–1676 Violence on both sides increases as English settlements spread.

Missouri R.

1680–1692
Pueblo Revolt

POWHATAN
1622–1644 Jamestown
1587 Roanoke I.
CROATAN

Colorado R.

1540 Cibola
1599 Acoma Revolt
1680 Santa Fe
PUEBLO

GUALE
1576, 1597 Guale Rebellions

CHOCTAW

Mississippi R.

PACIFIC OCEAN

Rio Grande

1540 Mabila
APALACHEE
1647 Apalachee Revolt
1567, 1584 Potano Wars

ATLANTIC OCEAN
30°N

KARANKAWA

3 1685 Remains of French settlement destroyed in revenge for theft of Indian canoes.

1685–1688 Fort St.-Louis

Gulf of Mexico

120°W   90°W   80°W

European Settlements in North America

Europeans settled in lands claimed by earlier explorers.

★ The Spanish settled in areas originally claimed by Columbus, Ponce de León, de Soto, and Coronado.

★ The French and Dutch settled farther north in areas first explored by Cartier and Hudson.

★ English and Swedish colonists settled in previously unclaimed lands along the Atlantic coast.

★ Some colonists sought freedom in a new land. Others were committed to long terms of hard labor. Still others came to make their fortunes and return to Europe.

"...to give light to those who were in darkness, and to procure wealth which all men desire."

—BERNAL DIAZ DEL CASTILLO
ON THE GOALS OF THE SPANISH CONQUERORS
OF INDIAN CIVILIZATIONS

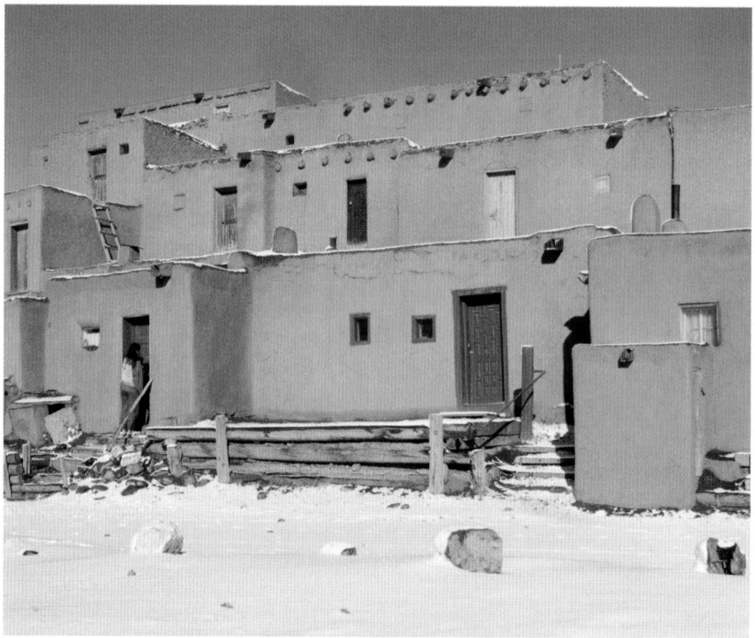

A Taos Pueblo is more than 200 years older than nearby Santa Fe, the oldest Spanish settlement in the area. It survives as home to descendants of its Pueblo Indian builders.

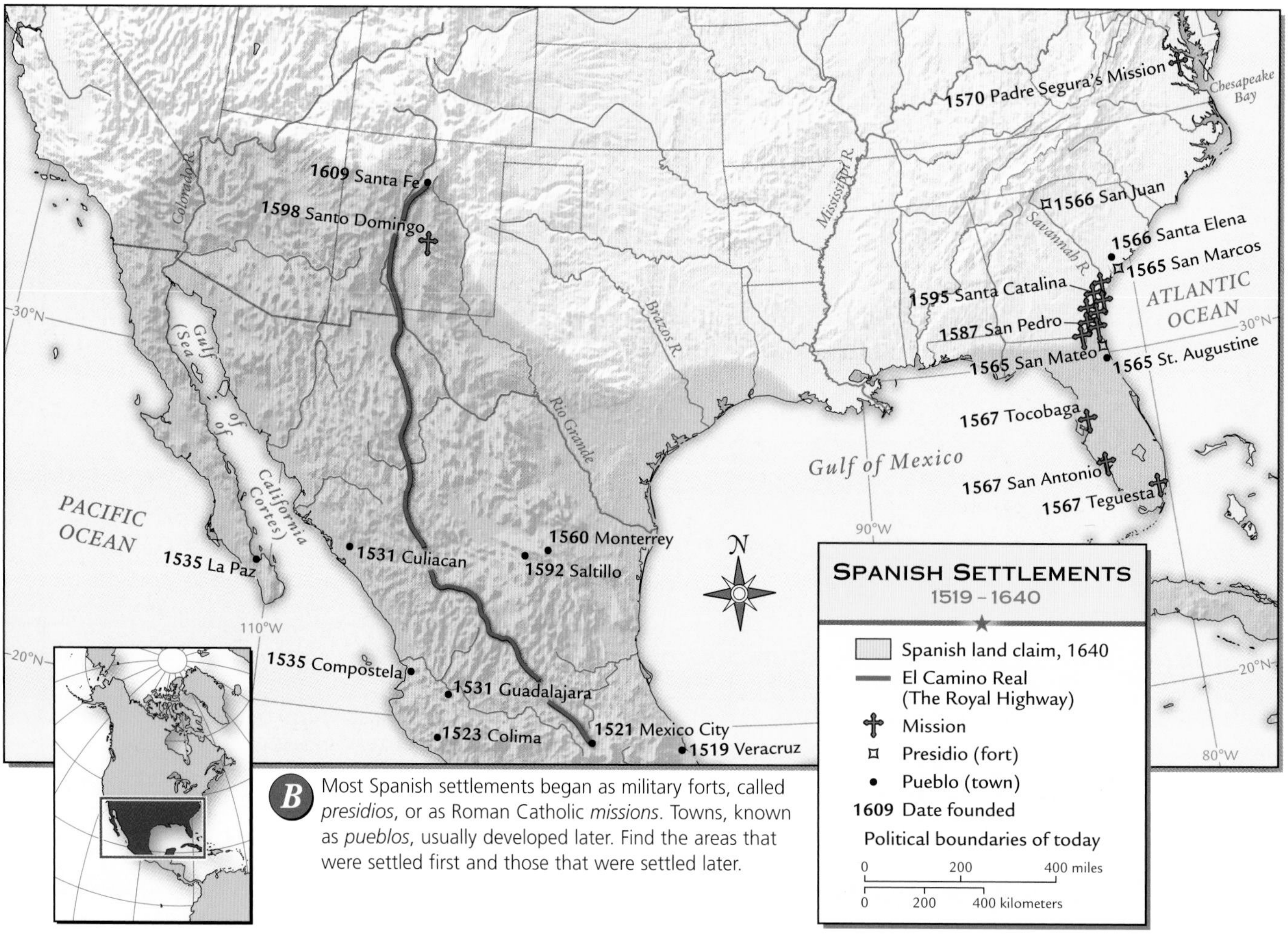

1570 Padre Segura's Mission
Chesapeake Bay
1609 Santa Fe
1598 Santo Domingo
Colorado R.
Mississippi R.
1566 San Juan
Savannah R.
1566 Santa Elena
1565 San Marcos
1595 Santa Catalina
1587 San Pedro
1565 San Mateo
1565 St. Augustine
ATLANTIC OCEAN
30°N
Brazos R.
Rio Grande
Gulf (Sea of Cortes) of California
1567 Tocobaga
Gulf of Mexico
1567 San Antonio
1567 Teguesta
PACIFIC OCEAN
1535 La Paz
1531 Culiacan
1560 Monterrey
1592 Saltillo
90°W
110°W
N
20°N
1535 Compostela
1531 Guadalajara
1523 Colima
1521 Mexico City
1519 Veracruz
80°W
SPANISH SETTLEMENTS
1519–1640
Spanish land claim, 1640
El Camino Real (The Royal Highway)
Mission
Presidio (fort)
Pueblo (town)
1609 Date founded
Political boundaries of today
0 200 400 miles
0 200 400 kilometers

B Most Spanish settlements began as military forts, called *presidios*, or as Roman Catholic *missions*. Towns, known as *pueblos*, usually developed later. Find the areas that were settled first and those that were settled later.

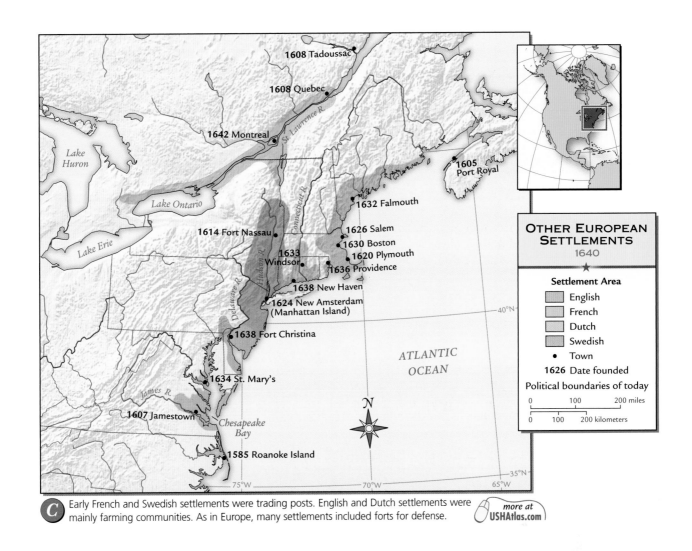

C Early French and Swedish settlements were trading posts. English and Dutch settlements were mainly farming communities. As in Europe, many settlements included forts for defense.

more at USHAtlas.com

OTHER EUROPEAN SETTLEMENTS
1640

Settlement Area
- English
- French
- Dutch
- Swedish
- • Town
- **1626** Date founded

Political boundaries of today

0   100   200 miles
0   100   200 kilometers

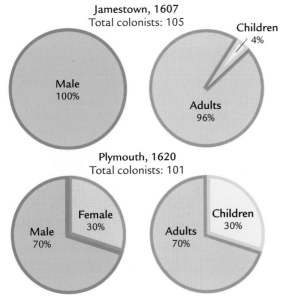

Jamestown, 1607
Total colonists: 105

Male 100%

Children 4%
Adults 96%

Plymouth, 1620
Total colonists: 101

Male 70%
Female 30%

Adults 70%
Children 30%

D **EARLY COLONISTS**

Some *colonies*, such as Jamestown, were founded with the goal of gaining wealth. In others, such as Plymouth, the main goal was to start a new life in a new land. Compare these distinct groups of original settlers.

E Just as they had in England, the colonists at Plymouth planted gardens and built board houses—some with thatched roofs—like those at the reconstructed historical site above. Log cabins were introduced by Swedish settlers.

The Thirteen British Colonies

By 1750 there were 13 British colonies along the Atlantic coast south of New France.

★ In the New England Colonies, people lived and worked in fishing villages, port cities, and small towns surrounded by modest family farms.

★ In the Middle Colonies, farms were larger and farmland more productive. Lively *urban* centers were home to prosperous merchants and skilled artisans.

★ In the Southern Colonies, the large plantations near the coast grew single crops for trade at nearby port cities. Smaller towns and farms dotted the foothills farther west.

New France
(Fr.)

St. Lawrence R.

NEW ENGLAND COLONIES
(claimed by NY & NH)

❶ 1626 New Netherland is founded; English gain control in 1664 and rename it New York.

Lake Ontario

L. Erie

Schenectady

1626 New York

MIDDLE COLONIES

1682 Pennsylvania

1620 **Massachusetts**

Nova Scotia (Br.)

1688 **New Hampshire**

Falmouth

Exeter ★ Portsmouth
Gloucester
Salem
Albany   Boston ★   1620
Providence **Massachusetts**
★1636 1636
Hartford ★ Newport
New Haven ★ **Rhode Island**
★ **Connecticut**

Hudson R.

Perth Amboy ★
Trenton ★
1664 **New Jersey**
Philadelphia ★ Burlington
Lancaster ● ● Wilmington
Baltimore ● ★ New Castle
Annapolis ★ ● Dover
1638 **Delaware**

❷ 1638 New Sweden is founded along the Delaware River. English gain control in 1664.

1607 Virginia
St. Mary's ● ★ 1633 **Maryland**
Richmond ●
● Williamsburg
Jamestown ★

Chesapeake Bay

SOUTHERN COLONIES

1653 North Carolina

New Bern ★

ATLANTIC OCEAN

N

1663 South Carolina
● Wilmington

Savannah R.

1732 Georgia

★ Charles Town

Florida (Sp.)

● Savannah

● St. Augustine

THIRTEEN COLONIES 1750
★

— Regional division
— Colonial boundary
- - - Indefinite boundary
★ Colonial capital
1607 Date founded

0   100   200 miles
0   100   200 kilometers

A

In 1750 few colonies had definite western boundaries. Those not blocked by other colonies continued to expand as settlers moved west into new territory.

Potomac R.
Delaware R.
APPALACHIAN MTS.
★ Trenton
★ Wilmington
Baltimore
Washington
James R.
Richmond
PIEDMONT
COASTAL PLAIN
Raleigh ≈
Columbia ≈
Savannah R.
Augusta ≈
Macon ≈

FALL LINE SETTLEMENTS
★

Land Regions
 Plains and lowland
 Plateau
 Highland
≈ City on Fall Line

0   100   200 miles
0   100   200 kilometers

B

Waterfalls and rapids along the edge of the *Piedmont* created a barrier to navigation called the *Fall Line*. Trading towns grew where goods to be carried past the falls were unloaded from boats.

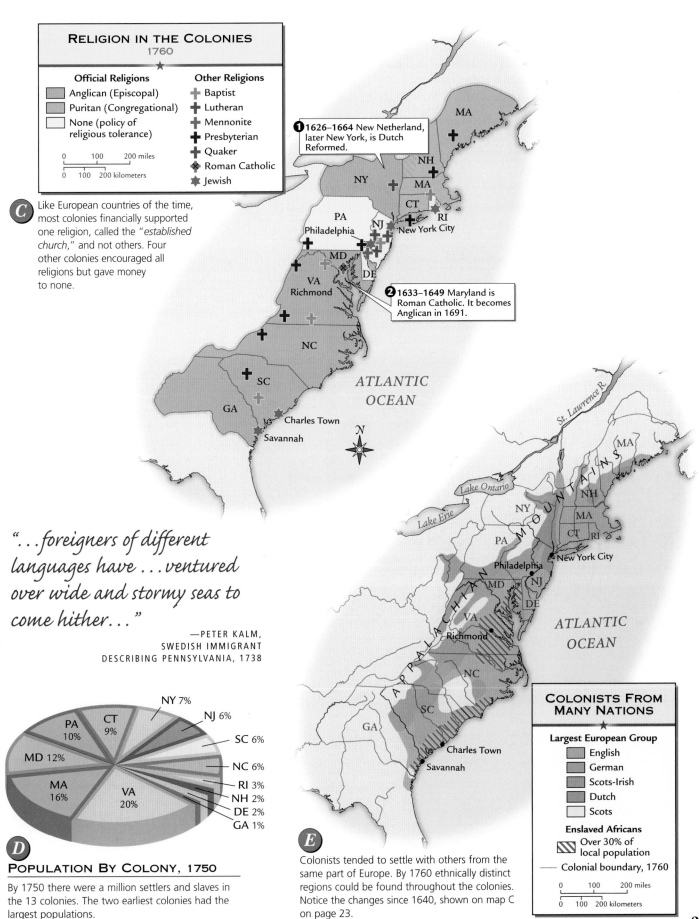

RELIGION IN THE COLONIES
1760
★

Official Religions
- ▨ Anglican (Episcopal)
- ▨ Puritan (Congregational)
- ☐ None (policy of religious tolerance)

Other Religions
- ✚ Baptist
- ✚ Lutheran
- ✚ Mennonite
- ✚ Presbyterian
- ✚ Quaker
- ✦ Roman Catholic
- ★ Jewish

0   100   200 miles
0   100   200 kilometers

C Like European countries of the time, most colonies financially supported one religion, called the *"established church,"* and not others. Four other colonies encouraged all religions but gave money to none.

❶ **1626–1664** New Netherland, later New York, is Dutch Reformed.

❷ **1633–1649** Maryland is Roman Catholic. It becomes Anglican in 1691.

MA
NH
NY
MA
CT
RI
PA
Philadelphia
NJ
New York City
MD
DE
VA
Richmond
NC
SC
GA
Charles Town
Savannah

ATLANTIC OCEAN

N

"...foreigners of different languages have ...ventured over wide and stormy seas to come hither..."

—PETER KALM,
SWEDISH IMMIGRANT
DESCRIBING PENNSYLVANIA, 1738

D

NY 7%
NJ 6%
CT 9%
PA 10%
SC 6%
MD 12%
NC 6%
RI 3%
MA 16%
NH 2%
VA 20%
DE 2%
GA 1%

POPULATION BY COLONY, 1750

By 1750 there were a million settlers and slaves in the 13 colonies. The two earliest colonies had the largest populations.

E Colonists tended to settle with others from the same part of Europe. By 1760 ethnically distinct regions could be found throughout the colonies. Notice the changes since 1640, shown on map C on page 23.

St. Lawrence R.
MA
Lake Ontario
NH
Lake Erie
NY
MA
CT
RI
PA
Philadelphia
New York City
MD
NJ
DE
VA
Richmond
NC
SC
GA
Charles Town
Savannah

ATLANTIC OCEAN

COLONISTS FROM MANY NATIONS
★

Largest European Group
- ▨ English
- ▨ German
- ▨ Scots-Irish
- ▨ Dutch
- ☐ Scots

Enslaved Africans
- ▨ Over 30% of local population
- — Colonial boundary, 1760

0   100   200 miles
0   100   200 kilometers

Slavery in the Americas

More than 11 million Africans were sold into slavery in the Americas. Most were put to work on plantations in the West Indies and Brazil.

★ In North America, the Southern Colonies copied the plantation system, which relied on slave labor.

★ By 1760 slaves were held in all 13 colonies, but slavery remained concentrated on plantations and in large cities.

★ Although far outnumbered by slaves, many people of African descent gained their freedom and continued to live in the colonies.

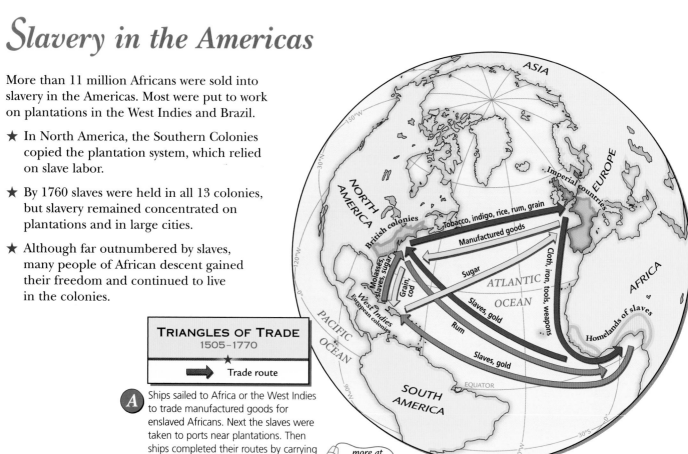

TRIANGLES OF TRADE
1505–1770
★
→ Trade route

A Ships sailed to Africa or the West Indies to trade manufactured goods for enslaved Africans. Next the slaves were taken to ports near plantations. Then ships completed their routes by carrying plantation crops to their home ports.

more at USHAtlas.com

B Slaves on plantations dug pits for planting sugar cane and later harvested it with large knives. Then they crushed and boiled the cane in mills where temperatures reached 140°F. Millions died after leading short lives of brutal labor.

more at USHAtlas.com

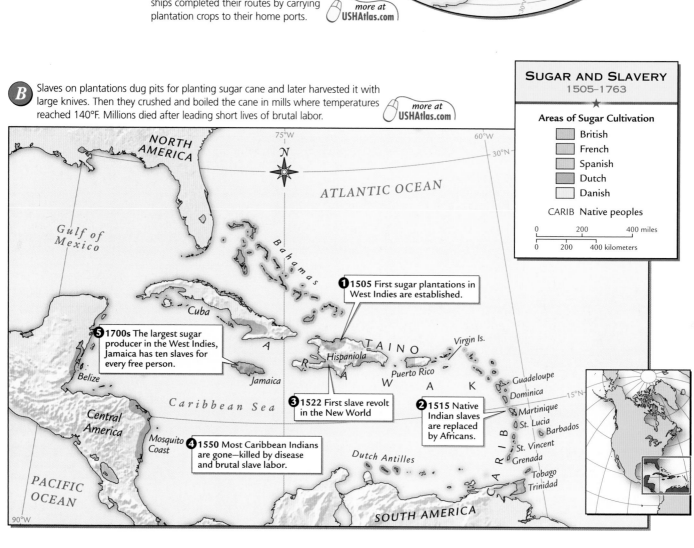

SUGAR AND SLAVERY
1505–1763
★
Areas of Sugar Cultivation
- British
- French
- Spanish
- Dutch
- Danish

CARIB Native peoples

0   200   400 miles
0   200   400 kilometers

1 1505 First sugar plantations in West Indies are established.

5 1700s The largest sugar producer in the West Indies, Jamaica has ten slaves for every free person.

3 1522 First slave revolt in the New World

2 1515 Native Indian slaves are replaced by Africans.

4 1550 Most Caribbean Indians are gone—killed by disease and brutal slave labor.

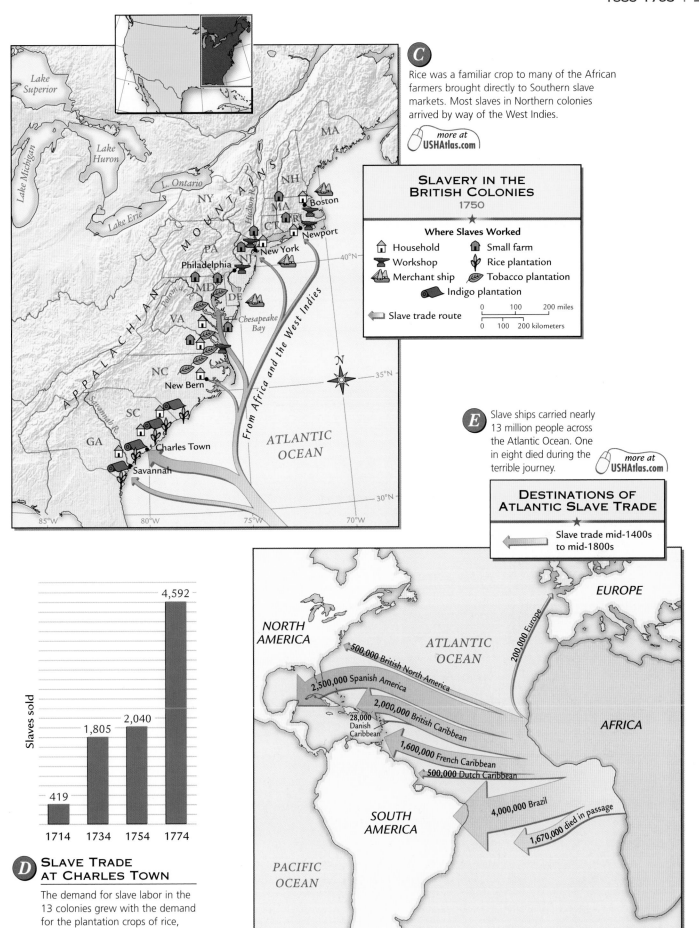

C Rice was a familiar crop to many of the African farmers brought directly to Southern slave markets. Most slaves in Northern colonies arrived by way of the West Indies.

more at USHAtlas.com

SLAVERY IN THE BRITISH COLONIES
1750

Where Slaves Worked

🏠 Household   🏚 Small farm

⚒ Workshop   🌿 Rice plantation

⛵ Merchant ship   🍃 Tobacco plantation

📜 Indigo plantation

⬅ Slave trade route

0   100   200 miles
0   100   200 kilometers

E Slave ships carried nearly 13 million people across the Atlantic Ocean. One in eight died during the terrible journey.

more at USHAtlas.com

DESTINATIONS OF ATLANTIC SLAVE TRADE

⬅ Slave trade mid-1400s to mid-1800s

200,000 Europe

500,000 British North America

2,500,000 Spanish America

2,000,000 British Caribbean

28,000 Danish Caribbean

1,600,000 French Caribbean

500,000 Dutch Caribbean

4,000,000 Brazil

1,670,000 died in passage

Slaves sold

4,592

2,040

1,805

419

1714   1734   1754   1774

D SLAVE TRADE AT CHARLES TOWN

The demand for slave labor in the 13 colonies grew with the demand for the plantation crops of rice, indigo, and tobacco.

Revolution and the New Nation

1754–1820s

1754–1763
French and Indian War ends in victory for Britain.

1764
Sugar Act is first of new taxes imposed on colonists.

1750   1760   1770

The French and Indian War Changes America

The bitter rivalry between France and Britain led to war over their competing claims in North America.

★ Huron and Algonkin Indians fought with the French. Colonists and Iroquois Indians fought with the British.

★ Britain won the war and took control of French territory east of the Mississippi River.

★ In the Proclamation of 1763, Britain reserved all lands west of the Appalachians for Native Americans.

★ Colonists faced new British taxes and tighter British control after the war. Many colonists grew rebellious.

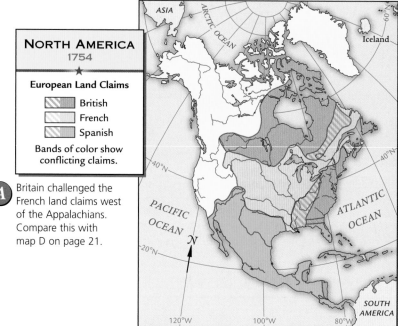

NORTH AMERICA
1754
★
European Land Claims

	British
	French
	Spanish

Bands of color show conflicting claims.

A Britain challenged the French land claims west of the Appalachians. Compare this with map D on page 21.

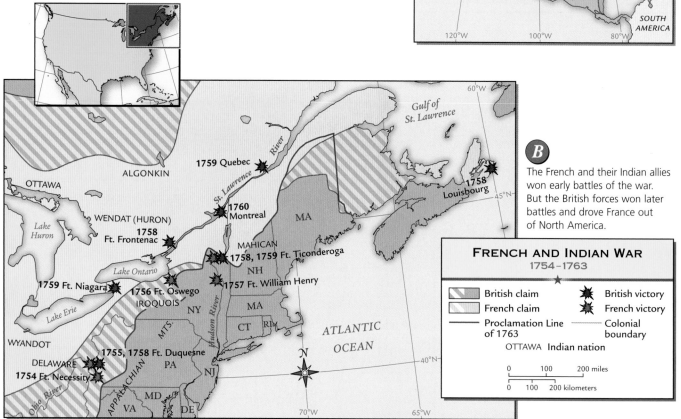

B The French and their Indian allies won early battles of the war. But the British forces won later battles and drove France out of North America.

FRENCH AND INDIAN WAR
1754–1763
★

British claim	✦ British victory
French claim	✦ French victory
—— Proclamation Line of 1763	—— Colonial boundary
OTTAWA Indian nation	

0   100   200 miles
0   100   200 kilometers

1783
United States expands beyond Appalachians to Mississippi River.

1787
Northwest Territory laid out for settlement.

1803
Louisiana Territory bought by United States.

1775–1781
Revolutionary War wins U.S. independence from Great Britain.

1788
U.S. Constitution ratified.

1792
Kentucky becomes first state west of Appalachians.

1812–1815
War of 1812 fought against Britain.

1823
Monroe Doctrine bans new colonies in the Americas.

| 1780 | 1790 | 1800 | 1810 | 1820 | 1830 |

1776
Declaration of Independence signed in Philadelphia.

1790
Slaves and free blacks total 19% of U.S. population.

1821
Mexico gains independence from Spain.

YEAR	TAX LAW	ITEMS TAXED
1764	Sugar Act	Molasses
1765	Stamp Act	Newspapers, dice, playing cards, legal documents
1767	Townshend Act	Imported paint, lead, glass, paper, tea

D BRITISH TAXES ON COLONISTS

After the French and Indian War, Britain taxed colonists for the first time. Taxes were meant to pay for defense of the colonies and to assert British control over colonists and colonial trade.

more at USHAtlas.com

NORTH AMERICA
1763

European Land Claims
- British
- French
- Spanish
- Russian
- Proclamation Line of 1763

C Indians fought colonists who moved west. In 1763 Britain set the Proclamation Line and banned settlement west of it to avoid another war.

E The 1773 Tea Act gave special privileges to the British East India Company and threatened colonial merchants, especially in Boston. Colonists, some dressed as Indians, boarded the company's ships and dumped the tea into Boston Harbor. Their protest became known as the Boston Tea Party.

1773

F TEA IMPORTED FROM BRITAIN

To protest the Tea Act and avoid paying taxes, some colonists chose to *boycott* British imports. The demand for tea and other British goods quickly dropped.

1774

1775

739,221 lbs.

73,274 lbs.

22,198 lbs.

29

Patriots Fight the Revolutionary War

Colonial rebellion grew into the American Revolution, the war for independence from Great Britain.

★ French, Spanish, and Dutch forces helped the Patriots fight Britain.

★ On the British side were American Loyalists, Hessian (German) troops, and Indians west of the colonies.

★ Slaves fought in both the Patriot and British armies in exchange for offers of freedom.

★ After six years of fighting on land and at sea, the Patriots won the war and Great Britain lost its 13 colonies.

more at USHAtlas.com

A

At first the Revolutionary War was fought mostly in New England and the Middle Colonies. Later the war shifted to the Southern Colonies. The British surrendered after losing battles on sea at Virginia Capes and on land at Yorktown.

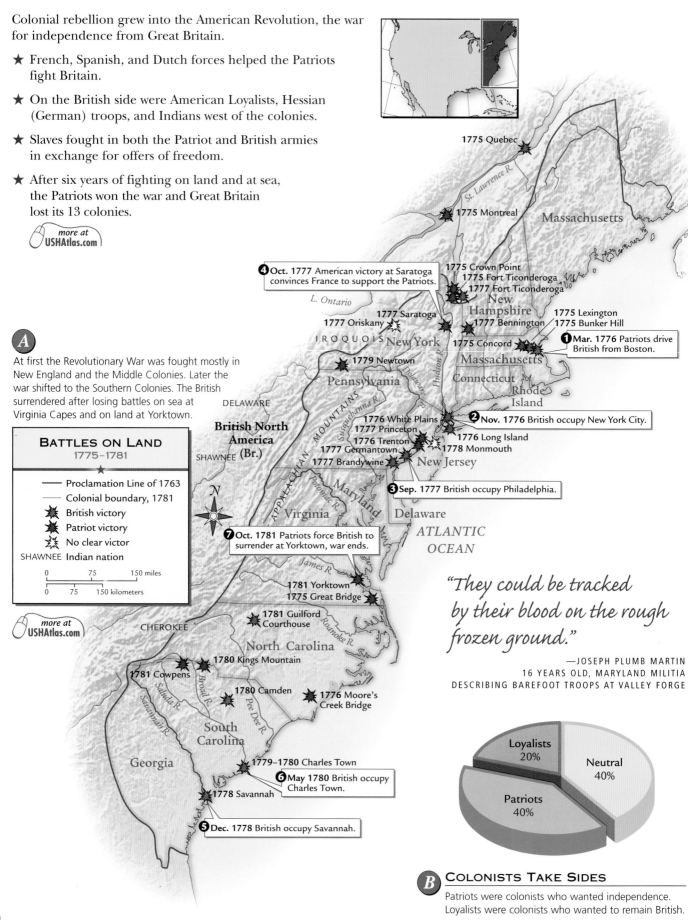

BATTLES ON LAND
1775–1781

- Proclamation Line of 1763
- Colonial boundary, 1781
- ✳ British victory
- ✳ Patriot victory
- ✳ No clear victor
- SHAWNEE Indian nation

0   75   150 miles
0   75   150 kilometers

more at USHAtlas.com

1775 Quebec

1775 Montreal

Massachusetts

❹ Oct. 1777 American victory at Saratoga convinces France to support the Patriots.

1775 Crown Point
1775 Fort Ticonderoga
1777 Fort Ticonderoga
New Hampshire

1775 Lexington
1775 Bunker Hill

1777 Saratoga
1777 Oriskany
1777 Bennington

1775 Concord

❶ Mar. 1776 Patriots drive British from Boston.

IROQUOIS   New York
Massachusetts
Connecticut

1779 Newtown

Rhode Island

Pennsylvania

1776 White Plains
1776 Princeton
1776 Trenton
1777 Germantown
1777 Brandywine

❷ Nov. 1776 British occupy New York City.

1776 Long Island
1778 Monmouth

DELAWARE

British North America (Br.)

SHAWNEE

New Jersey

❸ Sep. 1777 British occupy Philadelphia.

Maryland

Delaware

ATLANTIC OCEAN

❼ Oct. 1781 Patriots force British to surrender at Yorktown, war ends.

Virginia

1781 Yorktown
1775 Great Bridge

1781 Guilford Courthouse

CHEROKEE

North Carolina

1780 Kings Mountain

1781 Cowpens

1780 Camden

1776 Moore's Creek Bridge

South Carolina

Georgia

1779–1780 Charles Town

❻ May 1780 British occupy Charles Town.

1778 Savannah

❺ Dec. 1778 British occupy Savannah.

"They could be tracked by their blood on the rough frozen ground."

—JOSEPH PLUMB MARTIN
16 YEARS OLD, MARYLAND MILITIA
DESCRIBING BAREFOOT TROOPS AT VALLEY FORGE

Loyalists 20%
Neutral 40%
Patriots 40%

B COLONISTS TAKE SIDES

Patriots were colonists who wanted independence. Loyalists were colonists who wanted to remain British.

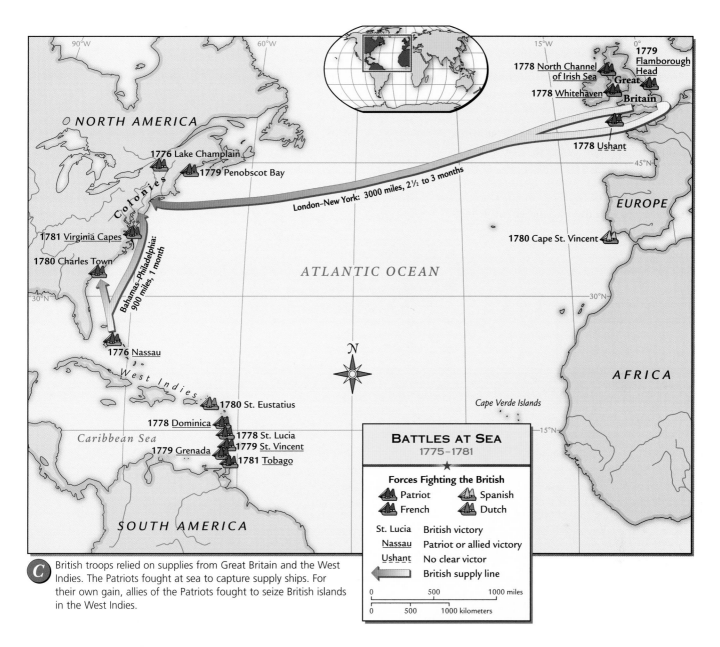

 map labels:

90°W · 60°W · 15°W · 0°

1778 North Channel of Irish Sea

1779 Flamborough Head

1778 Whitehaven

Great Britain

NORTH AMERICA

1776 Lake Champlain

1779 Penobscot Bay

1778 Ushant

45°N

Colonies

EUROPE

London–New York: 3000 miles, 2½ to 3 months

1781 Virginia Capes

1780 Cape St. Vincent

1780 Charles Town

Bahamas–Philadelphia: 900 miles, 1 month

30°N

30°N

ATLANTIC OCEAN

1776 Nassau

West Indies

N

AFRICA

1780 St. Eustatius

1778 Dominica

Caribbean Sea

1778 St. Lucia

Cape Verde Islands

1779 Grenada

1779 St. Vincent

1781 Tobago

15°N

SOUTH AMERICA

BATTLES AT SEA
1775–1781

★

Forces Fighting the British

🚢	Patriot	🚢	Spanish
🚢	French	🚢	Dutch

St. Lucia British victory

Nassau Patriot or allied victory

Ushant No clear victor

⬅ British supply line

0 · 500 · 1000 miles

0 · 500 · 1000 kilometers

C British troops relied on supplies from Great Britain and the West Indies. The Patriots fought at sea to capture supply ships. For their own gain, allies of the Patriots fought to seize British islands in the West Indies.

D At Flamborough Head and elsewhere, warships fought with cannons at close range.

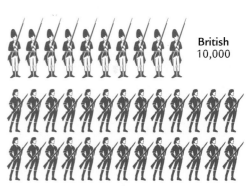

British
10,000

Patriots
25,700

E **SOLDIERS' DEATHS**

Patriot troops outnumbered the British but were poorly fed and clothed. Only 28 percent of those who died were killed in battle. The rest died from disease, of exposure, or as prisoners.

more at
USHAtlas.com

31

A New Nation: The United States of America

In 1783 the Treaty of Paris officially recognized the United States as an independent country.

★ The new nation gained all British land west of the Appalachians, east of the Mississippi River, and south of the Great Lakes.

★ In 1781 the states were loosely organized under the Articles of Confederation. The new country could not collect taxes, so it could not afford to carry out its responsibilities.

★ In 1788 the Constitution replaced the Articles of Confederation, uniting the states under a stronger *federal* government.

more at
USHAtlas.com

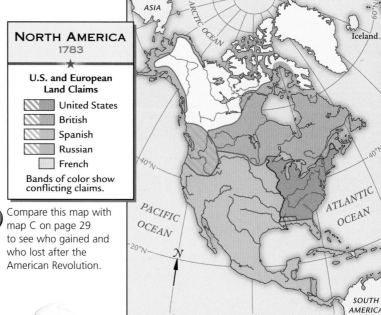

NORTH AMERICA
1783
★
U.S. and European Land Claims

▨	United States
▨	British
▨	Spanish
▨	Russian
☐	French

Bands of color show conflicting claims.

A Compare this map with map C on page 29 to see who gained and who lost after the American Revolution.

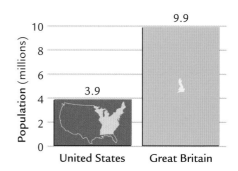

C **A SMALL POPULATION**

In 1790 the United States was a big country with a small population. Tiny Great Britain had more than twice as many people.

United States 3.9 — Great Britain 9.9
Population (millions)

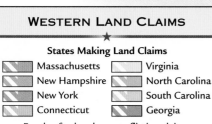

WESTERN LAND CLAIMS
★
States Making Land Claims

▨ Massachusetts	☐ Virginia
▨ New Hampshire	☐ North Carolina
▨ New York	☐ South Carolina
☐ Connecticut	▨ Georgia

Bands of color show conflicting claims.
Political boundaries of 1781

0   200   400 miles
0   200   400 kilometers

B Eight states made competing claims on western lands on the basis of their old colonial *charters*. Other states refused to ratify the Articles of Confederation until such claims were dropped.

British North America (Br.)

MA
NH
NY
MA
CT
RI
PA
NJ
MD
DE
ATLANTIC OCEAN
VA
NC
SC
GA
Louisiana (Sp.)
W. Florida (Br.)
E. Florida (Br.)
Gulf of Mexico

ASIA
ARCTIC OCEAN
Iceland
PACIFIC OCEAN
ATLANTIC OCEAN
SOUTH AMERICA
N
120°W   100°W   80°W
60°N   40°N   20°N

D State and European claims on western lands ignored the Native Americans who had lived throughout North America for centuries.

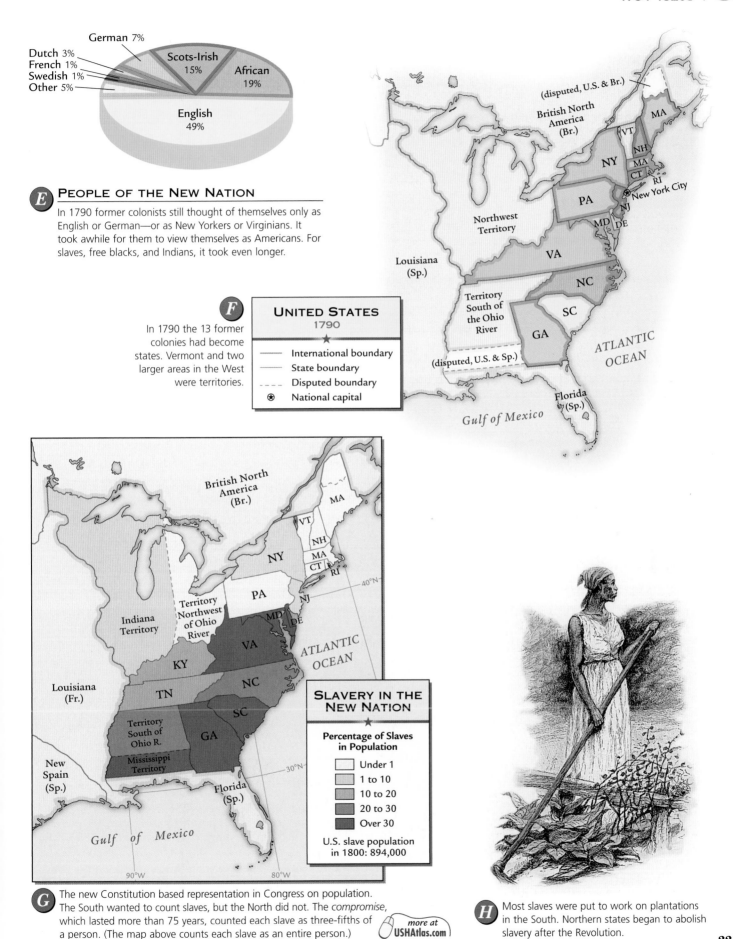

German 7%
Dutch 3%
French 1%
Swedish 1%
Other 5%

Scots-Irish
15%

African
19%

English
49%

E PEOPLE OF THE NEW NATION

In 1790 former colonists still thought of themselves only as English or German—or as New Yorkers or Virginians. It took awhile for them to view themselves as Americans. For slaves, free blacks, and Indians, it took even longer.

F

In 1790 the 13 former colonies had become states. Vermont and two larger areas in the West were territories.

UNITED STATES
1790
★

——— International boundary
——— State boundary
- - - - Disputed boundary
⊛ National capital

(disputed, U.S. & Br.)

British North America (Br.)

MA
VT
NY
NH
MA
CT
RI
⊛ New York City
PA
NJ
MD
DE
VA
NC
SC
GA
ATLANTIC OCEAN

Northwest Territory

Louisiana (Sp.)

Territory South of the Ohio River

(disputed, U.S. & Sp.)

Florida (Sp.)

Gulf of Mexico

British North America (Br.)

MA
VT
NY
NH
MA
CT
RI
PA
NJ
MD
DE
VA
NC
SC
GA
ATLANTIC OCEAN

Indiana Territory

Territory Northwest of Ohio River

40°N

KY
TN
Territory South of Ohio R.
Mississippi Territory

Louisiana (Fr.)

New Spain (Sp.)

Florida (Sp.)

30°N

Gulf of Mexico

90°W   80°W

SLAVERY IN THE NEW NATION
★

Percentage of Slaves in Population

Under 1
1 to 10
10 to 20
20 to 30
Over 30

U.S. slave population in 1800: 894,000

G The new Constitution based representation in Congress on population. The South wanted to count slaves, but the North did not. The *compromise*, which lasted more than 75 years, counted each slave as three-fifths of a person. (The map above counts each slave as an entire person.)

more at USHAtlas.com

H Most slaves were put to work on plantations in the South. Northern states began to abolish slavery after the Revolution.

33

A Growing Population Spreads West

In 1775 Daniel Boone helped build the Wilderness Road, the first wagon road across the Appalachians. Other wagon roads leading west soon followed.

★ After the Revolution, people headed west across the mountains, looking for affordable land to settle.

★ Despite Indian resistance to American claims, newly surveyed land was soon dotted with farms, schools, and towns.

★ By road and river, growing numbers of settlers pushed the frontier westward to the Mississippi River.

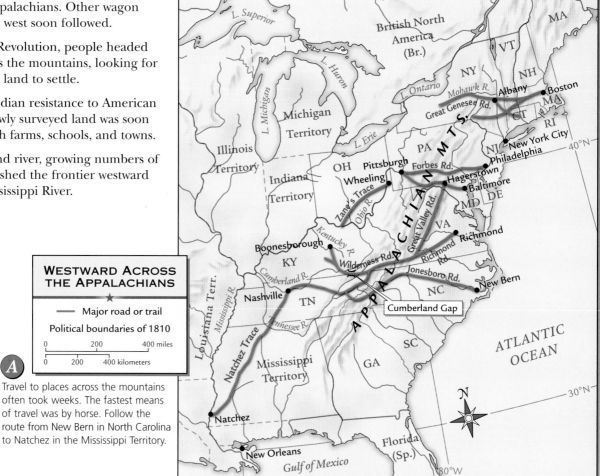

WESTWARD ACROSS THE APPALACHIANS
★

—— Major road or trail

Political boundaries of 1810

0   200   400 miles
0   200   400 kilometers

A Travel to places across the mountains often took weeks. The fastest means of travel was by horse. Follow the route from New Bern in North Carolina to Natchez in the Mississippi Territory.

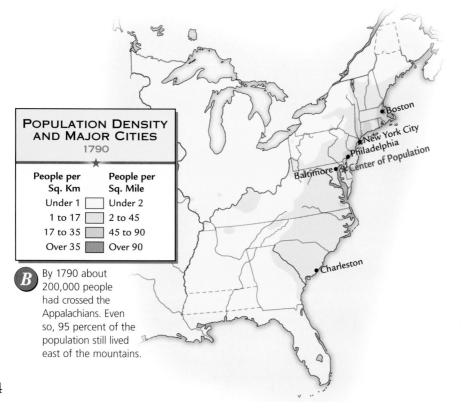

POPULATION DENSITY AND MAJOR CITIES
1790
★

People per Sq. Km		People per Sq. Mile	
Under 1		Under 2	
1 to 17		2 to 45	
17 to 35		45 to 90	
Over 35		Over 90	

B By 1790 about 200,000 people had crossed the Appalachians. Even so, 95 percent of the population still lived east of the mountains.

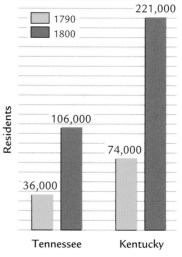

C POPULATION BOOM

Once an area in the territories had 60,000 settlers, it could apply for statehood. Kentucky became a state in 1792, Tennessee in 1796.

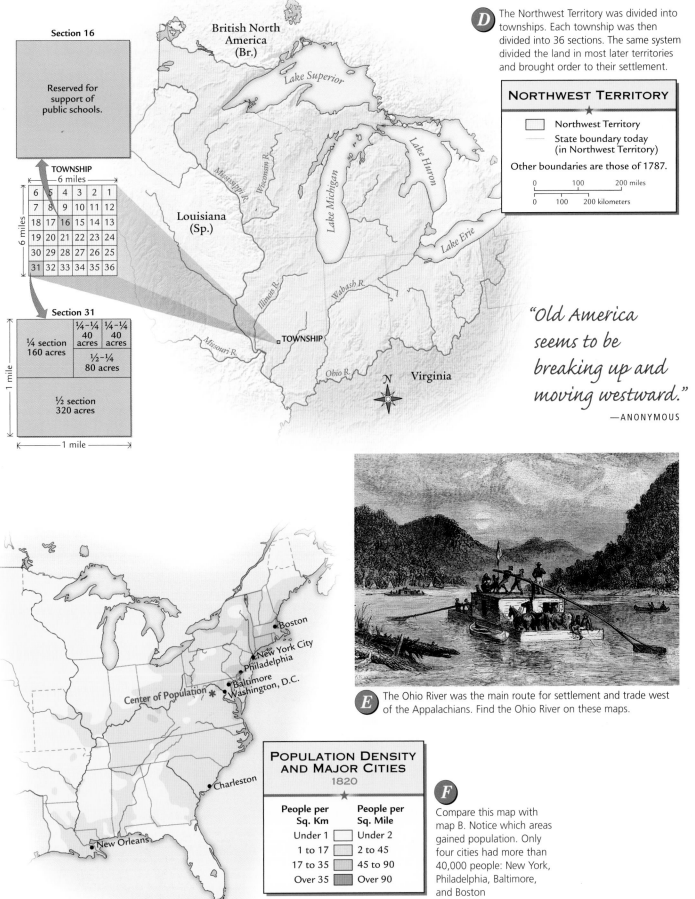

Section 16

Reserved for support of public schools.

TOWNSHIP

6 miles

6	5	4	3	2	1
7	8	9	10	11	12
18	17	16	15	14	13
19	20	21	22	23	24
30	29	28	27	26	25
31	32	33	34	35	36

6 miles

Section 31

1 mile

¼ section 160 acres	¼–¼ 40 acres	¼–¼ 40 acres
	½–¼ 80 acres	
½ section 320 acres		

1 mile

D The Northwest Territory was divided into townships. Each township was then divided into 36 sections. The same system divided the land in most later territories and brought order to their settlement.

NORTHWEST TERRITORY
★

☐ Northwest Territory
— State boundary today (in Northwest Territory)

Other boundaries are those of 1787.

0   100   200 miles
0   100   200 kilometers

British North America (Br.)

Lake Superior

Louisiana (Sp.)

Wisconsin R.
Mississippi R.
Lake Michigan
Lake Huron
Lake Erie

Illinois R.
Wabash R.
■ TOWNSHIP

Missouri R.
Ohio R.

N

Virginia

"Old America seems to be breaking up and moving westward."
—ANONYMOUS

E The Ohio River was the main route for settlement and trade west of the Appalachians. Find the Ohio River on these maps.

Boston
New York City
Philadelphia
Baltimore
Washington, D.C.
Center of Population ✳
Charleston
New Orleans

POPULATION DENSITY AND MAJOR CITIES
1820
★

People per Sq. Km	People per Sq. Mile
Under 1	Under 2
1 to 17	2 to 45
17 to 35	45 to 90
Over 35	Over 90

F Compare this map with map B. Notice which areas gained population. Only four cities had more than 40,000 people: New York, Philadelphia, Baltimore, and Boston

Neighbors Gain Their Independence

In the early 1800s, the spirit of revolution swept from the United States through the rest of the Americas.

★ Mexico and several other colonies broke away from Spain. Haiti won independence from France.

★ Russia, Austria, and Prussia feared revolution and offered to help Spain and France regain their colonies.

★ President James Monroe warned Europe that the Americas were off-limits to future colonization.

★ His policy, known as the "Monroe Doctrine," established the United States as the dominant country of the Americas.

A New Spain's last missions were built in California. Most missions had not only a church but a courtyard lined with workshops, storerooms, and places to cook, eat, and sleep. Fields, stables, and water were usually nearby.

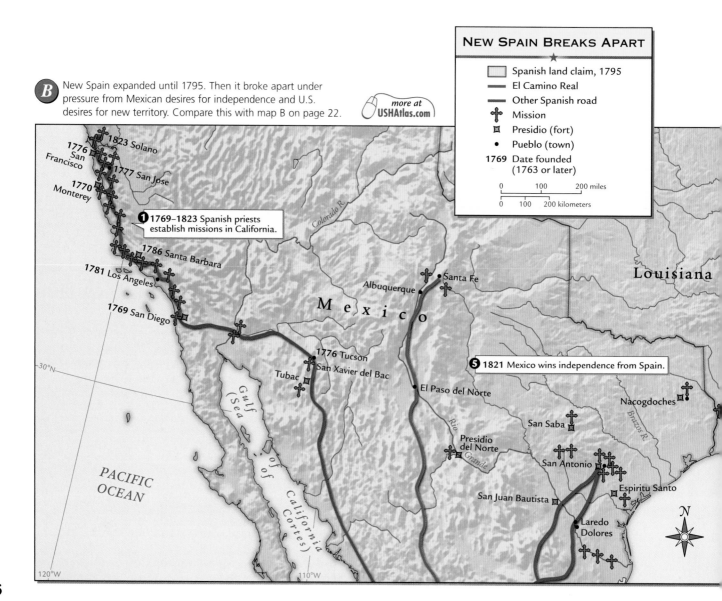

B New Spain expanded until 1795. Then it broke apart under pressure from Mexican desires for independence and U.S. desires for new territory. Compare this with map B on page 22.

more at USHAtlas.com

NEW SPAIN BREAKS APART
★
- Spanish land claim, 1795
- El Camino Real
- Other Spanish road
- ✝ Mission
- Presidio (fort)
- • Pueblo (town)
- **1769** Date founded (1763 or later)

0   100   200 miles
0 100   200 kilometers

1823 Solano
1776 San Francisco
1777 San Jose
1770 Monterey

1 1769–1823 Spanish priests establish missions in California.

1786 Santa Barbara
1781 Los Angeles
1769 San Diego

Colorado R.

Albuquerque • Santa Fe

M e x i c o

1776 Tucson
San Xavier del Bac
Tubac

Louisiana

5 1821 Mexico wins independence from Spain.

• El Paso del Norte

Nacogdoches

San Saba

Rio Grande

Presidio del Norte

Brazos R.

San Antonio

San Juan Bautista

Espiritu Santo

~30°N

PACIFIC OCEAN

Gulf (Sea) of California (Cortes)

Laredo
Dolores

120°W   110°W   🧭 N

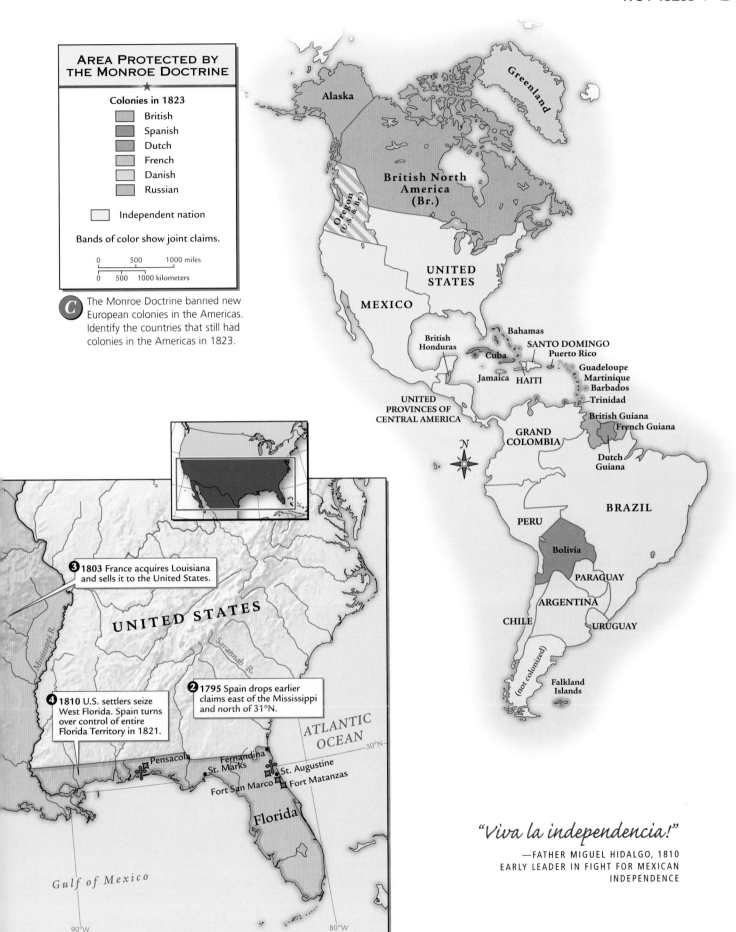

AREA PROTECTED BY THE MONROE DOCTRINE

★

Colonies in 1823

British
Spanish
Dutch
French
Danish
Russian

Independent nation

Bands of color show joint claims.

| 0 | 500 | 1000 miles |
| 0 | 500 | 1000 kilometers |

C The Monroe Doctrine banned new European colonies in the Americas. Identify the countries that still had colonies in the Americas in 1823.

Alaska

Greenland

British North America (Br.)

Oregon (U.S. & Br.)

UNITED STATES

MEXICO

British Honduras

Bahamas

Cuba

Jamaica

HAITI

SANTO DOMINGO
Puerto Rico

Guadeloupe
Martinique
Barbados

Trinidad

UNITED PROVINCES OF CENTRAL AMERICA

GRAND COLOMBIA

British Guiana
French Guiana

Dutch Guiana

PERU

BRAZIL

Bolivia

PARAGUAY

CHILE

ARGENTINA

URUGUAY

(not colonized)

Falkland Islands

❸ 1803 France acquires Louisiana and sells it to the United States.

UNITED STATES

Mississippi R.

Savannah R.

❷ 1795 Spain drops earlier claims east of the Mississippi and north of 31°N.

❹ 1810 U.S. settlers seize West Florida. Spain turns over control of entire Florida Territory in 1821.

ATLANTIC OCEAN

30°N

Pensacola

Fernandina
St. Marks

St. Augustine

Fort San Marco

Fort Matanzas

Florida

Gulf of Mexico

90°W

80°W

"Viva la independencia!"

—FATHER MIGUEL HIDALGO, 1810
EARLY LEADER IN FIGHT FOR MEXICAN INDEPENDENCE

Expansion and Reform
1801–1861

| | | 1803 **Louisiana Purchase** doubles size of U.S. | 1804–1806 **Lewis and Clark** explore Louisiana Territory. | 1812–1815 **War of 1812** between U.S. and Britain. |

1800 **1810** **1820**

1801 **Thomas Jefferson** becomes third U.S. President.

1806–1807 **Pike** explores western Great Plains.

1821 **Mexico gains independence** from Spain.

Growing With the Louisiana Territory

The Louisiana Purchase was the first step in the expansion of the country during the 1800s.

★ When the United States bought the Louisiana Territory from France in 1803, the size of the country doubled.

★ In 1804–1806, an expedition led by Meriwether Lewis and William Clark explored the new territory.

★ Information they gathered about the route and its people, terrain, plants, and wildlife guided later exploration and settlement.

A Much of the Louisiana Territory consisted of the Great Plains. In 1803 they were inhabited by Native Americans such as these hunters painted by George Catlin.

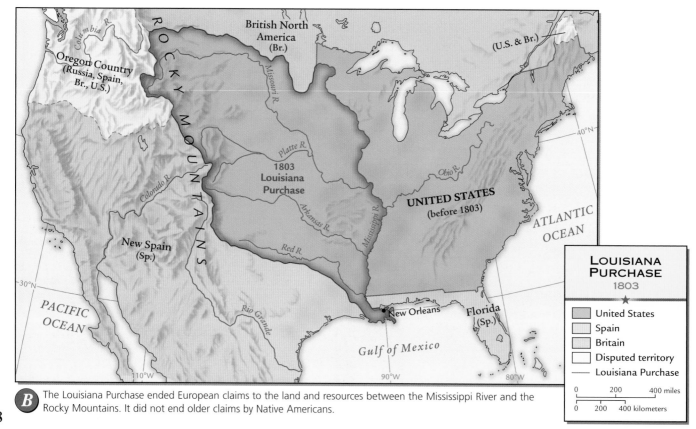

LOUISIANA PURCHASE
1803
★

- United States
- Spain
- Britain
- Disputed territory
- Louisiana Purchase

0   200   400 miles
0   200   400 kilometers

B The Louisiana Purchase ended European claims to the land and resources between the Mississippi River and the Rocky Mountains. It did not end older claims by Native Americans.

38

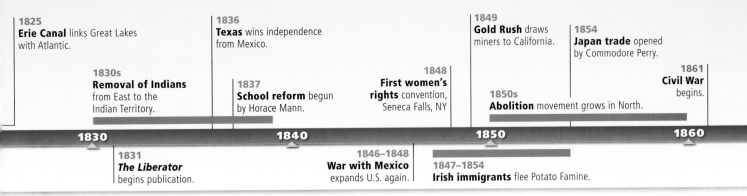

1825	1836	1849	1854
Erie Canal links Great Lakes with Atlantic.	**Texas** wins independence from Mexico.	**Gold Rush** draws miners to California.	**Japan trade** opened by Commodore Perry.

1830s
Removal of Indians from East to the Indian Territory.

1837
School reform begun by Horace Mann.

1848
First women's rights convention, Seneca Falls, NY

1850s
Abolition movement grows in North.

1861
Civil War begins.

1830   **1840**   **1850**   **1860**

1831
The Liberator begins publication.

1846–1848
War with Mexico expands U.S. again.

1847–1854
Irish immigrants flee Potato Famine.

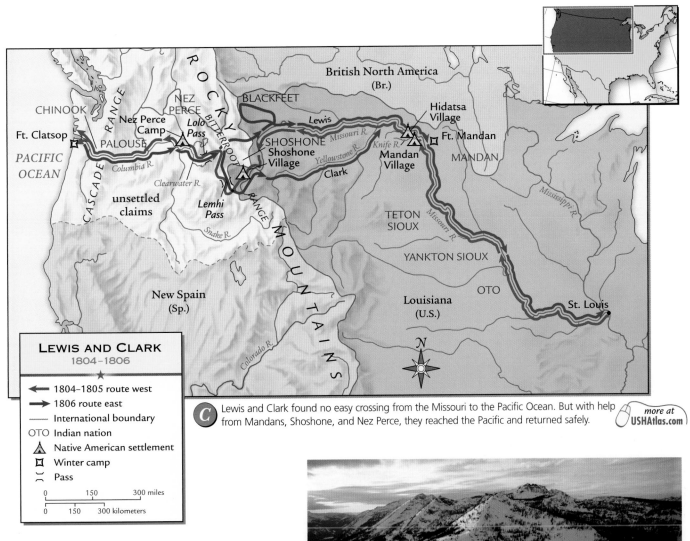

LEWIS AND CLARK
1804–1806
★

⬅ 1804–1805 route west
➡ 1806 route east
— International boundary
OTO Indian nation
▲ Native American settlement
⌂ Winter camp
) (Pass

0   150   300 miles
0   150   300 kilometers

C Lewis and Clark found no easy crossing from the Missouri to the Pacific Ocean. But with help from Mandans, Shoshone, and Nez Perce, they reached the Pacific and returned safely.

"I discovered immense ranges of high mountains still to the West..."

—CAPTAIN MERIWETHER LEWIS, AUGUST 12, 1805
DESCRIBING THE VIEW FROM LEMHI PASS
ON THE CONTINENTAL DIVIDE

D When the Lewis and Clark expedition began to climb the Rockies, they hoped to see an easy route to the Pacific Coast once they reached the top. All they saw were more mountains.

39

War of 1812 and Indian Resettlement

In 1812 the United States went to war with Great Britain over the seizure of American ships trading in Europe.

★ Organized by the Shawnee leader Tecumseh, a confederation of eastern American Indian tribes had been fighting U.S. expansion. Now they joined forces with the British.

★ In 1814 the Treaty of Ghent officially ended the war. Neither country lost or gained territory, but the British gave up attempts to stop U.S. expansion.

★ Indians lost the most. By 1840 the United States gained control of more than 100 million acres of Indian land.

B The Battle of New Orleans, the most famous American victory of the War of 1812, was fought after the war was officially over. Neither side knew that a peace treaty had been signed weeks before.

A

British interference with U.S. shipping and the expansion of U.S. settlement led to the War of 1812. Both issues affected the Great Lakes and the Gulf Coast, where many battles of the war took place.

more at USHAtlas.com

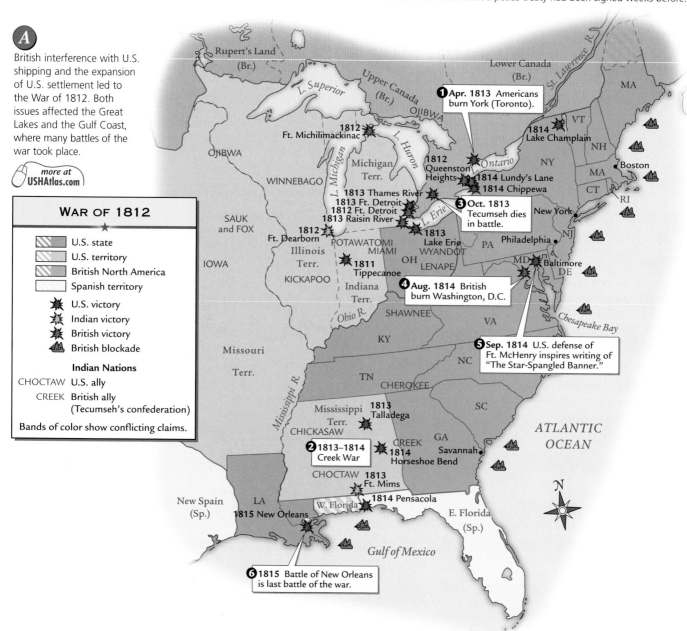

WAR OF 1812
★

- U.S. state
- U.S. territory
- British North America
- Spanish territory
- ✸ U.S. victory
- ✸ Indian victory
- ✸ British victory
- British blockade

Indian Nations

CHOCTAW — U.S. ally

CREEK — British ally (Tecumseh's confederation)

Bands of color show conflicting claims.

1 Apr. 1813 Americans burn York (Toronto).

3 Oct. 1813 Tecumseh dies in battle.

4 Aug. 1814 British burn Washington, D.C.

5 Sep. 1814 U.S. defense of Ft. McHenry inspires writing of "The Star-Spangled Banner."

2 1813–1814 Creek War

6 1815 Battle of New Orleans is last battle of the war.

Rupert's Land (Br.)

Lower Canada (Br.)

Upper Canada (Br.)

St. Lawrence R.

L. Superior

OJIBWA

MA

VT

1814 Lake Champlain

NH

1812 Ft. Michilimackinac

L. Huron

Michigan Terr.

1812 Queenston Heights

NY

Boston

OJIBWA

L. Ontario

1814 Lundy's Lane

MA

WINNEBAGO

L. Michigan

1813 Thames River
1813 Ft. Detroit
1812 Ft. Detroit
1813 Raisin River

1814 Chippewa

CT

RI

SAUK and FOX

L. Erie

New York

NJ

1812 Ft. Dearborn

POTAWATOMI

1813 Lake Erie

PA

Philadelphia

IOWA

Illinois Terr.

MIAMI

OH

WYANDOT

LENAPE

MD

Baltimore

DE

KICKAPOO

1811 Tippecanoe

Indiana Terr.

Ohio R.

SHAWNEE

VA

Chesapeake Bay

Missouri Terr.

KY

NC

ATLANTIC OCEAN

TN

CHEROKEE

SC

Mississippi R.

Mississippi Terr.

1813 Talladega

CHICKASAW

CREEK

GA

Savannah

1814 Horseshoe Bend

CHOCTAW

1813 Ft. Mims

New Spain (Sp.)

LA

W. Florida

1814 Pensacola

E. Florida (Sp.)

1815 New Orleans

Gulf of Mexico

N

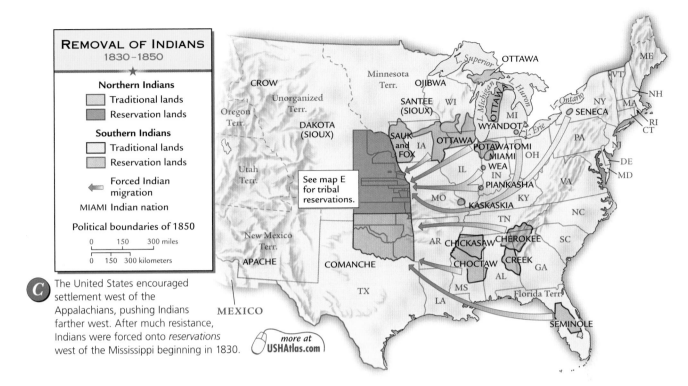

REMOVAL OF INDIANS
1830–1850

★

Northern Indians
Traditional lands
Reservation lands

Southern Indians
Traditional lands
Reservation lands

← Forced Indian migration

MIAMI Indian nation

Political boundaries of 1850

0   150   300 miles
0   150   300 kilometers

See map E for tribal reservations.

more at
USHAtlas.com

C The United States encouraged settlement west of the Appalachians, pushing Indians farther west. After much resistance, Indians were forced onto *reservations* west of the Mississippi beginning in 1830.

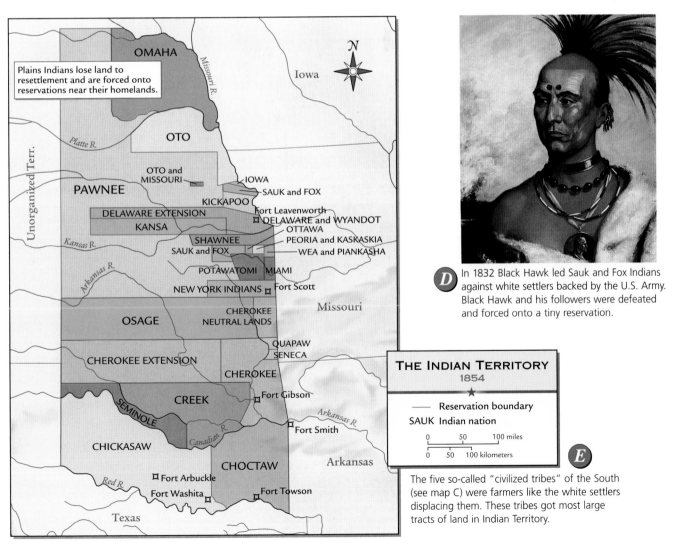

Plains Indians lose land to resettlement and are forced onto reservations near their homelands.

N

OMAHA

OTO

OTO and MISSOURI

PAWNEE

IOWA
SAUK and FOX
KICKAPOO
Fort Leavenworth
DELAWARE EXTENSION
DELAWARE and WYANDOT
KANSA
OTTAWA
SHAWNEE
PEORIA and KASKASKIA
SAUK and FOX
WEA and PIANKASHA
POTAWATOMI   MIAMI
NEW YORK INDIANS   Fort Scott

OSAGE
CHEROKEE NEUTRAL LANDS
Missouri

QUAPAW
SENECA
CHEROKEE EXTENSION
CHEROKEE

CREEK
Fort Gibson
SEMINOLE
Fort Smith

CHICKASAW
CHOCTAW
Arkansas

Fort Arbuckle
Fort Washita   Fort Towson

Texas

Unorganized Terr.

Platte R.
Kansas R.
Arkansas R.
Missouri R.
Arkansas R.
Canadian R.
Red R.

D In 1832 Black Hawk led Sauk and Fox Indians against white settlers backed by the U.S. Army. Black Hawk and his followers were defeated and forced onto a tiny reservation.

THE INDIAN TERRITORY
1854

★

— Reservation boundary

SAUK Indian nation

0   50   100 miles
0   50   100 kilometers

E The five so-called "civilized tribes" of the South (see map C) were farmers like the white settlers displacing them. These tribes got most large tracts of land in Indian Territory.

Exploration Opens the West

Between 1790 and 1820, the United States doubled its size and added ten new states.

★ The larger country offered new opportunities to the white settlers who replaced the Indians.

★ During the first half of the 1800s, Americans blazed new trails, gathered information, and scouted the West for places to settle.

★ By 1850, Americans had settled nearly all the land east of the Mississippi River and along the western coast of the Gulf of Mexico. Few settlers had moved farther west onto the vast, treeless Great Plains.

A In 1820 Captain Stephen Long described the western plains as the "Great American Desert." Few settlers disturbed the people and wildlife of the plains for years afterward.

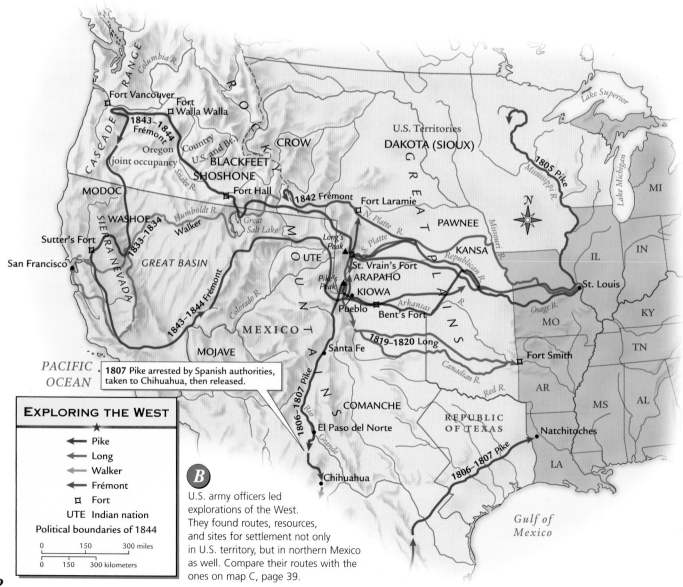

EXPLORING THE WEST

★

◄— Pike
◄— Long
◄— Walker
◄— Frémont
⌂ Fort
UTE Indian nation
Political boundaries of 1844

0 — 150 — 300 miles
0 — 150 — 300 kilometers

1807 Pike arrested by Spanish authorities, taken to Chihuahua, then released.

B U.S. army officers led explorations of the West. They found routes, resources, and sites for settlement not only in U.S. territory, but in northern Mexico as well. Compare their routes with the ones on map C, page 39.

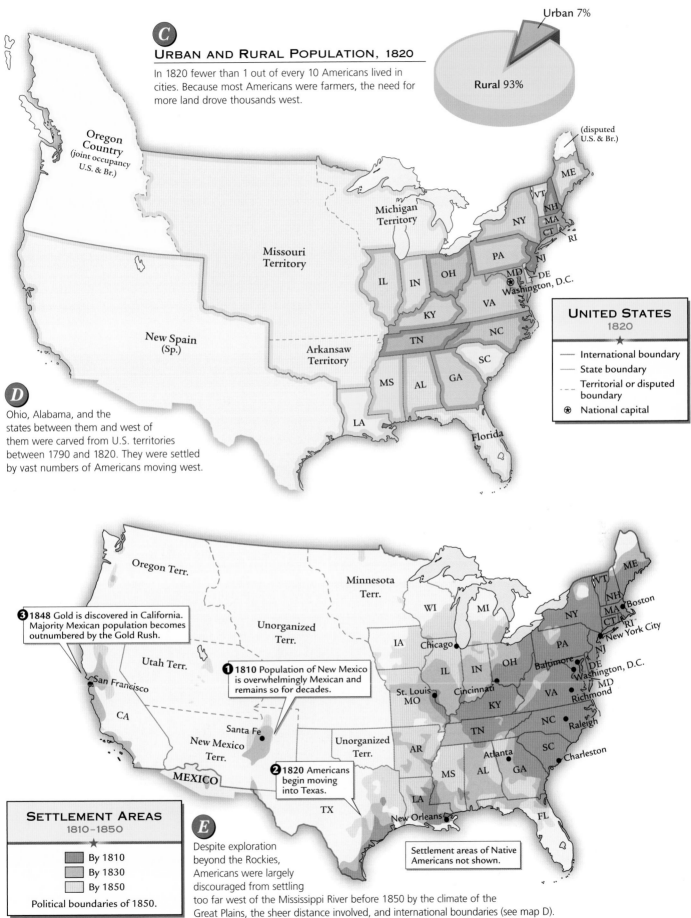

C

URBAN AND RURAL POPULATION, 1820

In 1820 fewer than 1 out of every 10 Americans lived in cities. Because most Americans were farmers, the need for more land drove thousands west.

Urban 7%

Rural 93%

D

Ohio, Alabama, and the states between them and west of them were carved from U.S. territories between 1790 and 1820. They were settled by vast numbers of Americans moving west.

UNITED STATES
1820
★
— International boundary
— State boundary
--- Territorial or disputed boundary
⊛ National capital

❸ 1848 Gold is discovered in California. Majority Mexican population becomes outnumbered by the Gold Rush.

❶ 1810 Population of New Mexico is overwhelmingly Mexican and remains so for decades.

❷ 1820 Americans begin moving into Texas.

SETTLEMENT AREAS
1810–1850
★
By 1810
By 1830
By 1850
Political boundaries of 1850.

E

Despite exploration beyond the Rockies, Americans were largely discouraged from settling too far west of the Mississippi River before 1850 by the climate of the Great Plains, the sheer distance involved, and international boundaries (see map D).

Settlement areas of Native Americans not shown.

Travel in a Growing Nation

The great size of the growing United States made overland transportation difficult and expensive.

★ In the early 1800s, travel by steamboat was the fastest and least expensive way to get around.

★ During the 1820s and 1830s, canals were built to link eastern cities to the Great Lakes and western rivers.

★ In the 1840s, railroads improved travel again, and by 1860 railroad lines ran through most of the eastern United States.

NATURAL WATERWAYS
★

United States, 1825
Inland boat service
Coastal steamboat service

0   200   400 miles
0   200   400 kilometers

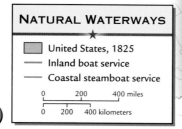

A Because there were few passable roads in the young nation, heavy goods going long distances usually were transported on waterways. Compare this map with map B on page 24.

B Robert Fulton invented the first successful steamboat, the *Clermont*, in 1807. Steamboats soon dominated eastern waterways. By 1860 they also were the primary mode of travel on western rivers.

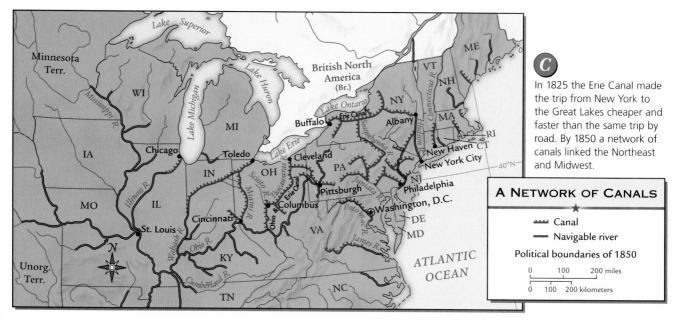

C In 1825 the Erie Canal made the trip from New York to the Great Lakes cheaper and faster than the same trip by road. By 1850 a network of canals linked the Northeast and Midwest.

A NETWORK OF CANALS
★

Canal
Navigable river

Political boundaries of 1850

0   100   200 miles
0   100   200 kilometers

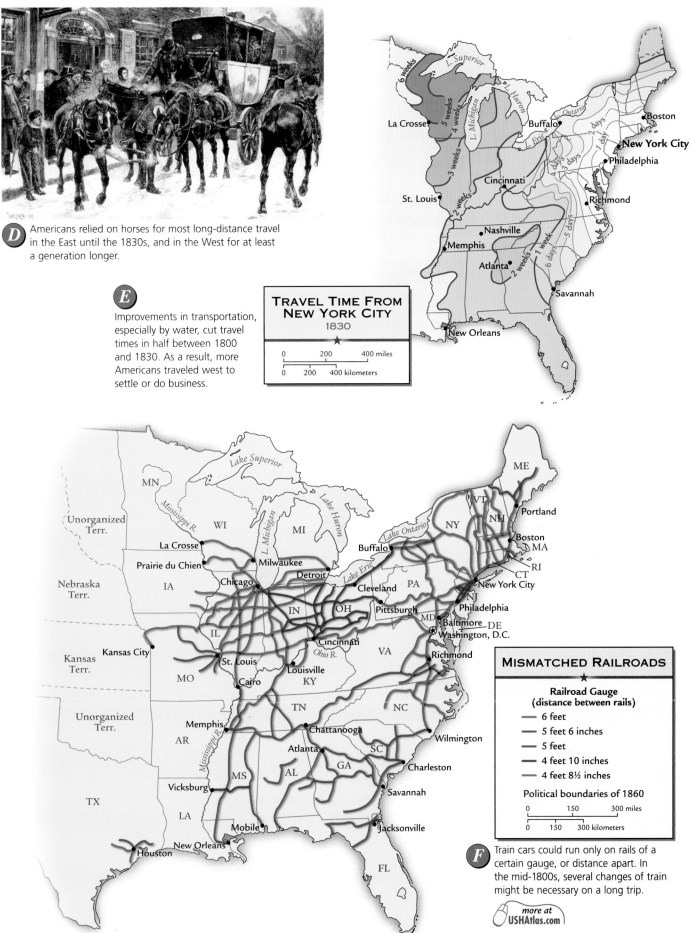

D Americans relied on horses for most long-distance travel in the East until the 1830s, and in the West for at least a generation longer.

E Improvements in transportation, especially by water, cut travel times in half between 1800 and 1830. As a result, more Americans traveled west to settle or do business.

TRAVEL TIME FROM NEW YORK CITY
1830

★

0   200   400 miles

0   200   400 kilometers

MISMATCHED RAILROADS

★

Railroad Gauge
(distance between rails)

— 6 feet
— 5 feet 6 inches
— 5 feet
— 4 feet 10 inches
— 4 feet 8½ inches

Political boundaries of 1860

0   150   300 miles

0   150   300 kilometers

F Train cars could run only on rails of a certain gauge, or distance apart. In the mid-1800s, several changes of train might be necessary on a long trip.

more at
USHAtlas.com

45

America Expands to the Pacific

In the 1840s, the United States sought land from Texas, Mexico, and Britain so that it could expand to the Pacific.

★ Texas had won independence from Mexico in 1836. The United States *annexed* it in 1845.

★ In 1848, victory in the War with Mexico gave the northern third of Mexico to the United States.

★ Farther north, the United States gained the southern half of Oregon Country in an 1846 agreement with Britain.

Unorganized Terr.

Arkansas River

N

UNITED STATES

TN

AR

MS

❸ 1845 Texas annexed by United States

Santa Fe

APACHE

COMANCHE

Red River

Clarksville

CADDO

❶ Mar. 2, 1836 Republic of Texas declares independence.

El Paso

REPUBLIC OF TEXAS

Sabine R.

LA

Rio Grande

Nacogdoches

Mississippi River

Chihuahua

Feb. 23–Mar. 6, 1836
The Alamo
Dec. 11, 1835
San Antonio

Washington

Nueces R.

San Felipe de Austin

Apr. 21, 1836
San Jacinto

❷ Apr. 22, 1836 Mexican army surrenders to Texas.

Corpus Christi

MEXICO

Gulf of Mexico

Matamoros

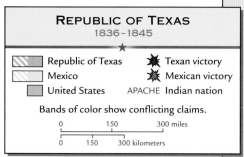

REPUBLIC OF TEXAS
1836–1845
★

▨	Republic of Texas	✸	Texan victory
☐	Mexico	✸	Mexican victory
▨	United States	APACHE	Indian nation

Bands of color show conflicting claims.

0   150   300 miles
0   150   300 kilometers

A In 1820 slavery was banned in most U.S. territories. The next year Americans from slave states began to move to Texas. They won independence from Mexico in 1836, and in 1845 the United States annexed Texas as a slave state.

more at USHAtlas.com

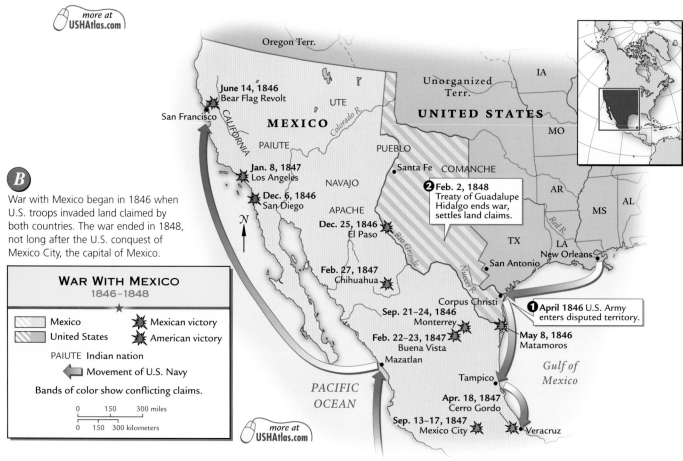

Oregon Terr.

IA

June 14, 1846
Bear Flag Revolt

UTE

Unorganized Terr.

San Francisco

CALIFORNIA

MEXICO

Colorado R.

UNITED STATES

MO

PAIUTE

PUEBLO

Jan. 8, 1847
Los Angeles

NAVAJO

Santa Fe

COMANCHE

AR

❷ Feb. 2, 1848
Treaty of Guadalupe Hidalgo ends war, settles land claims.

AL

Dec. 6, 1846
San Diego

APACHE

MS

Dec. 25, 1846
El Paso

N

Rio Grande

TX

Red R.

LA

New Orleans

B

War with Mexico began in 1846 when U.S. troops invaded land claimed by both countries. The war ended in 1848, not long after the U.S. conquest of Mexico City, the capital of Mexico.

Feb. 27, 1847
Chihuahua

Nueces R.

San Antonio

Corpus Christi

❶ April 1846 U.S. Army enters disputed territory.

Sep. 21–24, 1846
Monterrey

May 8, 1846
Matamoros

Feb. 22–23, 1847
Buena Vista

Mazatlan

Tampico

Gulf of Mexico

WAR WITH MEXICO
1846–1848
★

▨	Mexico	✸	Mexican victory
▨	United States	✸	American victory
PAIUTE	Indian nation		
⬅	Movement of U.S. Navy		

Bands of color show conflicting claims.

0   150   300 miles
0   150   300 kilometers

more at USHAtlas.com

PACIFIC OCEAN

Apr. 18, 1847
Cerro Gordo

Sep. 13–17, 1847
Mexico City

Veracruz

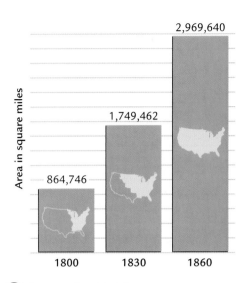

2,969,640

1,749,462

864,746

Area in square miles

1800   1830   1860

C Mexican *vaqueros*, or cowboys, developed ranching methods suitable for the Southwest, which their English-speaking neighbors later adopted. *Vaqueros* were among the 75,000 Mexican residents of lands acquired by the United States during the 1840s.

D LAND AREA OF THE UNITED STATES

The United States tripled in size between 1800 and 1860. Many Americans believed it fulfilled their "Manifest Destiny" to inhabit the continent from the Atlantic to the Pacific.

5 1846 Split by Oregon Treaty; Britain gets northern part

1 1818 Split by Convention of 1818. U.S. exchanges land north of the 49th parallel for land south of it.

3 1842 Webster-Ashburton Treaty with Britain

Oregon Country

Red River Basin

Columbia R.

L. Superior

L. Michigan

L. Huron

L. Ontario

L. Erie

Missouri R.

PACIFIC OCEAN

Great Salt Lake

Mexican Cession

See callout 2

Colorado R.

Ohio R.

ATLANTIC OCEAN

4 1845 Annexed by Act of U.S. Congress

6 1848 Ceded by Treaty of Guadalupe Hidalgo

Gadsden Purchase

Texas Annexation

Mississippi R.

7 1853 From Mexico

Florida Cession

2 1819 Adams-Onis Treaty with Spain

AMERICAN EXPANSION
1818–1853
★

State boundaries of today

0   250   500 miles

0   250   500 kilometers

E The United States gained most of its western land in four steps between 1845 and 1853. Each acquisition was different: an annexation, a peaceful treaty, a treaty ending a war, and a purchase.

more at
USHAtlas.com

West Across the Rockies

Until the 1860s, trails provided the only routes for settlers, traders, soldiers, freight, and mail bound for the West.

★ Westward journeys covered great distances at walking speed. Water was scarce, help far away.

★ During the 1840s, wagon trails saw heavy use from farmers seeking land, miners seeking gold, and *Mormons* seeking religious freedom.

★ Increasing western settlement soon demanded better trails for freight and, briefly, for the Pony Express.

A *Emigrants* on the Oregon Trail traveled nearly half a year before they reached their destination. In this reenactment, a wagon train nears mountains after crossing the vast plains.

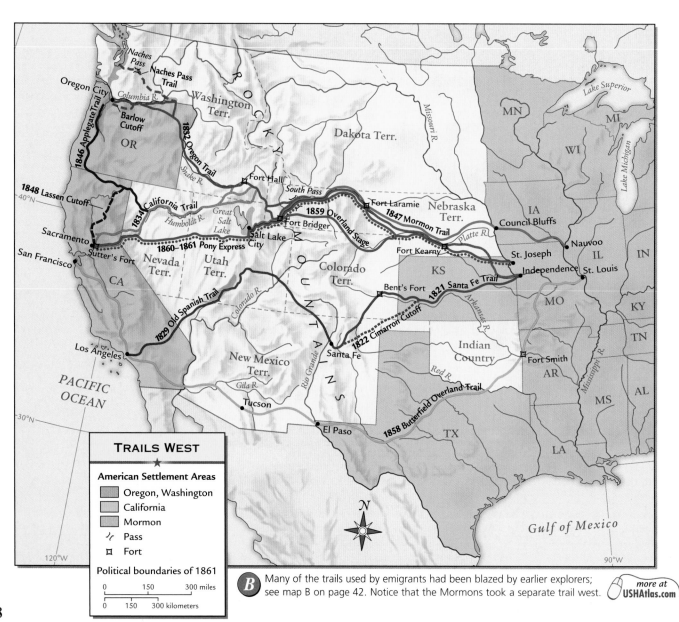

TRAILS WEST
★
American Settlement Areas
- Oregon, Washington
- California
- Mormon
- Pass
- Fort

Political boundaries of 1861

0   150   300 miles
0   150   300 kilometers

B Many of the trails used by emigrants had been blazed by earlier explorers; see map B on page 42. Notice that the Mormons took a separate trail west.

more at USHAtlas.com

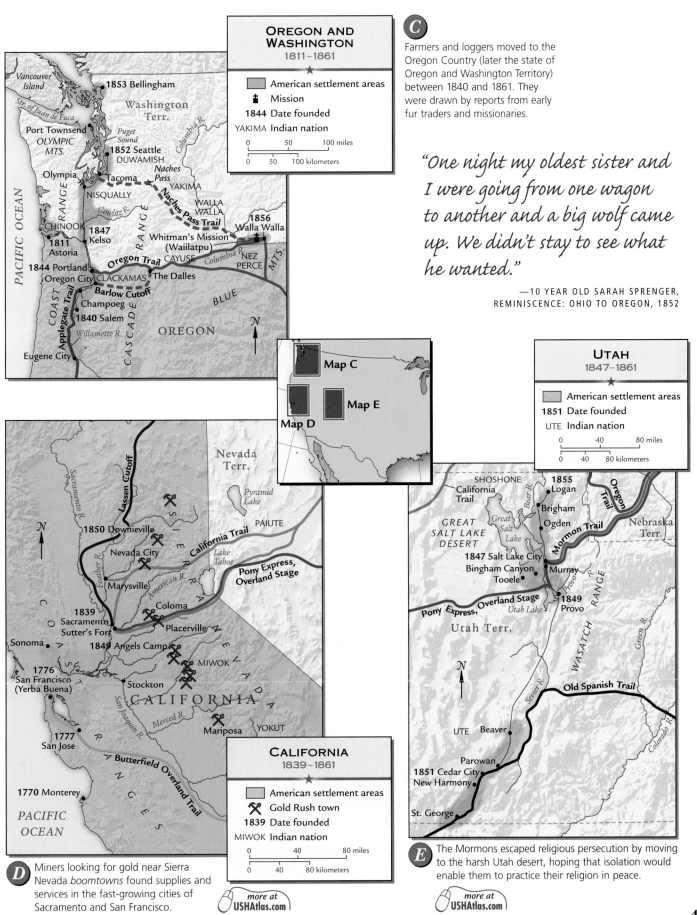

OREGON AND WASHINGTON
1811–1861

☆

☐ American settlement areas
⚑ Mission
1844 Date founded
YAKIMA Indian nation

0   50   100 miles
0   50   100 kilometers

C Farmers and loggers moved to the Oregon Country (later the state of Oregon and Washington Territory) between 1840 and 1861. They were drawn by reports from early fur traders and missionaries.

"One night my oldest sister and I were going from one wagon to another and a big wolf came up. We didn't stay to see what he wanted."

—10 YEAR OLD SARAH SPRENGER,
REMINISCENCE: OHIO TO OREGON, 1852

Map C
Map E
Map D

UTAH
1847–1861

☆

☐ American settlement areas
1851 Date founded
UTE Indian nation

0   40   80 miles
0   40   80 kilometers

CALIFORNIA
1839–1861

☆

☐ American settlement areas
⚒ Gold Rush town
1839 Date founded
MIWOK Indian nation

0   40   80 miles
0   40   80 kilometers

D Miners looking for gold near Sierra Nevada *boomtowns* found supplies and services in the fast-growing cities of Sacramento and San Francisco.

E The Mormons escaped religious persecution by moving to the harsh Utah desert, hoping that isolation would enable them to practice their religion in peace.

more at USHAtlas.com

more at USHAtlas.com

Immigrants and Runaway Slaves

Opportunity in the growing United States was a beacon that drew people from other parts of the world.

★ Between 1820 and 1860, about 5.1 million *immigrants* came to the United States, most from Northern and Western Europe.

★ Freedom in the North and in Canada drew African American slaves escaping the South.

★ By the 1830s, reformers were supporting the *abolition* movement to abolish slavery and the *Underground Railroad* to aid escaped slaves.

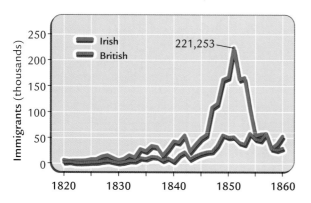

A IRISH AND BRITISH IMMIGRANTS

Immigrants from *rural* Ireland came to America to escape poverty. Their numbers soared to unprecedented levels in the 1840s and 1850s after the Irish potato crop failed.

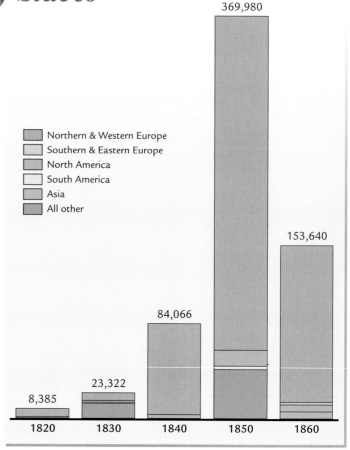

Northern & Western Europe
Southern & Eastern Europe
North America
South America
Asia
All other

B IMMIGRANT ORIGINS

Most immigrants were from the same places as the original colonists (see graph E on page 33). Others often faced bigotry and discrimination. For example, in many U.S. cities Irish immigrants were denied jobs.

more at USHAtlas.com

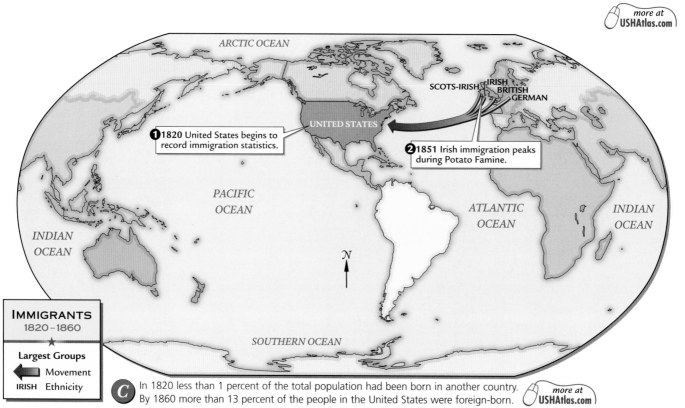

① 1820 United States begins to record immigration statistics.

② 1851 Irish immigration peaks during Potato Famine.

SCOTS-IRISH IRISH BRITISH GERMAN

UNITED STATES

ARCTIC OCEAN
PACIFIC OCEAN
ATLANTIC OCEAN
INDIAN OCEAN
INDIAN OCEAN
SOUTHERN OCEAN

N

IMMIGRANTS
1820–1860
★

Largest Groups
⬅ Movement
IRISH Ethnicity

C In 1820 less than 1 percent of the total population had been born in another country. By 1860 more than 13 percent of the people in the United States were foreign-born.

more at USHAtlas.com

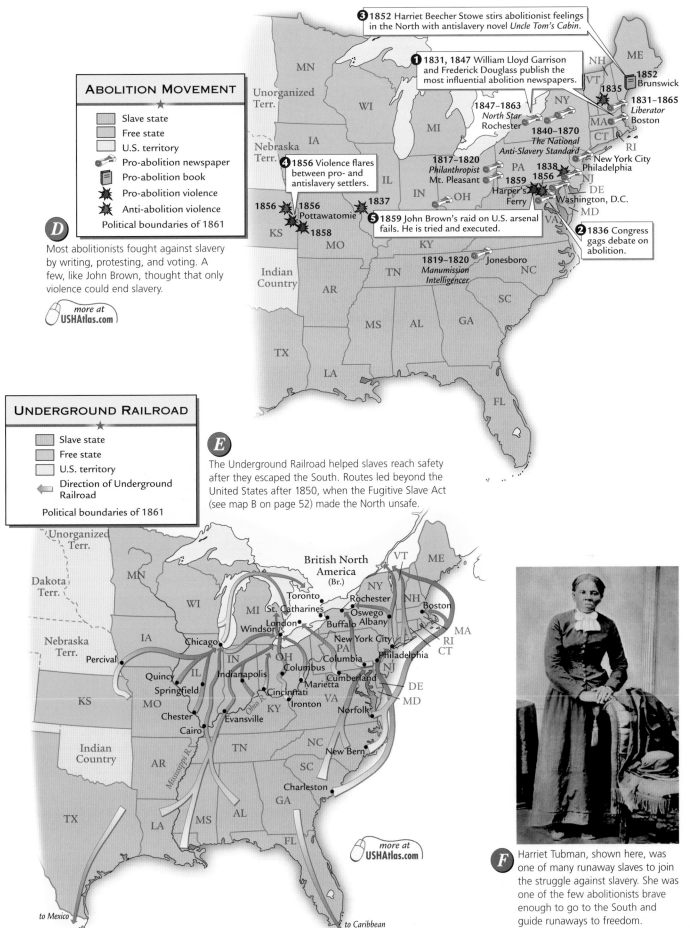

ABOLITION MOVEMENT

★

- Slave state
- Free state
- U.S. territory
- Pro-abolition newspaper
- Pro-abolition book
- Pro-abolition violence
- Anti-abolition violence
- Political boundaries of 1861

D Most abolitionists fought against slavery by writing, protesting, and voting. A few, like John Brown, thought that only violence could end slavery.

more at USHAtlas.com

3 1852 Harriet Beecher Stowe stirs abolitionist feelings in the North with antislavery novel *Uncle Tom's Cabin*.

1 1831, 1847 William Lloyd Garrison and Frederick Douglass publish the most influential abolition newspapers.

1852 Brunswick

1847–1863 *North Star* Rochester

1835

1831–1865 *Liberator* Boston

1840–1870 *The National Anti-Slavery Standard*

4 1856 Violence flares between pro- and antislavery settlers.

1817–1820 *Philanthropist* Mt. Pleasant

New York City
Philadelphia

1838
1856

1859
Harper's Ferry

1856
1856 Pottawatomie

1837

1858

5 1859 John Brown's raid on U.S. arsenal fails. He is tried and executed.

Washington, D.C.

2 1836 Congress gags debate on abolition.

1819–1820 *Manumission Intelligencer* Jonesboro

MN, Unorganized Terr., WI, IA, Nebraska Terr., IL, IN, OH, KS, MO, KY, Indian Country, AR, TN, NC, MS, AL, GA, SC, TX, LA, FL, NH, VT, ME, NY, MA, CT, RI, PA, NJ, DE, MD, VA

UNDERGROUND RAILROAD

★

- Slave state
- Free state
- U.S. territory
- Direction of Underground Railroad
- Political boundaries of 1861

E The Underground Railroad helped slaves reach safety after they escaped the South. Routes led beyond the United States after 1850, when the Fugitive Slave Act (see map B on page 52) made the North unsafe.

British North America (Br.)

Toronto, St. Catharines, Rochester, Oswego, London, Windsor, Buffalo, Albany, Chicago, New York City, Columbia, Philadelphia, Cumberland, Columbus, Marietta, Cincinnati, Indianapolis, Quincy, Springfield, Ironton, Norfolk, Percival, Chester, Evansville, Cairo, New Bern, Charleston

Unorganized Terr., Dakota Terr., MN, WI, MI, Nebraska Terr., IA, IN, OH, PA, VT, ME, NY, NH, MA, RI, CT, NJ, DE, MD, VA, KS, MO, KY, Indian Country, AR, TN, NC, SC, GA, TX, LA, MS, AL, FL

Ohio R., Mississippi R.

to Mexico

to Caribbean

more at USHAtlas.com

F Harriet Tubman, shown here, was one of many runaway slaves to join the struggle against slavery. She was one of the few abolitionists brave enough to go to the South and guide runaways to freedom.

Civil War and Reconstruction

1820–1877

1854
Republican Party
founded to oppose slavery
in the territories.

1860
Democratic Party divides into
antislavery and proslavery factions.

Republican candidate Abraham
Lincoln elected U.S. President.

South Carolina secedes from the
Union, first of 11 states to do so.

1820

1855

1820
Missouri Compromise
prohibits slavery north of 36°30′N.

1857
Dred Scott decision declares
blacks are not U.S. citizens.

Slavery Divides the Nation

The issue of slavery affected national decisions for decades. Congress twice compromised to satisfy both North and South, but without lasting success.

★ The Missouri Compromise divided new territories at 36°30′N. Slavery was banned north of this line and allowed south of it.

★ The Compromise of 1850 allowed territory gained from Mexico to decide on slavery by a vote of the residents, or *popular sovereignty*.

★ The Kansas-Nebraska Act allowed slavery in those two territories, even though they were north of 36°30′N.

★ In the Dred Scott case, the Supreme Court ruled that Congress had no power to prohibit slavery. This opened *all* territories to slavery.

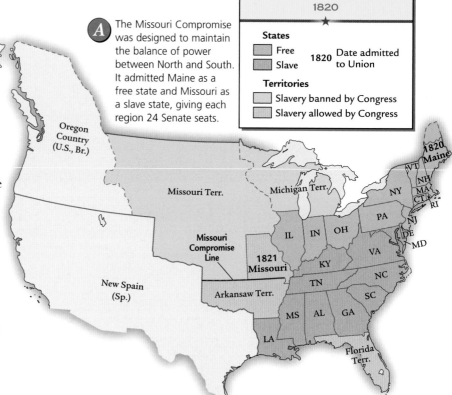

A The Missouri Compromise was designed to maintain the balance of power between North and South. It admitted Maine as a free state and Missouri as a slave state, giving each region 24 Senate seats.

MISSOURI COMPROMISE
1820

States
- Free
- Slave
- 1820 Date admitted to Union

Territories
- Slavery banned by Congress
- Slavery allowed by Congress

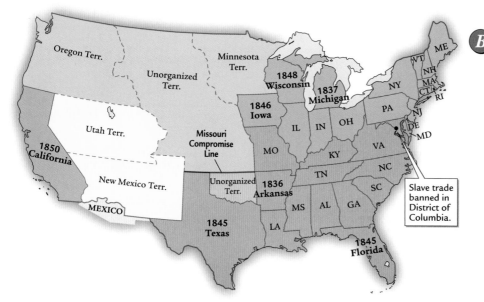

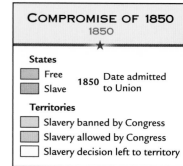

B New states gave the North a majority in the Senate. But the Compromise of 1850 permitted the residents of Utah and New Mexico to allow slavery. The related Fugitive Slave Act required that escaped slaves in the North be returned to their Southern owners.

COMPROMISE OF 1850
1850

States
- Free
- Slave
- 1850 Date admitted to Union

Territories
- Slavery banned by Congress
- Slavery allowed by Congress
- Slavery decision left to territory

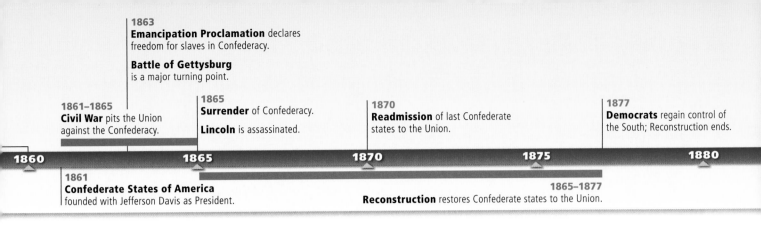

1863
Emancipation Proclamation declares freedom for slaves in Confederacy.

Battle of Gettysburg is a major turning point.

1861–1865
Civil War pits the Union against the Confederacy.

1865
Surrender of Confederacy.

Lincoln is assassinated.

1870
Readmission of last Confederate states to the Union.

1877
Democrats regain control of the South; Reconstruction ends.

1860 1865 1870 1875 1880

1861
Confederate States of America founded with Jefferson Davis as President.

1865–1877
Reconstruction restores Confederate states to the Union.

KANSAS–NEBRASKA ACT
1854
★

States
- Free
- Slave

Territories
- Slavery banned by Congress
- Slavery allowed by Congress
- Slavery decision left to territory

C After passage of the Kansas-Nebraska Act, forces for and against slavery clashed in Kansas. Soon the territory earned the nickname, "Bleeding Kansas."

DRED SCOTT DECISION
1857
★

States
- Free
- Slave

Territories
- Slavery allowed by Supreme Court

D Dred Scott was a slave who sued for his freedom. He lost his case when the Supreme Court decided that blacks were not U.S. citizens and had no rights in a federal court of law.

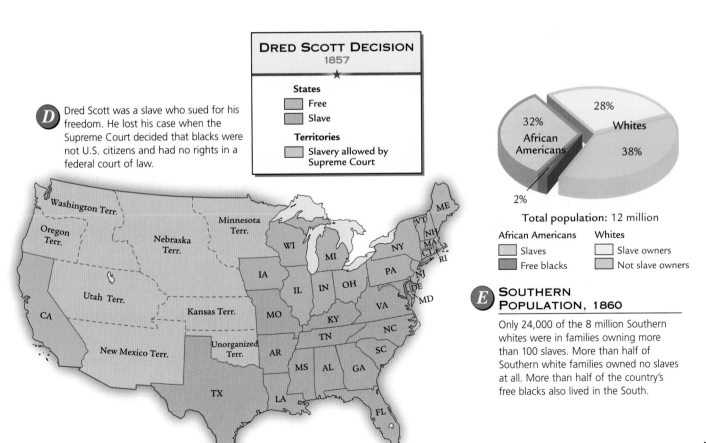

28%
Whites
38%

32%
African Americans

2%

Total population: 12 million

African Americans
- Slaves
- Free blacks

Whites
- Slave owners
- Not slave owners

E SOUTHERN POPULATION, 1860

Only 24,000 of the 8 million Southern whites were in families owning more than 100 slaves. More than half of Southern white families owned no slaves at all. More than half of the country's free blacks also lived in the South.

53

The United States Before the Civil War

By 1861 the United States stretched to the Pacific and consisted of 34 states and 8 organized territories.

★ The South covered a larger area, but the North was more populous and had more cities.

★ The North had a mixed economy based on a variety of crops and on manufacturing of many kinds.

★ The Southern economy relied on *cash crops* (crops grown for sale), especially cotton. Its plantations, in turn, relied on slaves.

A For Southerners, slavery was both an economic and a political issue. Without unpaid slave labor, few Southern cash crops could be grown and harvested at a profit. Compare this map with map C on page 27.

more at **USHAtlas.com**

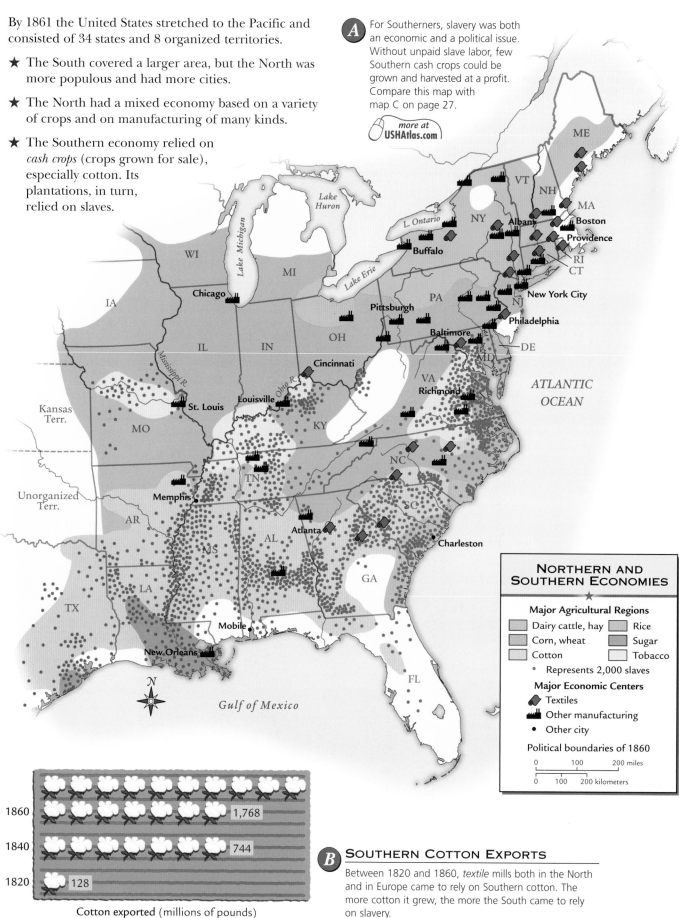

NORTHERN AND SOUTHERN ECONOMIES

★

Major Agricultural Regions

- Dairy cattle, hay
- Corn, wheat
- Cotton
- Rice
- Sugar
- Tobacco
- • Represents 2,000 slaves

Major Economic Centers

- Textiles
- Other manufacturing
- • Other city

Political boundaries of 1860

| 0 | 100 | 200 miles |
| 0 | 100 | 200 kilometers |

Cotton exported (millions of pounds)

1860 — 1,768
1840 — 744
1820 — 128

B **SOUTHERN COTTON EXPORTS**

Between 1820 and 1860, *textile* mills both in the North and in Europe came to rely on Southern cotton. The more cotton it grew, the more the South came to rely on slavery.

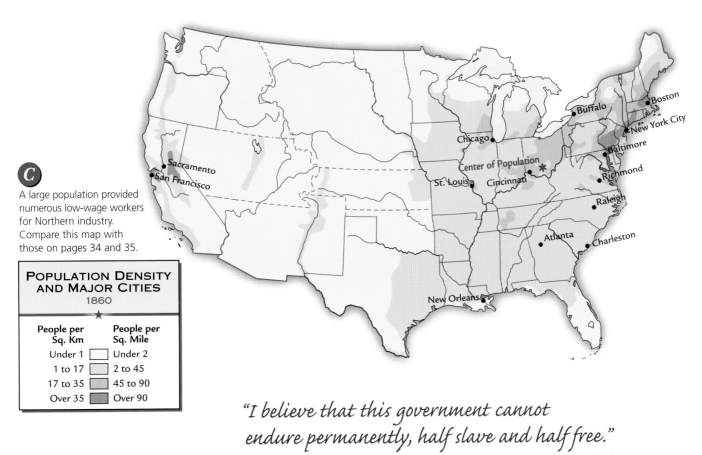

C

A large population provided numerous low-wage workers for Northern industry. Compare this map with those on pages 34 and 35.

POPULATION DENSITY AND MAJOR CITIES
1860
★

People per Sq. Km	People per Sq. Mile
Under 1	Under 2
1 to 17	2 to 45
17 to 35	45 to 90
Over 35	Over 90

"I believe that this government cannot endure permanently, half slave and half free."

–ABRAHAM LINCOLN, 1858
SPEECH TO REPUBLICAN STATE CONVENTION,
SPRINGFIELD, ILLINOIS

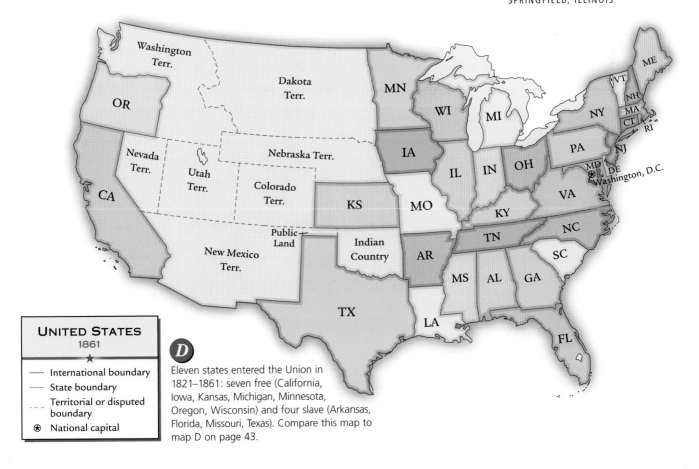

UNITED STATES
1861
★

— International boundary
— State boundary
--- Territorial or disputed boundary
⊛ National capital

D

Eleven states entered the Union in 1821–1861: seven free (California, Iowa, Kansas, Michigan, Minnesota, Oregon, Wisconsin) and four slave (Arkansas, Florida, Missouri, Texas). Compare this map to map D on page 43.

The Civil War Begins

The Civil War broke out in 1861 over the right of states to *secede*, or withdraw, from the United States.

★ Soon after Abraham Lincoln was elected President in 1860, 11 slave states seceded to form the Confederate States of America.

★ Lincoln believed that individual states could not leave the nation. The North fought to preserve the Union—the United States of America.

★ The Confederate army fought with skill and determination. It dealt the Union army many early defeats.

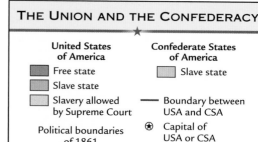

THE UNION AND THE CONFEDERACY

United States of America	Confederate States of America
■ Free state	■ Slave state
■ Slave state	
■ Slavery allowed by Supreme Court	— Boundary between USA and CSA
Political boundaries of 1861	⊛ Capital of USA or CSA

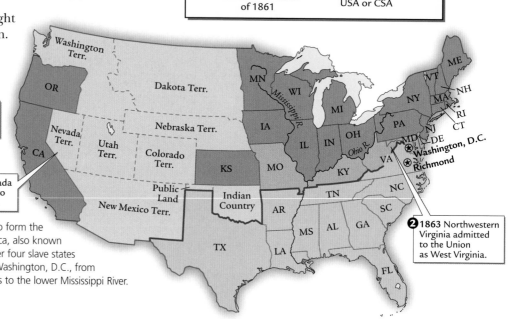

❶ **1862** Congress bans slavery in territories, ends slavery in District of Columbia.

❸ **1864** Nevada admitted to the Union.

A

Eleven slave states seceded to form the Confederate States of America, also known as the *Confederacy*. The other four slave states stayed in the Union, saving Washington, D.C., from isolation and providing access to the lower Mississippi River.

more at USHAtlas.com

❷ **1863** Northwestern Virginia admitted to the Union as West Virginia.

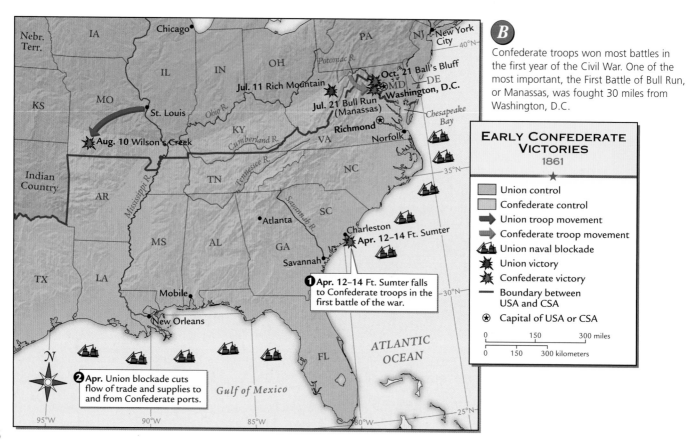

B

Confederate troops won most battles in the first year of the Civil War. One of the most important, the First Battle of Bull Run, or Manassas, was fought 30 miles from Washington, D.C.

Jul. 11 Rich Mountain
Oct. 21 Ball's Bluff
Jul. 21 Bull Run (Manassas)
Washington, D.C.
Aug. 10 Wilson's Creek
Richmond
Norfolk

EARLY CONFEDERATE VICTORIES
1861

■	Union control
■	Confederate control
➡	Union troop movement
➡	Confederate troop movement
⛴	Union naval blockade
✸	Union victory
✸	Confederate victory
—	Boundary between USA and CSA
⊛	Capital of USA or CSA

0   150   300 miles
0   150   300 kilometers

❶ **Apr. 12–14** Ft. Sumter falls to Confederate troops in the first battle of the war.

❷ **Apr.** Union blockade cuts flow of trade and supplies to and from Confederate ports.

Apr. 12–14 Ft. Sumter

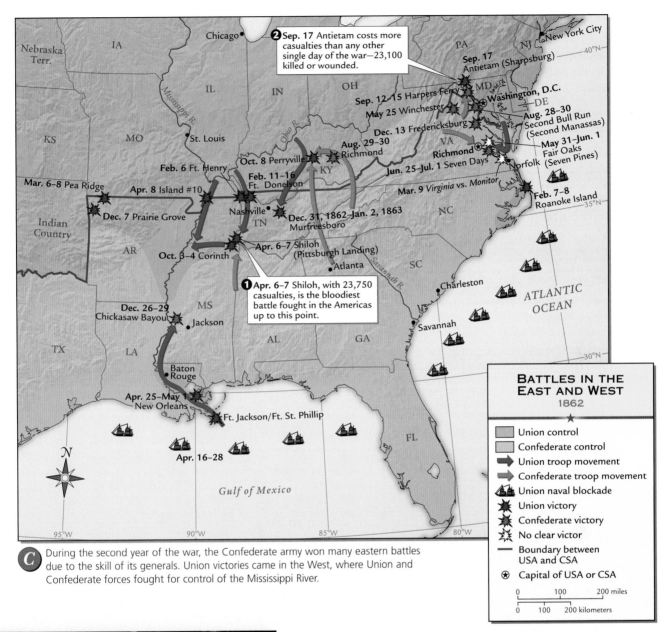

❷ **Sep. 17** Antietam costs more casualties than any other single day of the war—23,100 killed or wounded.

Sep. 17 Antietam (Sharpsburg)

Sep. 12–15 Harpers Ferry

May 25 Winchester

Dec. 13 Fredericksburg

Aug. 29–30 Richmond

Aug. 28–30 Second Bull Run (Second Manassas)

May 31–Jun. 1 Fair Oaks (Seven Pines)

Oct. 8 Perryville

Feb. 6 Ft. Henry

Feb. 11–16 Ft. Donelson

Mar. 6–8 Pea Ridge

Apr. 8 Island #10

Dec. 7 Prairie Grove

Nashville

Dec. 31, 1862–Jan. 2, 1863 Murfreesboro

Oct. 3–4 Corinth

Apr. 6–7 Shiloh (Pittsburgh Landing)

Atlanta

Jun. 25–Jul. 1 Seven Days

Richmond

Mar. 9 Virginia vs. Monitor

Norfolk

Feb. 7–8 Roanoke Island

❶ **Apr. 6–7** Shiloh, with 23,750 casualties, is the bloodiest battle fought in the Americas up to this point.

Dec. 26–29 Chickasaw Bayou

Jackson

Apr. 25–May 1 New Orleans

Baton Rouge

Ft. Jackson/Ft. St. Phillip

Apr. 16–28

Charleston

Savannah

ATLANTIC OCEAN

Gulf of Mexico

Nebraska Terr.

IA

Chicago

IL

IN

OH

PA

NJ

New York City

MD

Washington, D.C.

DE

VA

NC

SC

GA

AL

MS

LA

TX

AR

Indian Country

KS

MO

St. Louis

KY

TN

FL

BATTLES IN THE EAST AND WEST
1862

▮	Union control
▮	Confederate control
➡	Union troop movement
➡	Confederate troop movement
⛵	Union naval blockade
✸	Union victory
✸	Confederate victory
✷	No clear victor
—	Boundary between USA and CSA
✪	Capital of USA or CSA

0   100   200 miles
0   100   200 kilometers

Ⓒ During the second year of the war, the Confederate army won many eastern battles due to the skill of its generals. Union victories came in the West, where Union and Confederate forces fought for control of the Mississippi River.

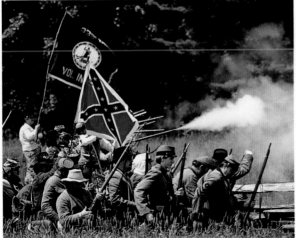

Ⓓ Confederate troops, called "rebels" by Northerners, wore gray uniforms, such as the ones in this battle reenactment. Union troops, called "Yankees" by Southerners, wore blue.

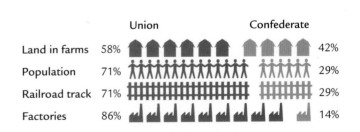

	Union		Confederate
Land in farms	58%		42%
Population	71%		29%
Railroad track	71%		29%
Factories	86%		14%

Ⓔ **UNION AND CONFEDERATE RESOURCES**

The resources of the Union made it better able to withstand a long, destructive conflict than the Confederacy, which had more troops with prior training and experience.

more at USHAtlas.com

The Civil War Continues

The Union gained decisive advantages in 1863.

★ On January 1 President Lincoln issued the Emancipation Proclamation, which declared slaves in the Confederacy free.

★ Union victories at Gettysburg and Vicksburg, along with the Union cutoff of Confederate trade, weakened the South's ability to fight.

★ The Confederacy had expected support from Britain and France. After the Emancipation Proclamation, the Europeans saw the war as a conflict over slavery and honored the Union *blockade*.

★ By 1864 the Confederate army was short of men and supplies, but it continued to fight.

A Many Civil War battles were fought in farm fields. Most soldiers, like the Union troops in this reenactment, arrived on foot.

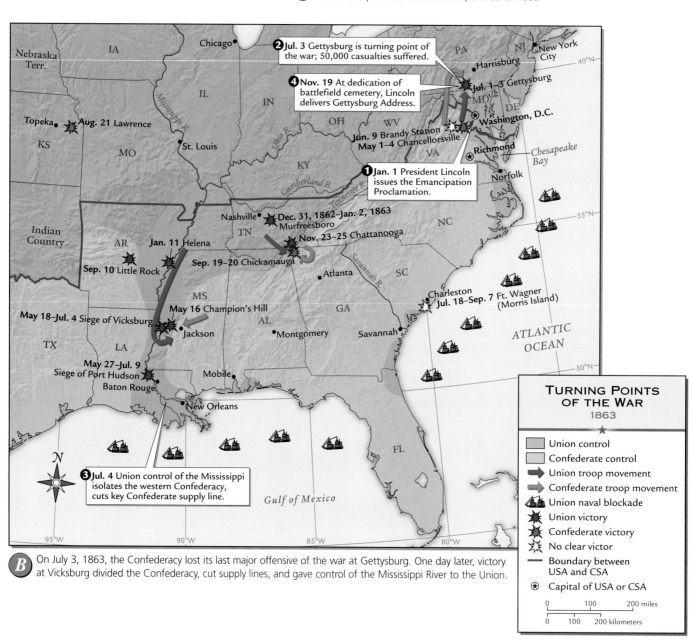

2 Jul. 3 Gettysburg is turning point of the war; 50,000 casualties suffered.

4 Nov. 19 At dedication of battlefield cemetery, Lincoln delivers Gettysburg Address.

Jul. 1–3 Gettysburg

Jun. 9 Brandy Station
May 1–4 Chancellorsville

1 Jan. 1 President Lincoln issues the Emancipation Proclamation.

Aug. 21 Lawrence

Dec. 31, 1862–Jan. 2, 1863 Murfreesboro

Nov. 23–25 Chattanooga

Jan. 11 Helena

Sep. 19–20 Chickamauga

Sep. 10 Little Rock

May 16 Champion's Hill

May 18–Jul. 4 Siege of Vicksburg

Charleston
Jul. 18–Sep. 7 Ft. Wagner (Morris Island)

May 27–Jul. 9 Siege of Port Hudson
Baton Rouge

3 Jul. 4 Union control of the Mississippi isolates the western Confederacy, cuts key Confederate supply line.

TURNING POINTS OF THE WAR
1863
★

- Union control
- Confederate control
- ➡ Union troop movement
- ➡ Confederate troop movement
- Union naval blockade
- ✸ Union victory
- ✸ Confederate victory
- ✸ No clear victor
- — Boundary between USA and CSA
- ✹ Capital of USA or CSA

| 0 | 100 | 200 miles |
| 0 | 100 | 200 kilometers |

B On July 3, 1863, the Confederacy lost its last major offensive of the war at Gettysburg. One day later, victory at Vicksburg divided the Confederacy, cut supply lines, and gave control of the Mississippi River to the Union.

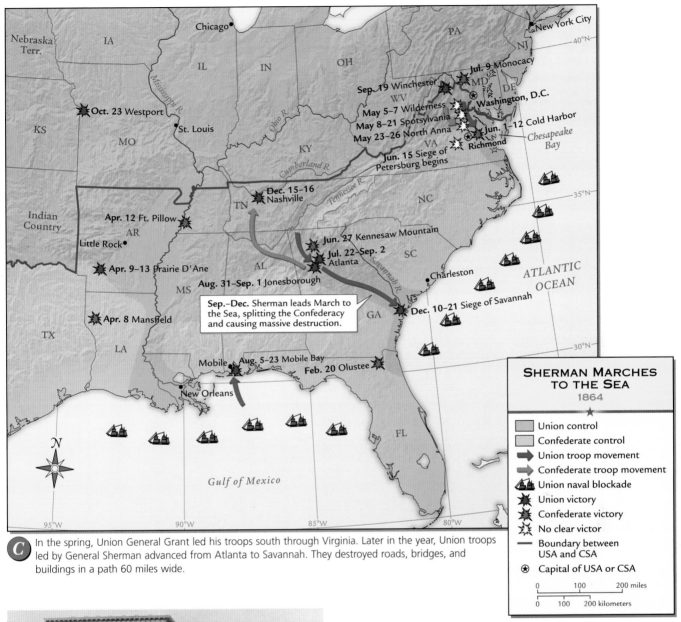

Chicago
New York City
Nebraska Terr.
IA
IL
IN
OH
PA
NJ
40°N
Jul. 9 Monocacy
MD
Sep. 19 Winchester
DE
WV
Washington, D.C.
May 5–7 Wilderness
May 8–21 Spotsylvania
Jun. 1–12 Cold Harbor
Oct. 23 Westport
May 23–26 North Anna
Chesapeake Bay
St. Louis
KS
VA
Richmond
MO
Jun. 15 Siege of Petersburg begins
35°N
KY
Cumberland R.
Ohio R.
Mississippi R.
Tennessee R.
NC
Dec. 15–16 Nashville
Indian Country
TN
Apr. 12 Ft. Pillow
AR
Jun. 27 Kennesaw Mountain
Little Rock
SC
Apr. 9–13 Prairie D'Ane
Jul. 22–Sep. 2 Atlanta
AL
Charleston
ATLANTIC OCEAN
MS
Aug. 31–Sep. 1 Jonesborough
Savannah R.
Apr. 8 Mansfield
Sep.–Dec. Sherman leads March to the Sea, splitting the Confederacy and causing massive destruction.
GA
Dec. 10–21 Siege of Savannah
TX
LA
30°N
Mobile
Aug. 5–23 Mobile Bay
Feb. 20 Olustee
New Orleans
FL
Gulf of Mexico
N
95°W
90°W
85°W
80°W

C In the spring, Union General Grant led his troops south through Virginia. Later in the year, Union troops led by General Sherman advanced from Atlanta to Savannah. They destroyed roads, bridges, and buildings in a path 60 miles wide.

SHERMAN MARCHES TO THE SEA
1864

- ☐ Union control
- ☐ Confederate control
- ➡ Union troop movement
- ➡ Confederate troop movement
- ⛴ Union naval blockade
- ✸ Union victory
- ✸ Confederate victory
- ✸ No clear victor
- — Boundary between USA and CSA
- ⊛ Capital of USA or CSA

0   100   200 miles
0   100   200 kilometers

D Charleston, South Carolina, was one of many Southern cities damaged during the war. Most Northern cities were far from the fighting and suffered no physical damage.

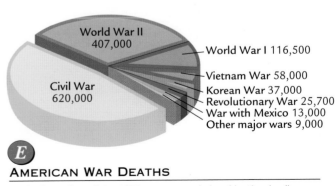

World War II 407,000
World War I 116,500
Civil War 620,000
Vietnam War 58,000
Korean War 37,000
Revolutionary War 25,700
War with Mexico 13,000
Other major wars 9,000

E

AMERICAN WAR DEATHS

Medical practices of the 1800s were overwhelmed by the deadly *tactics* and weapons of the Civil War. Loss of blood, shock, and infection cost thousands of lives. Disease cost many more.

more at USHAtlas.com

The War Ends, Reconstruction Follows

In April 1865 General Lee surrendered his Confederate army to Grant. Other Confederate generals soon surrendered too, and the Civil War ended.

★ During *Reconstruction*, former Confederate states had to accept new constitutional amendments before they could re-enter the Union.

★ The 13th, 14th, and 15th Amendments ended slavery and extended the vote and other rights of citizenship to all men regardless of "race, color, or condition of previous servitude." *more at USHAtlas.com*

★ By 1877 all Union forces had left the South. Former Confederates had regained power, and soon afterward blacks were denied their newly won rights.

B The 13th Amendment to the Constitution ended slavery in the United States. Having few alternatives, most former slaves, like the *sharecropper* family in this hand-painted photo, continued to work on Southern farms.

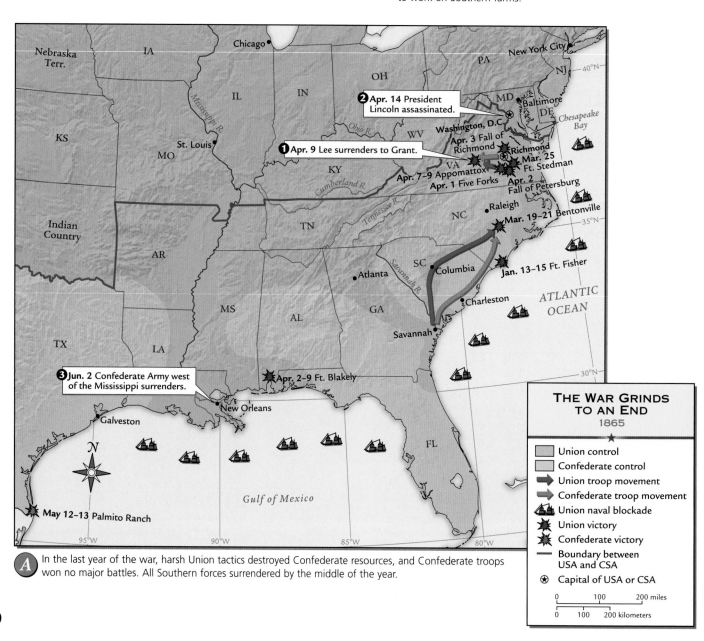

A In the last year of the war, harsh Union tactics destroyed Confederate resources, and Confederate troops won no major battles. All Southern forces surrendered by the middle of the year.

THE WAR GRINDS TO AN END
1865
★

- Union control
- Confederate control
- ➡ Union troop movement
- ➡ Confederate troop movement
- Union naval blockade
- Union victory
- Confederate victory
- Boundary between USA and CSA
- ✪ Capital of USA or CSA

0   100   200 miles
0   100   200 kilometers

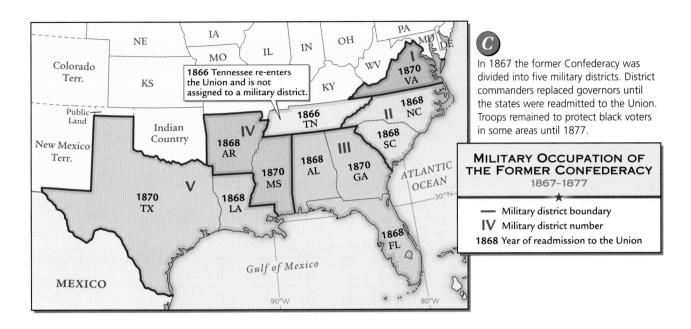

1866 Tennessee re-enters the Union and is not assigned to a military district.

C

In 1867 the former Confederacy was divided into five military districts. District commanders replaced governors until the states were readmitted to the Union. Troops remained to protect black voters in some areas until 1877.

MILITARY OCCUPATION OF THE FORMER CONFEDERACY
1867–1877
★
— Military district boundary
IV Military district number
1868 Year of readmission to the Union

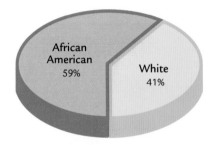

D **SOUTH CAROLINA POPULATION, 1870**

African American 59%

White 41%

Southern whites feared loss of political power if blacks had the chance to vote. Blacks outnumbered whites in three former Confederate states, and nearly equaled their numbers in three others.

E

In 1870 Hiram Revels of Mississippi became the first African American elected to the U.S. Senate. During Reconstruction many blacks were elected to state and federal offices.

POLITICAL POWER STRUGGLE
★
Membership in U.S. Congress
Democratic majority
Republican majority
Evenly divided

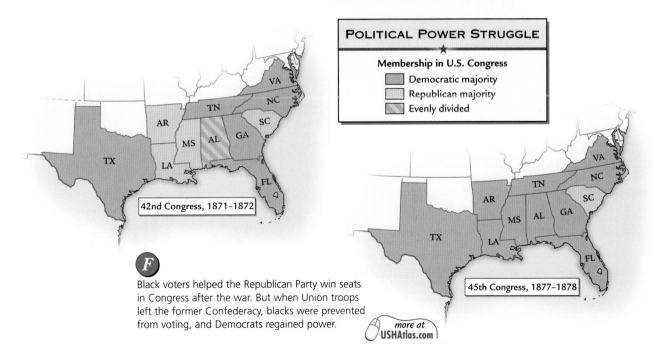

42nd Congress, 1871–1872

45th Congress, 1877–1878

F

Black voters helped the Republican Party win seats in Congress after the war. But when Union troops left the former Confederacy, blacks were prevented from voting, and Democrats regained power.

more at USHAtlas.com

ERA 6

Development of the Industrial United States

1865–1900

1869
Union Pacific and Central Pacific link East and West.

1866
Sedalia Trail brings Texas cattle to Missouri railhead.

1865
Civil War ends.

1860   1865   1870

Early 1860s
Chinese immigrants in California begin work on Central Pacific Railroad.

1867
Alaska purchased from Russia.

Immigration Swells the Work Force

After the Civil War, immigration increased so much that total U.S. population rose despite wartime losses.

★ Immigrants provided a vast new pool of labor for the rapidly industrializing nation. They built railroads, worked in mines and factories, and farmed the Great Plains.

★ By 1890 almost one out of every seven people in the United States was foreign-born.

"Give me your tired, your poor, your huddled masses yearning to breathe free..."

—INSCRIPTION AT THE BASE OF THE STATUE OF LIBERTY FROM THE POEM, "NEW WORLD COLOSSUS," BY EMMA LAZARUS, 1883

A **IMMIGRANT ORIGINS**

Most immigrants still came from Northern and Western Europe, but the numbers from Southern and Eastern Europe were increasing. Compare this graph with graph B on page 50.

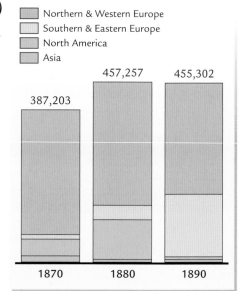

- Northern & Western Europe
- Southern & Eastern Europe
- North America
- Asia

387,203 — 1870
457,257 — 1880
455,302 — 1890

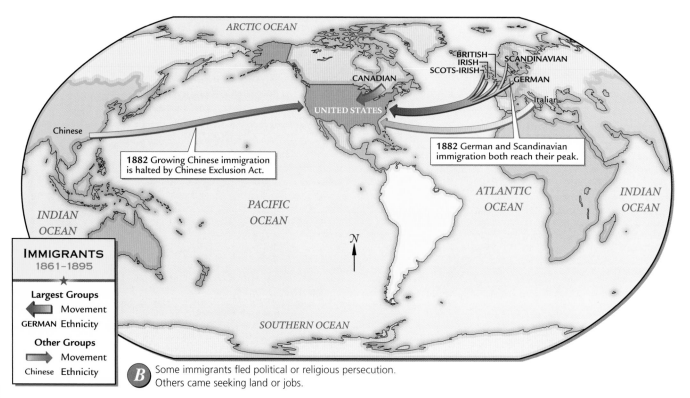

ARCTIC OCEAN

BRITISH
IRISH
SCOTS-IRISH
SCANDINAVIAN

CANADIAN

GERMAN

UNITED STATES

Italian

Chinese

1882 Growing Chinese immigration is halted by Chinese Exclusion Act.

1882 German and Scandinavian immigration both reach their peak.

INDIAN OCEAN

PACIFIC OCEAN

ATLANTIC OCEAN

INDIAN OCEAN

N

SOUTHERN OCEAN

IMMIGRANTS
1861–1895

Largest Groups
← Movement
GERMAN Ethnicity

Other Groups
→ Movement
Chinese Ethnicity

B Some immigrants fled political or religious persecution. Others came seeking land or jobs.

1873
Steel production increases with first large-scale plant.

1876
Custer is defeated by Sioux at Little Bighorn.

Telephone is invented.

1880
Cattle outnumber buffalo on the western range.

Late 1880s
Railroads in Texas end long cattle drives.

1890
Wounded Knee Massacre marks end of Indian wars.

1894
U.S. factory production is highest in world.

1900
U.S. coal production is highest in world.

| 1875 | 1880 | 1885 | 1890 | 1895 | 1900 |

1874
Gold in Dakota Territory brings miners, new clashes with Indians.

1882
Immigration reaches highest total of the century.

1898
Alaska Gold Rush draws miners north.

LARGEST IMMIGRANT GROUPS BY STATE
1890

★

Origin of Largest Foreign-born Group

- Germany
- England
- Ireland
- Norway
- Mexico
- Canada
- Caribbean
- China

C Foreign-born residents often settled in the same states as others from their homelands. Notice which group of immigrants was largest in more states than any other group.

D Most Chinese immigrants became railroad laborers, but others worked as farmers, peddlers, and local merchants.

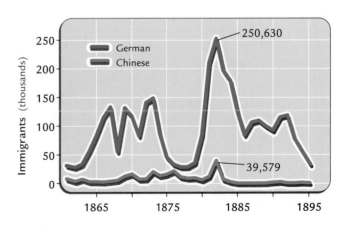

Immigrants (thousands)

250,630

■ German
■ Chinese

39,579

1865 1875 1885 1895

E **GERMAN AND CHINESE IMMIGRANTS**

Political upheaval in Germany sent huge numbers of Germans to the United States in the early 1880s. Chinese immigrants outnumbered all others of non-European ancestry until 1882, when the Chinese Exclusion Act was passed.

more at USHAtlas.com

63

Railroads Transform the West

The first *transcontinental* railroad was completed in 1869. It cut cross-country travel time from 26 days to 7 days.

★ Federal subsidies helped pay for Western railroads. Railroads, in turn, made it easier to settle the West.

★ Trains carried cattle to Eastern markets and supplies to Western settlers.

★ Railroad expansion helped destroy the buffalo (formally called the North American bison). Cattle replaced buffalo on the range and provided meat for fast-growing Eastern cities.

B Building Western railroads was hard, hot work. Most of the labor was performed by Chinese and Irish immigrants.

1860 — 30,626

1870 — 52,922

1880 — 93,262

1890 — 166,703

Railroad track (miles)

A MILES OF RAILROAD TRACK

After 1860 all railroad track was the same gauge, or width: 4 feet, 8½ inches. Now a single train could go anywhere track had been laid. The growing U.S. steel industry provided all the track railroads needed to expand.

more at USHAtlas.com

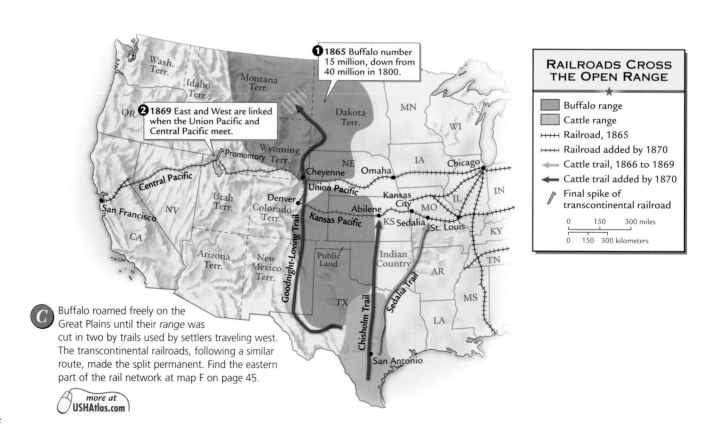

❶ 1865 Buffalo number 15 million, down from 40 million in 1800.

❷ 1869 East and West are linked when the Union Pacific and Central Pacific meet.

RAILROADS CROSS THE OPEN RANGE

★

▨ Buffalo range
▨ Cattle range
├┼┼┼ Railroad, 1865
├┼┼┼ Railroad added by 1870
⇐ Cattle trail, 1866 to 1869
⬅ Cattle trail added by 1870
⚑ Final spike of transcontinental railroad

0   150   300 miles
0   150   300 kilometers

C Buffalo roamed freely on the Great Plains until their *range* was cut in two by trails used by settlers traveling west. The transcontinental railroads, following a similar route, made the split permanent. Find the eastern part of the rail network at map F on page 45.

more at USHAtlas.com

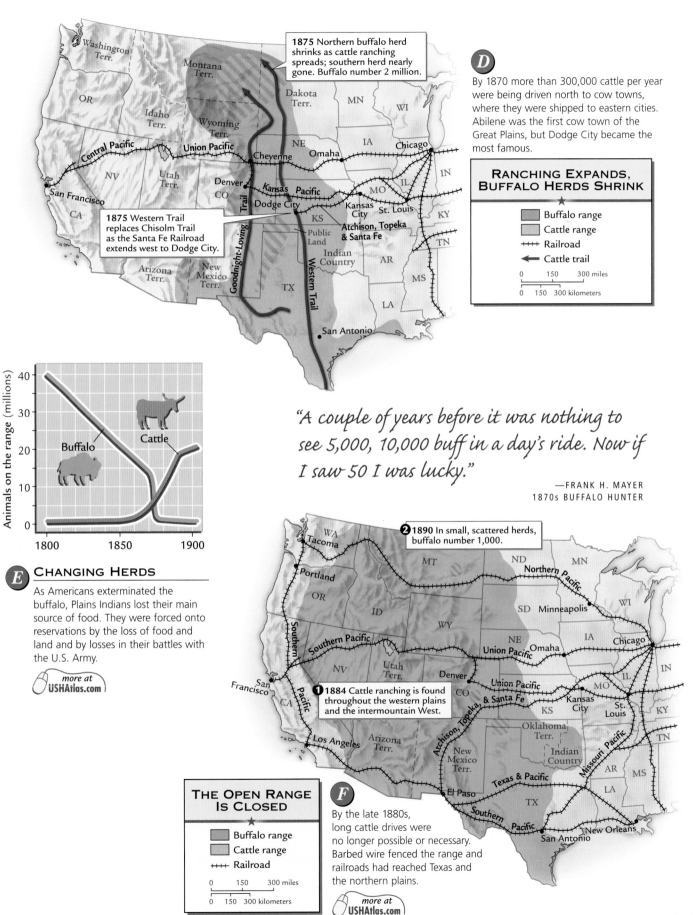

1875 Northern buffalo herd shrinks as cattle ranching spreads; southern herd nearly gone. Buffalo number 2 million.

1875 Western Trail replaces Chisolm Trail as the Santa Fe Railroad extends west to Dodge City.

D

By 1870 more than 300,000 cattle per year were being driven north to cow towns, where they were shipped to eastern cities. Abilene was the first cow town of the Great Plains, but Dodge City became the most famous.

RANCHING EXPANDS, BUFFALO HERDS SHRINK

★

- Buffalo range
- Cattle range
- ++++ Railroad
- ← Cattle trail

0   150   300 miles
0   150   300 kilometers

"A couple of years before it was nothing to see 5,000, 10,000 buff in a day's ride. Now if I saw 50 I was lucky."

—FRANK H. MAYER
1870s BUFFALO HUNTER

E CHANGING HERDS

As Americans exterminated the buffalo, Plains Indians lost their main source of food. They were forced onto reservations by the loss of food and land and by losses in their battles with the U.S. Army.

more at USHAtlas.com

Animals on the range (millions)

Buffalo
Cattle

1800   1850   1900

❷ **1890** In small, scattered herds, buffalo number 1,000.

❶ **1884** Cattle ranching is found throughout the western plains and the intermountain West.

THE OPEN RANGE IS CLOSED

★

- Buffalo range
- Cattle range
- ++++ Railroad

0   150   300 miles
0   150   300 kilometers

F

By the late 1880s, long cattle drives were no longer possible or necessary. Barbed wire fenced the range and railroads had reached Texas and the northern plains.

more at USHAtlas.com

Using Indian Lands to Feed the Nation

After the Civil War, nearly 250,000 Indians lived on the western prairies and the Great Plains, a region Eastern settlers believed useless for farming.

★ To encourage citizens to settle the Plains, the Homestead Act of 1862 offered settlers 160 acres of free land.

★ Indians fought these intruders but were weakened by the loss of the buffalo. By 1880 the army had forced most Plains Indians onto reservations.

★ By 1900, 500,000 settlers farmed the Plains, growing food to help feed the cities of the East.

A The Great Plains was once called the "Great American Desert." It was believed that the land west of the 100th meridian was too dry to farm.

RAINFALL

Millimeters per Year	Inches per Year
0 to 250	0 to 10
250 to 500	10 to 20
500 to 1000	20 to 40
1000 to 2000	40 to 80
Over 2000	Over 80

Political boundaries of 1880

"The West begins where the average annual rainfall drops below twenty inches."

—BERNARD DE VOTO
U.S. HISTORIAN

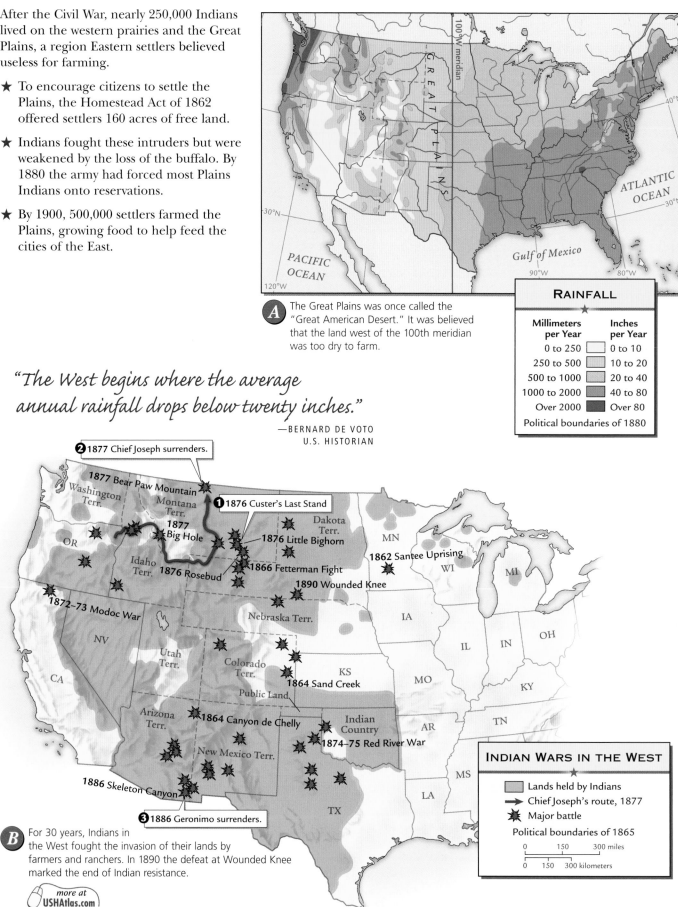

❷ 1877 Chief Joseph surrenders.
1877 Bear Paw Mountain
❶ 1876 Custer's Last Stand
1877 Big Hole
1876 Little Bighorn
1862 Santee Uprising
1876 Rosebud
1866 Fetterman Fight
1890 Wounded Knee
1872–73 Modoc War
1864 Sand Creek
Public Land
1864 Canyon de Chelly
1874–75 Red River War
1886 Skeleton Canyon
❸ 1886 Geronimo surrenders.

INDIAN WARS IN THE WEST

Lands held by Indians
→ Chief Joseph's route, 1877
✸ Major battle
Political boundaries of 1865

0   150   300 miles
0   150   300 kilometers

B For 30 years, Indians in the West fought the invasion of their lands by farmers and ranchers. In 1890 the defeat at Wounded Knee marked the end of Indian resistance.

more at USHAtlas.com

66

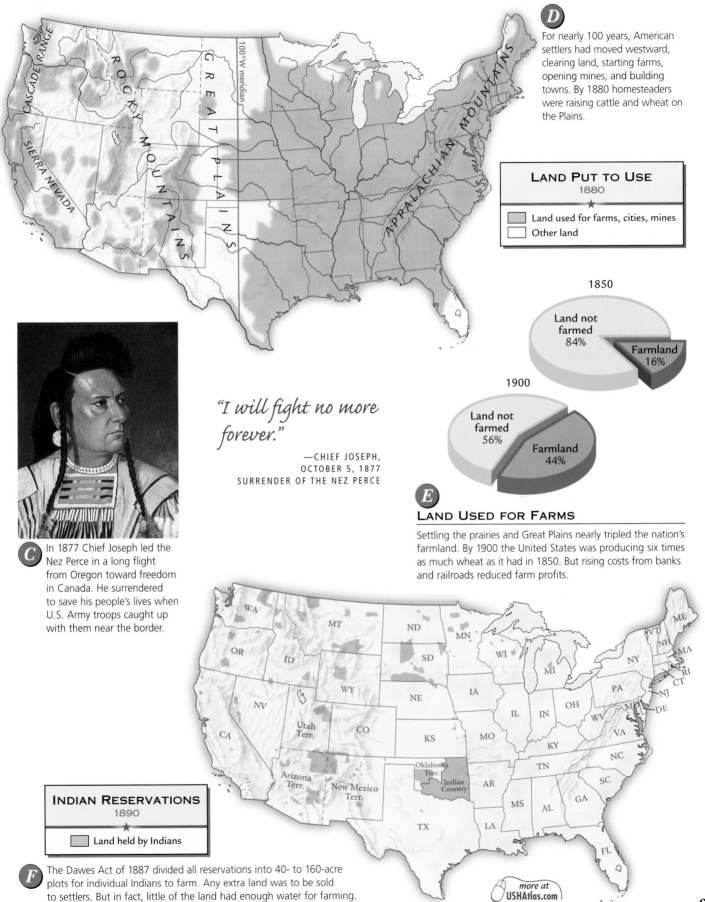

D

For nearly 100 years, American settlers had moved westward, clearing land, starting farms, opening mines, and building towns. By 1880 homesteaders were raising cattle and wheat on the Plains.

LAND PUT TO USE
1880
★

Land used for farms, cities, mines

Other land

1850

Land not farmed 84%

Farmland 16%

1900

Land not farmed 56%

Farmland 44%

E

LAND USED FOR FARMS

Settling the prairies and Great Plains nearly tripled the nation's farmland. By 1900 the United States was producing six times as much wheat as it had in 1850. But rising costs from banks and railroads reduced farm profits.

"I will fight no more forever."

—CHIEF JOSEPH,
OCTOBER 5, 1877
SURRENDER OF THE NEZ PERCE

C In 1877 Chief Joseph led the Nez Perce in a long flight from Oregon toward freedom in Canada. He surrendered to save his people's lives when U.S. Army troops caught up with them near the border.

INDIAN RESERVATIONS
1890
★

Land held by Indians

F The Dawes Act of 1887 divided all reservations into 40- to 160-acre plots for individual Indians to farm. Any extra land was to be sold to settlers. But in fact, little of the land had enough water for farming.

more at
USHAtlas.com

Mining the Raw Materials for Industry

Whenever gold was discovered in the United States, miners arrived from all over the world. Few became rich, but many stayed to settle the land.

★ Less glamorous metals such as copper and lead provided valuable resources for Eastern factories.

★ When lone miners had used up surface mines, mining companies took over with underground mining equipment.

★ Purchased in 1867, Alaska went largely unnoticed for 30 years—until gold was discovered in the nearby Yukon Territory.

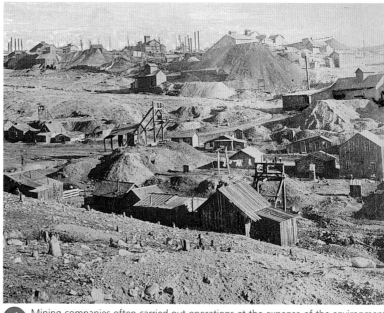

A Mining companies often carried out operations at the expense of the environment. Mining by-products poisoned water and soil at the mines, downstream, and in nearby boomtowns such as Leadville, Colorado, shown in the photo above.

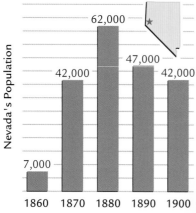

Nevada's Population

62,000
47,000
42,000
42,000
7,000

1860 1870 1880 1890 1900

B BOOM AND BUST IN NEVADA

Nevada's population boomed with the discovery of silver. But when the price of silver dropped, so did the population.

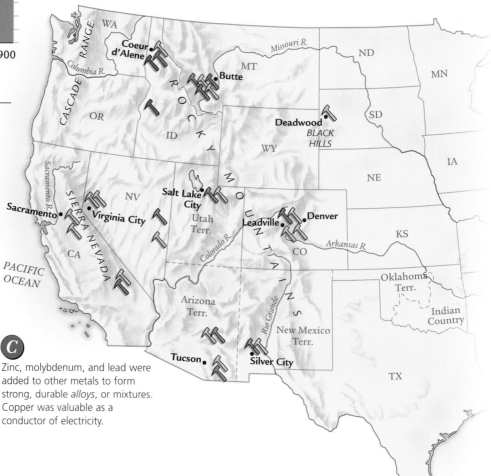

C Zinc, molybdenum, and lead were added to other metals to form strong, durable *alloys*, or mixtures. Copper was valuable as a conductor of electricity.

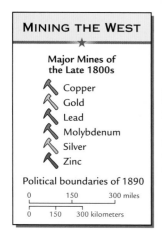

MINING THE WEST
★
Major Mines of the Late 1800s

- Copper
- Gold
- Lead
- Molybdenum
- Silver
- Zinc

Political boundaries of 1890

0   150   300 miles
0   150   300 kilometers

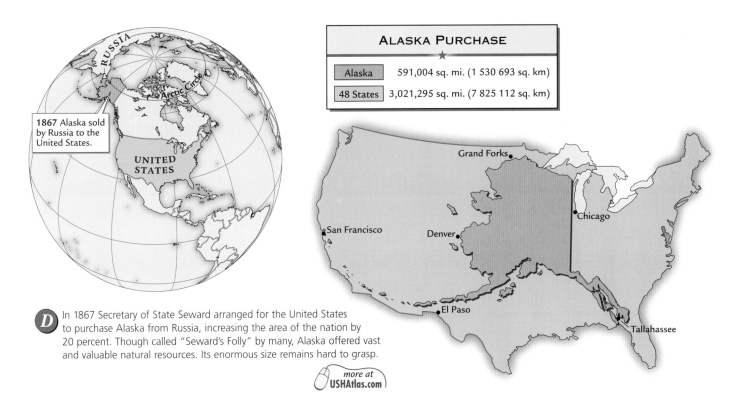

1867 Alaska sold by Russia to the United States.

ALASKA PURCHASE
★

| Alaska | 591,004 sq. mi. (1 530 693 sq. km) |
| 48 States | 3,021,295 sq. mi. (7 825 112 sq. km) |

D In 1867 Secretary of State Seward arranged for the United States to purchase Alaska from Russia, increasing the area of the nation by 20 percent. Though called "Seward's Folly" by many, Alaska offered vast and valuable natural resources. Its enormous size remains hard to grasp.

more at USHAtlas.com

"Gold is as plentiful as sawdust."
—ADVERTISEMENT FOR A STEAMER TO KLONDIKE COUNTRY
THE *SEATTLE DAILY TIMES*
JULY 14, 1897

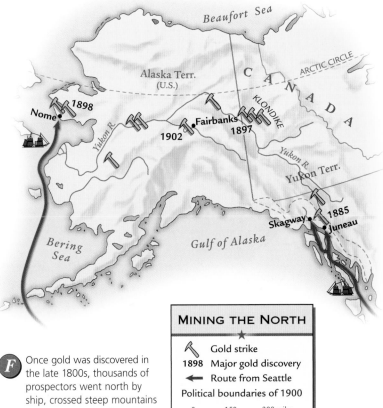

E Miners such as these discovered that Alaska was more than ice and snow. Mining is still one of Alaska's leading industries.

MINING THE NORTH
★

⚒ Gold strike
1898 Major gold discovery
← Route from Seattle
Political boundaries of 1900

| 0 | 150 | 300 miles |
| 0 | 150 | 300 kilometers |

F Once gold was discovered in the late 1800s, thousands of prospectors went north by ship, crossed steep mountains on foot, then built boats to carry them to mining camps near the Yukon River.

Becoming an Industrial Nation

By 1900 there were five times as many industrial workers as before the Civil War, and the United States was first in the world in factory production.

★ Miners and industrial workers often worked dangerous 10-hour days, six days a week, for low pay. *Labor unions* sought better conditions.

★ Coal powered locomotives and factories. It was also used to transform iron into steel.

★ Steel was used to build machinery, railroads, steamships, and tall buildings.

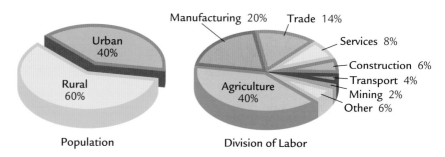

Population

Urban 40%
Rural 60%

Division of Labor

Manufacturing 20%
Trade 14%
Services 8%
Construction 6%
Transport 4%
Mining 2%
Other 6%
Agriculture 40%

A POPULATION AND LABOR, 1900

Compare the graph of urban and rural population with graph C on page 43. Industry introduced immigrants and longtime residents to new kinds of work and to life in the big city.

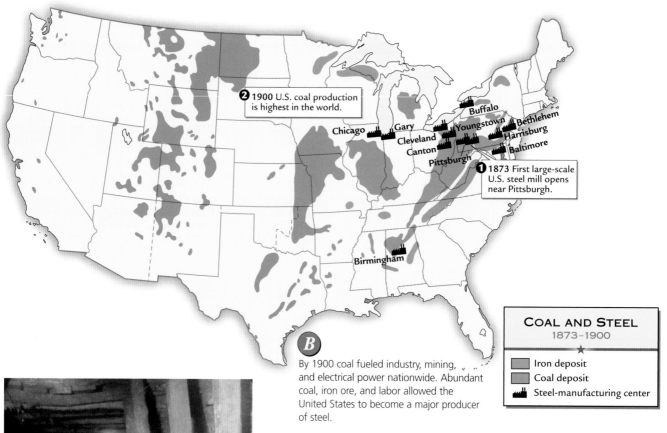

❷ 1900 U.S. coal production is highest in the world.

Buffalo
Chicago
Gary
Youngstown
Bethlehem
Cleveland
Harrisburg
Canton
Pittsburgh
Baltimore

❶ 1873 First large-scale U.S. steel mill opens near Pittsburgh.

Birmingham

B

By 1900 coal fueled industry, mining, and electrical power nationwide. Abundant coal, iron ore, and labor allowed the United States to become a major producer of steel.

COAL AND STEEL
1873–1900
★
Iron deposit
Coal deposit
Steel-manufacturing center

C

Many coal miners were immigrants. Cave-ins, explosions, and disease made their work much more dangerous than work in factories, on railroads, and in other kinds of mines.

"…there is seldom a day in the coal fields that some woman is not widowed by the mines."

—EARL W. MAYO, 1900
FRANK LESLIE'S POPULAR MONTHLY

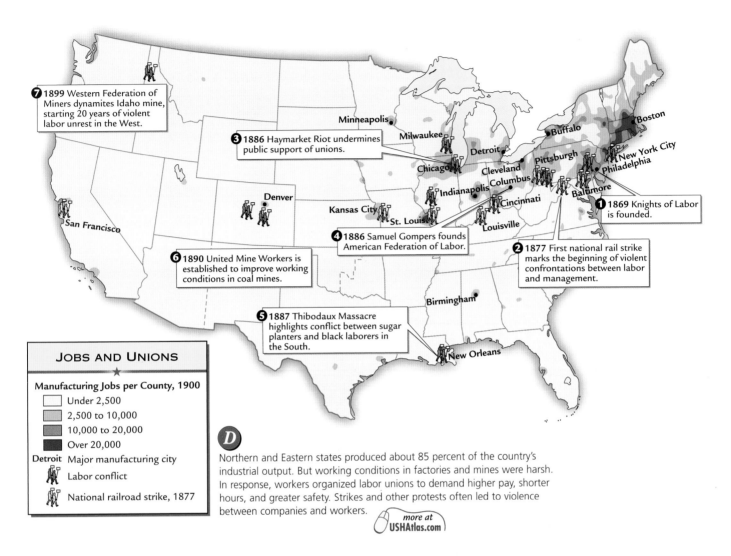

1899 Western Federation of Miners dynamites Idaho mine, starting 20 years of violent labor unrest in the West.

3 1886 Haymarket Riot undermines public support of unions.

1 1869 Knights of Labor is founded.

4 1886 Samuel Gompers founds American Federation of Labor.

2 1877 First national rail strike marks the beginning of violent confrontations between labor and management.

6 1890 United Mine Workers is established to improve working conditions in coal mines.

5 1887 Thibodaux Massacre highlights conflict between sugar planters and black laborers in the South.

JOBS AND UNIONS

Manufacturing Jobs per County, 1900

Under 2,500

2,500 to 10,000

10,000 to 20,000

Over 20,000

Detroit Major manufacturing city

Labor conflict

National railroad strike, 1877

D Northern and Eastern states produced about 85 percent of the country's industrial output. But working conditions in factories and mines were harsh. In response, workers organized labor unions to demand higher pay, shorter hours, and greater safety. Strikes and other protests often led to violence between companies and workers.

more at USHAtlas.com

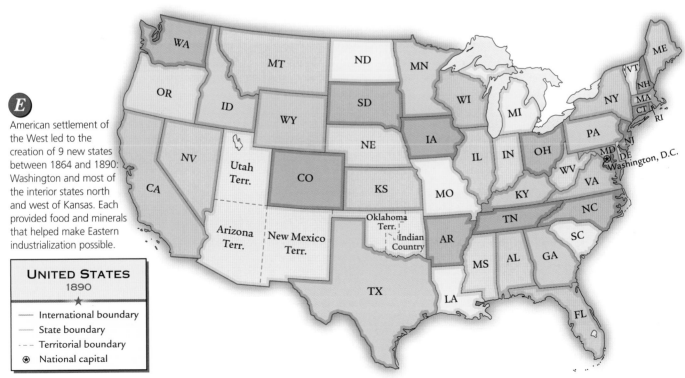

E American settlement of the West led to the creation of 9 new states between 1864 and 1890: Washington and most of the interior states north and west of Kansas. Each provided food and minerals that helped make Eastern industrialization possible.

UNITED STATES
1890

International boundary

State boundary

Territorial boundary

National capital

ERA 7

Emergence of Modern America
1890–1930

1898
Spanish-American War involves America in Cuba and Philippines.

Hawaii becomes a U.S. possession.

| **1890** | **1895** | **1900** |

Late 1800s
Jim Crow laws passed to limit rights of African Americans.

1890
Three **National Parks** are established in California.

The Spanish-American War and World Power

The United States became recognized as a world power after the Spanish-American War.

★ The Spanish-American War was fought over the independence of Cuba, a Spanish colony for 400 years.

★ After the *Maine*, a U.S. warship, exploded in Havana harbor, Americans called for U.S. intervention in Cuba.

★ U.S. victories over Spain brought independence to Cuba and made the Philippines and Puerto Rico U.S. territories.

Feb. 15 U.S.S. Maine explodes and ignites the war.

FIGHTING IN CUBA
1898

- Spanish possession
- American fleet movement
- Spanish fleet movement
- U.S. blockade
- Major battle site

| 0 | 150 | 300 miles |
| 0 | 150 | 300 kilometers |

A After the sinking of the *Maine*, the U.S. Navy blockaded Cuba, trapping the main Spanish fleet. When it tried to escape, the Americans sank all seven Spanish ships.

❶ 1898 Philippines becomes a U.S. territory.

❷ 1899–1902 Philippine insurrection fails to win independence from the United States.

FIGHTING IN THE PHILIPPINES
1898

- Spanish possession
- American fleet movement
- Major battle site
- British colony
- U.S. fleet

| 0 | 250 | 500 miles |
| 0 | 250 | 500 kilometers |

B The U.S. Navy destroyed a Spanish fleet in Manila, preventing Spain's ground forces from sailing to Cuba and helping the Spanish cause there.

Early 1900s
Immigrants from Southern and Eastern Europe pour into U.S. cities.

1915
Great Migration of Southern blacks begins.

1920
Women's vote becomes constitutional right.

1924
Indians become U.S. citizens.

1909
NAACP is founded.

1914–1918
World War consumes Europe.

1920–1933
Prohibition makes alcoholic drinks illegal.

1929
Great Depression begins.

1905   1910   1915   1920   1925   1930

1917
U.S. enters war, sends troops to France.

1924
Immigration from Southern and Eastern Europe limited by law.

C Theodore Roosevelt (center) poses with his Rough Riders after winning the battle at San Juan Hill in Cuba. A few years later, Roosevelt was elected President of the United States.

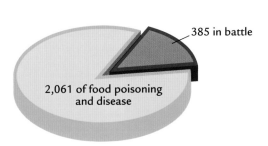

385 in battle

2,061 of food poisoning and disease

D **U.S. DEATHS IN THE SPANISH-AMERICAN WAR**

While the superiority of the U.S. Navy kept the number of battle deaths low, food poisoning from spoiled rations and tropical diseases such as malaria, dysentery, and yellow fever killed more than 2,000 troops.

E Victory over Spain led to U.S. acquisition of many Pacific islands. U.S. companies acquired Hawaii. These islands became way stations for expanding trade with Asia.

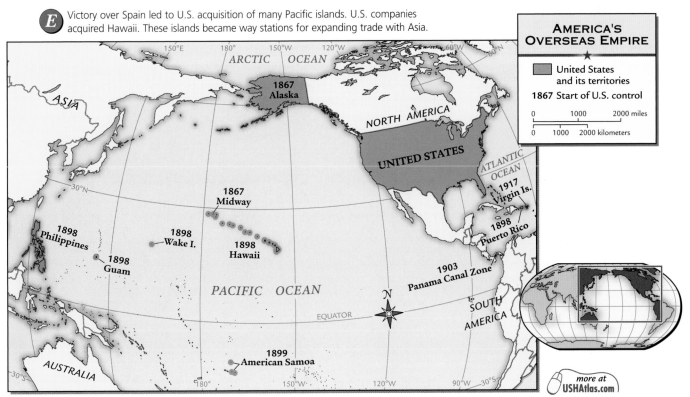

AMERICA'S OVERSEAS EMPIRE

☆
United States and its territories

1867 Start of U.S. control

0   1000   2000 miles
0   1000   2000 kilometers

ARCTIC OCEAN

ASIA

1867 Alaska

NORTH AMERICA

UNITED STATES

ATLANTIC OCEAN

1917 Virgin Is.

1867 Midway

1898 Philippines

1898 Wake I.

1898 Hawaii

1898 Guam

1898 Puerto Rico

1903 Panama Canal Zone

PACIFIC OCEAN

EQUATOR

SOUTH AMERICA

1899 American Samoa

AUSTRALIA

more at USHAtlas.com

Immigration and the Growth of Cities

Nearly 15 million immigrants entered the United States between 1895 and 1914, most of them Roman Catholics and Jews from Southern and Eastern Europe.

★ Many of the new immigrants were from Italy, Russia, and Poland. They tended to settle in large cities, such as Chicago and New York.

★ Settlement houses, such as Hull House in Chicago, helped immigrants adjust to life in America's cities.

★ The new immigrants made the population of the United States more diverse than that of any other nation in the world.

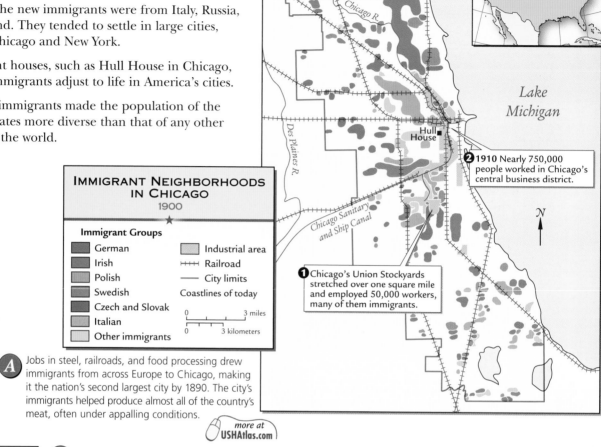

IMMIGRANT NEIGHBORHOODS IN CHICAGO
1900

Immigrant Groups
- German
- Irish
- Polish
- Swedish
- Czech and Slovak
- Italian
- Other immigrants
- Industrial area
- ++++ Railroad
- — City limits
- Coastlines of today

0   3 miles
0   3 kilometers

2 1910 Nearly 750,000 people worked in Chicago's central business district.

1 Chicago's Union Stockyards stretched over one square mile and employed 50,000 workers, many of them immigrants.

A Jobs in steel, railroads, and food processing drew immigrants from across Europe to Chicago, making it the nation's second largest city by 1890. The city's immigrants helped produce almost all of the country's meat, often under appalling conditions.

more at USHAtlas.com

B More and more immigrants came from Southern and Eastern Europe. Many Americans felt the newcomers were culturally inferior. In 1921 and 1924, Congress set new immigration *quotas*, or limits.

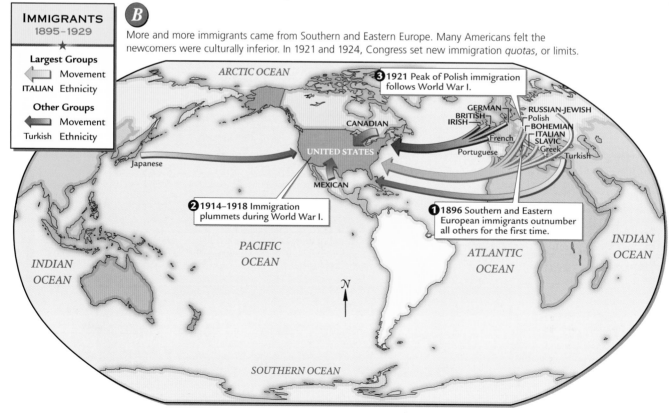

IMMIGRANTS 1895–1929

Largest Groups
← Movement
ITALIAN Ethnicity

Other Groups
← Movement
Turkish Ethnicity

3 1921 Peak of Polish immigration follows World War I.

2 1914–1918 Immigration plummets during World War I.

1 1896 Southern and Eastern European immigrants outnumber all others for the first time.

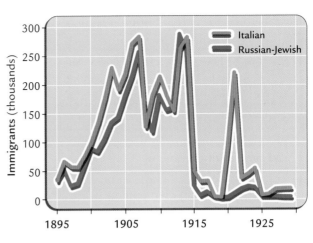

 C Once earlier immigrants saved enough money, they moved away from New York's Lower East Side. More recent immigrants from Southern and Eastern Europe, such as the ones in this colorized photo, moved in to replace them.

D ITALIAN AND RUSSIAN-JEWISH IMMIGRANTS

Southern Italians fleeing poverty and Russian Jews fleeing religious persecution were two of the largest immigrant groups in the years before World War I.

"Nowhere in the world are so many people crowded together on one square mile as here."

—JACOB RIIS
DESCRIPTION OF AN IMMIGRANT
NEIGHBORHOOD IN NEW YORK CITY
HOW THE OTHER HALF LIVES, 1890

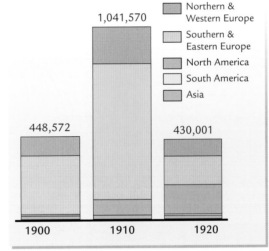

E IMMIGRANT ORIGINS

The start of World War I in 1914 cut off most immigration by Europeans. In 1917 newly required literacy tests cut immigration still further.

F

As cities grew, they began providing new services that people today take for granted, such as garbage collection, street lights, and public transportation. Most cities were still in the Northeast. Compare this map to map C on page 55.

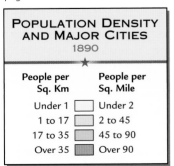

POPULATION DENSITY AND MAJOR CITIES
1890

People per Sq. Km	People per Sq. Mile
Under 1	Under 2
1 to 17	2 to 45
17 to 35	45 to 90
Over 35	Over 90

The United States Enters World War I

At first the United States resisted involvement in World War I, but eventually U.S. troops helped win the war.

★ Austria-Hungary had declared war on Serbia in 1914. The rest of Europe quickly took sides in the conflict.

★ On one side were the nations known as the Central Powers. On the other side were the Allies.

★ Much of the fighting was done from trenches dug along two battlefronts in Europe: the Western Front and the Eastern Front.

★ The United States joined the Allies in 1917. After another year of brutal trench warfare, the Central Powers surrendered.

"In one instant the entire front, as far as the eye could reach... was a sheet of flame."

—AMERICAN CORPORAL EUGENE KENNEDY
BATTLE OF ST. MIHIEL, SEPTEMBER 12–16, 1918

I WANT YOU
FOR U.S. ARMY
NEAREST RECRUITING STATION

A The familiar character Uncle Sam appeared on an Army recruiting poster in 1917.

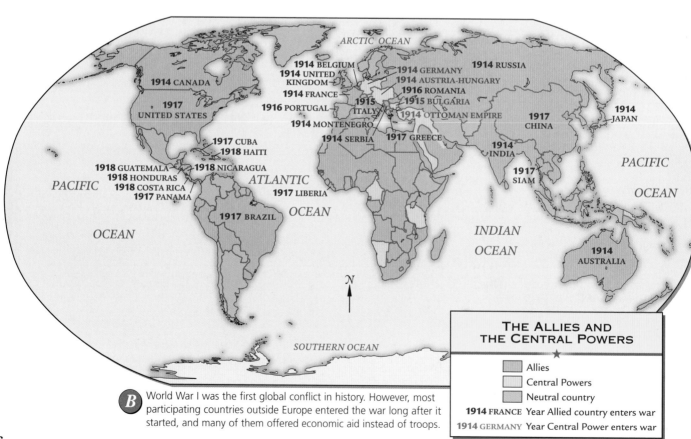

B World War I was the first global conflict in history. However, most participating countries outside Europe entered the war long after it started, and many of them offered economic aid instead of troops.

THE ALLIES AND THE CENTRAL POWERS

- Allies
- Central Powers
- Neutral country

1914 FRANCE Year Allied country enters war
1914 GERMANY Year Central Power enters war

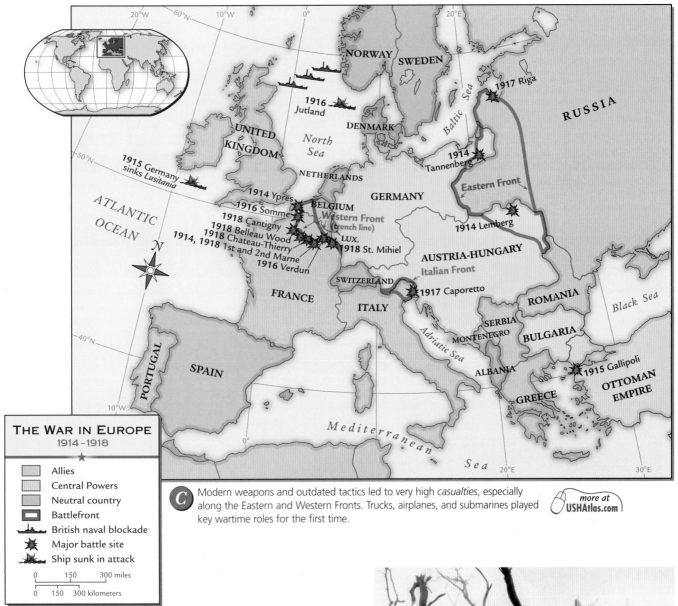

THE WAR IN EUROPE
1914–1918

- Allies
- Central Powers
- Neutral country
- Battlefront
- British naval blockade
- Major battle site
- Ship sunk in attack

0   150   300 miles
0   150   300 kilometers

C Modern weapons and outdated tactics led to very high *casualties*, especially along the Eastern and Western Fronts. Trucks, airplanes, and submarines played key wartime roles for the first time.

more at USHAtlas.com

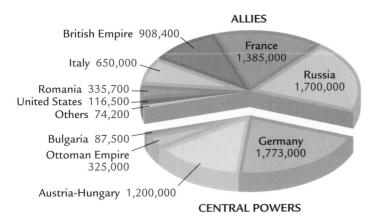

ALLIES

British Empire 908,400
Italy 650,000
France 1,385,000
Russia 1,700,000
Romania 335,700
United States 116,500
Others 74,200

Bulgaria 87,500
Ottoman Empire 325,000
Germany 1,773,000
Austria-Hungary 1,200,000

CENTRAL POWERS

D MILITARY DEATHS IN WORLD WAR I

Nearly 10 million Allied and Central Power soldiers died in the war. New weapons such as machine guns, mustard gas, and tanks increased the casualties. Compare with graph E on page 59.

E Machine guns, such as the one shown here, slaughtered attacking soldiers and prevented significant movement on the Western Front for three years.

A Widespread System of Segregation

By 1900 most African Americans were denied rights that most whites took for granted.

★ In a song from the early 1800s, Jim Crow was a derogatory name for a black man. Later it became the name for a system of discrimination.

★ *Jim Crow laws* rigidly enforced racial *segregation*, or separation. They restricted the rights of blacks who were forced to use separate accommodations, such as railroad cars, schools, and restrooms.

★ In 1896 the Supreme Court ruled that "separate but equal" accommodations were constitutional. But accommodations for blacks and whites were in fact rarely equal.

★ African Americans began moving to the North to escape discrimination in the South. New cultural expressions in literature and music blossomed in these new black communities.

"The problem of the Twentieth Century is the problem of the color line."

—W.E.B. DUBOIS, 1900
HISTORIAN AND SOCIOLOGIST

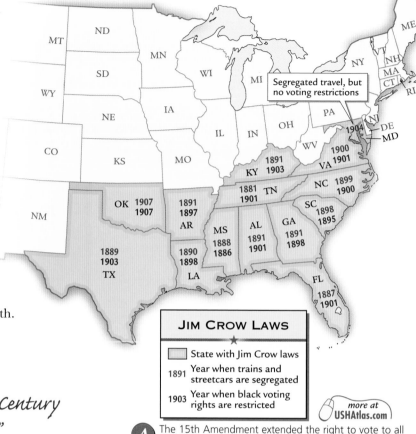

Segregated travel, but no voting restrictions

JIM CROW LAWS
★

	State with Jim Crow laws
1891	Year when trains and streetcars are segregated
1903	Year when black voting rights are restricted

more at USHAtlas.com

A The 15th Amendment extended the right to vote to all males over 21. In the South, however, poll taxes, literacy tests, prejudiced law enforcement, and violence kept most African American men from using their right to vote.

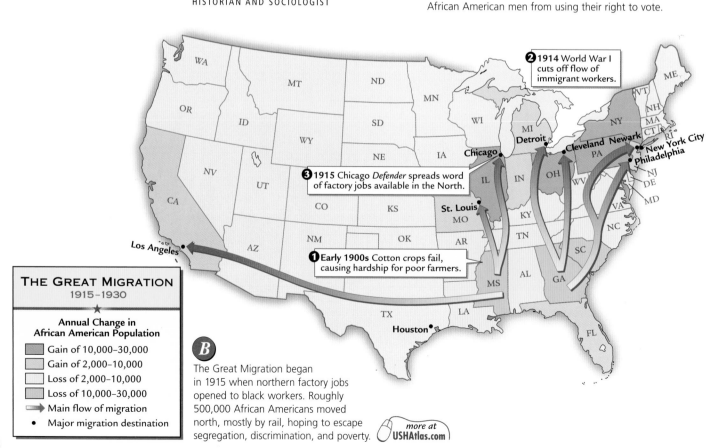

❷ 1914 World War I cuts off flow of immigrant workers.

❸ 1915 Chicago *Defender* spreads word of factory jobs available in the North.

❶ Early 1900s Cotton crops fail, causing hardship for poor farmers.

THE GREAT MIGRATION
1915–1930
★

Annual Change in African American Population

| | |
| Gain of 10,000–30,000 |
| Gain of 2,000–10,000 |
| Loss of 2,000–10,000 |
| Loss of 10,000–30,000 |
| ➡ Main flow of migration |
| • Major migration destination |

B The Great Migration began in 1915 when northern factory jobs opened to black workers. Roughly 500,000 African Americans moved north, mostly by rail, hoping to escape segregation, discrimination, and poverty.

more at USHAtlas.com

C BLACK MIGRATION

During World War I, African Americans moved to cities in the North and West to start new lives with jobs in war-related industries. Even outside the South, however, blacks still faced many forms of discrimination.

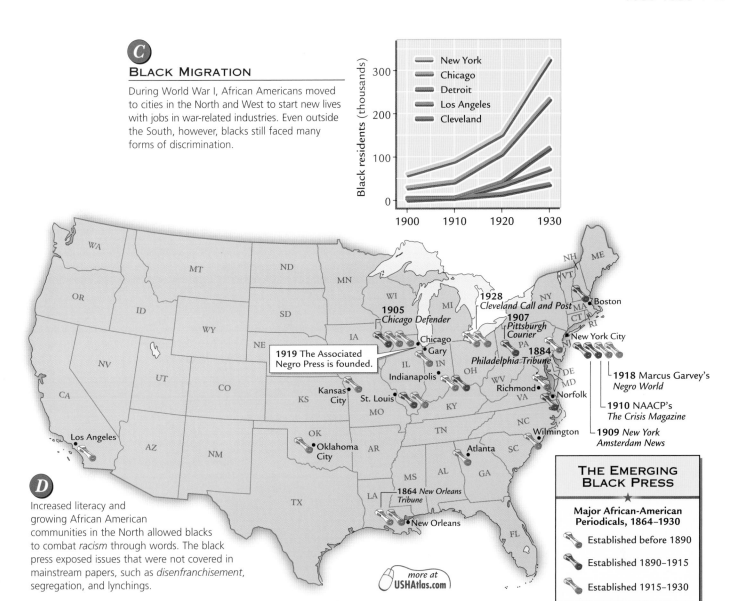

Chart: Black residents (thousands)
- New York
- Chicago
- Detroit
- Los Angeles
- Cleveland

y-axis: 0, 100, 200, 300
x-axis: 1900, 1910, 1920, 1930

1928 *Cleveland Call and Post*

1905 *Chicago Defender*

1907 *Pittsburgh Courier*

1919 The Associated Negro Press is founded.

1884 *Philadelphia Tribune*

Boston
New York City

1918 Marcus Garvey's *Negro World*

1910 NAACP's *The Crisis Magazine*

1909 *New York Amsterdam News*

Chicago
Gary
Indianapolis
Kansas City
St. Louis
Richmond
Norfolk
Wilmington
Los Angeles
Oklahoma City
Atlanta

1864 *New Orleans Tribune*
New Orleans

more at USHAtlas.com

D

Increased literacy and growing African American communities in the North allowed blacks to combat *racism* through words. The black press exposed issues that were not covered in mainstream papers, such as *disenfranchisement*, segregation, and lynchings.

THE EMERGING BLACK PRESS
★
Major African-American Periodicals, 1864–1930

- Established before 1890
- Established 1890–1915
- Established 1915–1930

E The 1920s were called the *Jazz Age*. African American musicians brought the new musical style from the South to cities such as Chicago and New York. Jazz bands like the one in this photo entertained white and black club-goers, radio listeners, and record buyers throughout the country.

F The *Harlem Renaissance*, a black literary movement in the 1920s and 1930s, fueled the creativity of numerous black authors. Langston Hughes, shown here, was one of the era's most gifted and prolific writers.

Reforms Change America

The 1910s and 1920s were decades of reform at both the state and national level.

★ After decades of effort, women gained the right to vote with the ratification the 19th Amendment in 1920.

★ The federal government began efforts to preserve our country's scenic beauty and natural wonders.

★ Between 1910 and 1930, states set limits on the amount and type of work children could perform.

★ In 1920 the 18th Amendment prohibited the sale and manufacture of alcoholic beverages.

A *Suffrage* is the right to vote. Women called *suffragists* had fought for that right since the 1850s. In the 1910s, woman suffrage rallies drew the attention of U.S. politicians and the support of suffragists worldwide.

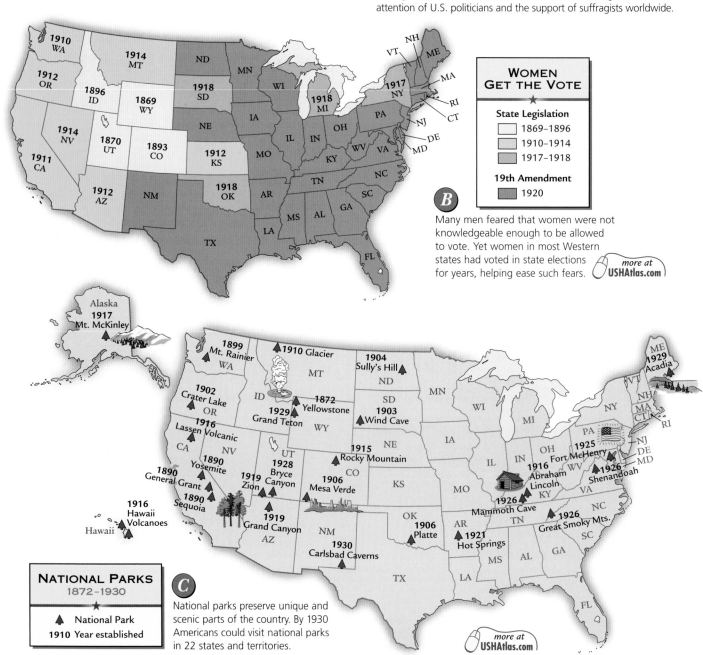

WOMEN GET THE VOTE
★
State Legislation
☐ 1869–1896
☐ 1910–1914
☐ 1917–1918

19th Amendment
☐ 1920

B Many men feared that women were not knowledgeable enough to be allowed to vote. Yet women in most Western states had voted in state elections for years, helping ease such fears. *more at* USHAtlas.com

NATIONAL PARKS
1872–1930
★
▲ National Park
1910 Year established

C National parks preserve unique and scenic parts of the country. By 1930 Americans could visit national parks in 22 states and territories.

more at USHAtlas.com

80

LIMITING CHILD LABOR

★

Maximum Hours of Daily Work per Child, by Law

■	No limit
■	11–12
■	10
■	9
■	8
■	Limits vary

D In 1890, 20 percent of the nation's children were employed full time. The first national child labor law was declared unconstitutional by the U.S. Supreme Court in 1918. Many states then set their own limits.

more at
USHAtlas.com

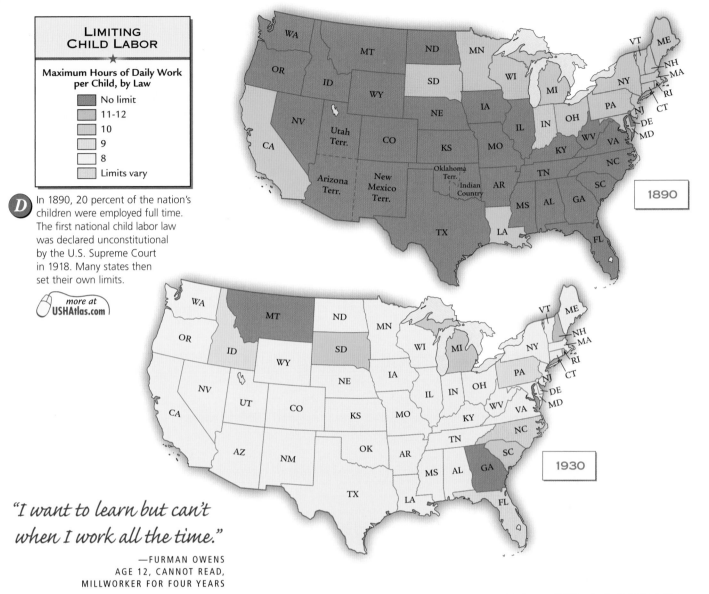

1890

1930

"I want to learn but can't when I work all the time."

—FURMAN OWENS
AGE 12, CANNOT READ,
MILLWORKER FOR FOUR YEARS

E Factories hired children because they were cheaper and less demanding than adults. Most money earned by child laborers, such as this one, went to help their families.

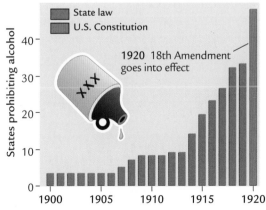

■	State law
■	U.S. Constitution

1920 18th Amendment goes into effect

States prohibiting alcohol

F **PROHIBITION**

In 1920 the temperance movement and others succeeded in having alcohol banned by the 18th Amendment. The ban was unpopular, however, and in 1933 the 21st Amendment repealed the 18th.

more at
USHAtlas.com

ERA 8

The Great Depression and World War II
1929-1945

1929–1940
Great Depression puts millions out of work.

1932
Franklin Roosevelt elected President of U.S.

1930

1933

1929
Stock market crashes.

1931
Japan seizes Manchuria.

1933
Hitler elected Chancellor of Germany.

Prosperity Ends, Immigration Slows

The stock market crash of 1929 introduced the Great Depression, worldwide economic hard times that lasted more than 10 years.

★ In the United States, immigration dropped to its lowest level in nearly 100 years.

★ At the same time, the Great Plains suffered an awful *drought*. The nation's breadbasket was called the "Dust Bowl" for its storms of blowing soil.

★ President Franklin D. Roosevelt's New Deal policy led to agencies that created jobs and helped the needy.

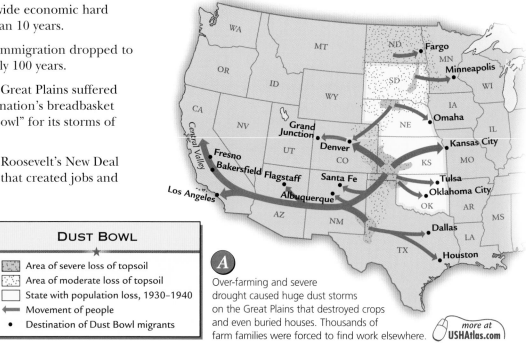

DUST BOWL
★

▨ Area of severe loss of topsoil
⠂ Area of moderate loss of topsoil
☐ State with population loss, 1930–1940
⬅ Movement of people
● Destination of Dust Bowl migrants

A Over-farming and severe drought caused huge dust storms on the Great Plains that destroyed crops and even buried houses. Thousands of farm families were forced to find work elsewhere. *more at* USHAtlas.com

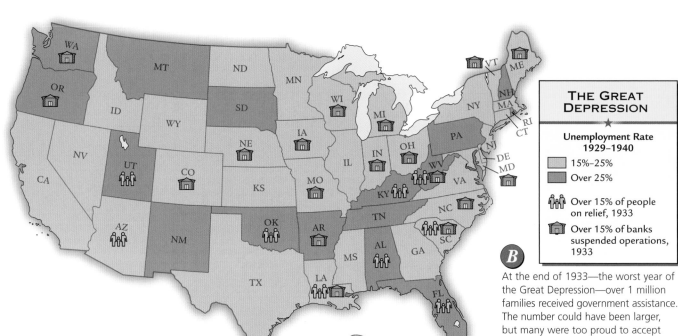

THE GREAT DEPRESSION
★

Unemployment Rate 1929–1940
☐ 15%–25%
▨ Over 25%

👪 Over 15% of people on relief, 1933

🏦 Over 15% of banks suspended operations, 1933

B At the end of 1933—the worst year of the Great Depression—over 1 million families received government assistance. The number could have been larger, but many were too proud to accept public help.

more at USHAtlas.com

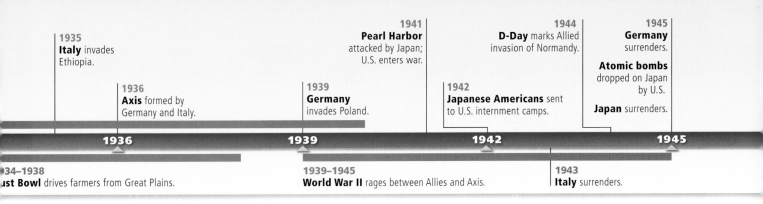

| 1935 **Italy** invades Ethiopia. | | 1941 **Pearl Harbor** attacked by Japan; U.S. enters war. | | 1944 **D-Day** marks Allied invasion of Normandy. | 1945 **Germany** surrenders. |

1936
Axis formed by Germany and Italy.

1939
Germany invades Poland.

1942
Japanese Americans sent to U.S. internment camps.

1945
Germany surrenders.

Atomic bombs dropped on Japan by U.S.

Japan surrenders.

1936 **1939** **1942** **1945**

...34–1938
...ust Bowl drives farmers from Great Plains.

1939–1945
World War II rages between Allies and Axis.

1943
Italy surrenders.

C Millions of Americans lost jobs, homes, businesses, and savings during the Depression. Bread lines and soup kitchens run by private charities offered help to those who had lost everything.

"Brother, can you spare a dime?"

—YIP HARBURG
FROM A POPULAR SONG OF
THE DEPRESSION ERA

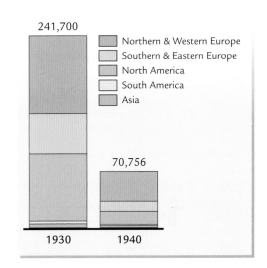

241,700

Northern & Western Europe
Southern & Eastern Europe
North America
South America
Asia

70,756

1930   1940

D **IMMIGRANT ORIGINS**

In the 1920s, federal quotas resulted in many prospective immigrants being turned away. During the Great Depression and World War II, the quotas went half-filled.

E During the Depression, few people immigrated to America. Many of those entering the country were Jews and others persecuted by German and Italian dictatorships.

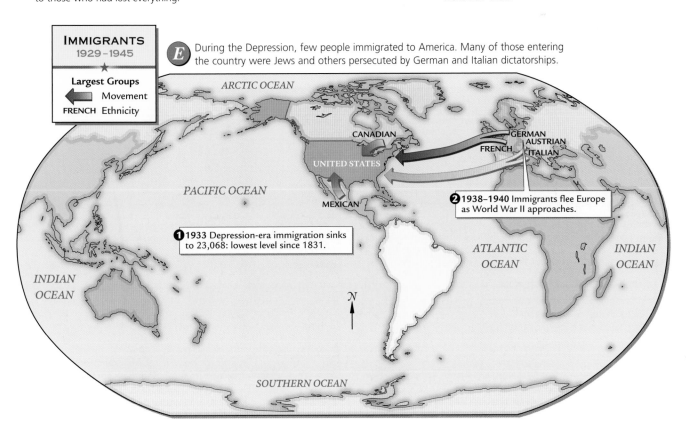

IMMIGRANTS
1929–1945

★

Largest Groups
← Movement
FRENCH Ethnicity

ARCTIC OCEAN

CANADIAN

UNITED STATES

GERMAN
AUSTRIAN
FRENCH
ITALIAN

PACIFIC OCEAN

MEXICAN

❶ 1933 Depression-era immigration sinks to 23,068: lowest level since 1831.

❷ 1938–1940 Immigrants flee Europe as World War II approaches.

ATLANTIC OCEAN

INDIAN OCEAN

INDIAN OCEAN

N

SOUTHERN OCEAN

Onset of World War II

The worldwide Depression helped promote militaristic governments in Germany, Italy, and Japan.

★ These countries soon began threatening their neighbors. When Germany invaded Poland in 1939, the world again went to war.

★ The United Kingdom and France led the Allies against the Axis Powers—Germany, Italy, and, later, Japan.

★ Though most Americans favored the Allies, the United States at first remained neutral.

1 1933 Hitler gains power.

2 1936 Germany defies 1919 treaty by returning troops to its Rhineland territory.

GERMAN AGGRESSION
★

- Germany, 1933
- Taken over by Germany, 1935–1939

0   250   500 miles
0   250   500 kilometers

A Adolf Hitler vowed to avenge the humiliations suffered by Germany after World War I. First Germany took back lands it had lost in World War I. Then it began seizing other countries.

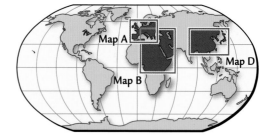

Map A
Map B
Map D

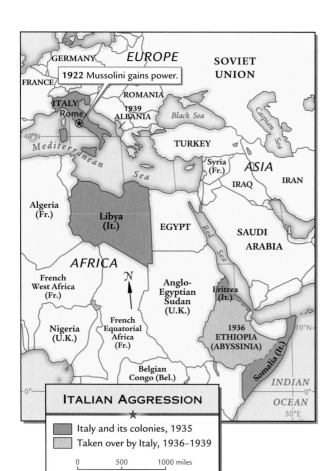

1922 Mussolini gains power.

ITALIAN AGGRESSION
★

- Italy and its colonies, 1935
- Taken over by Italy, 1936–1939

0   500   1000 miles
0   500   1000 kilometers

B Benito Mussolini came to power by promising Italians economic prosperity and military prestige. He pursued these goals through territorial expansion in Africa.

C In 1936 Benito Mussolini and Adolf Hitler, the dictators of Italy and Germany, formed the Axis to impose their military and political might on the world. Japan joined the Axis in 1940.

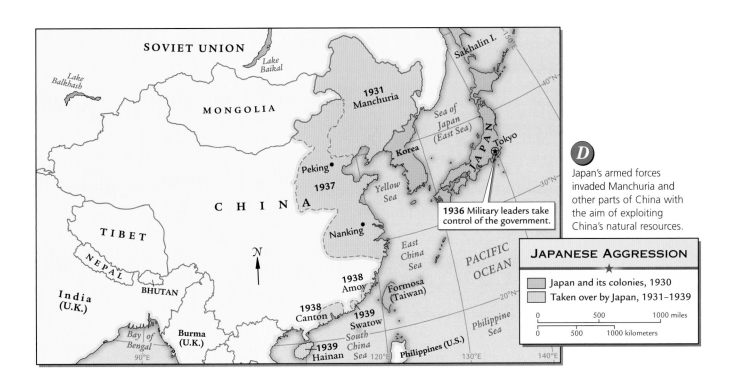

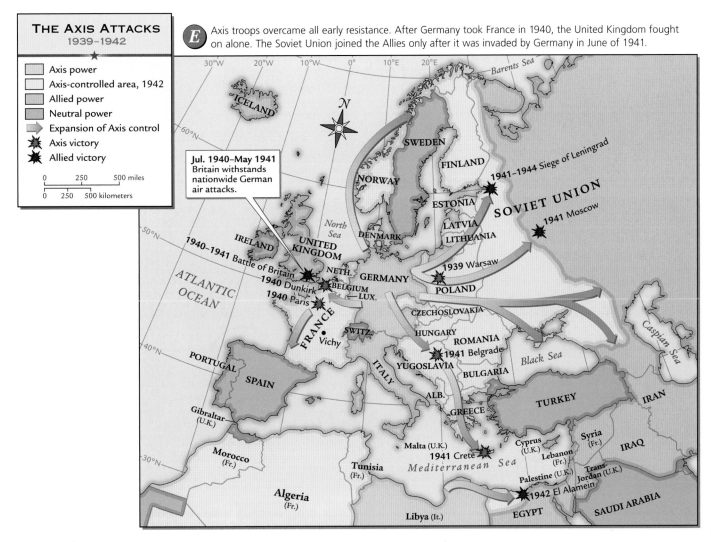

D Japan's armed forces invaded Manchuria and other parts of China with the aim of exploiting China's natural resources.

JAPANESE AGGRESSION

★

Japan and its colonies, 1930

Taken over by Japan, 1931–1939

0   500   1000 miles
0   500   1000 kilometers

THE AXIS ATTACKS
1939–1942

★

Axis power

Axis-controlled area, 1942

Allied power

Neutral power

Expansion of Axis control

Axis victory

Allied victory

0   250   500 miles
0   250   500 kilometers

E Axis troops overcame all early resistance. After Germany took France in 1940, the United Kingdom fought on alone. The Soviet Union joined the Allies only after it was invaded by Germany in June of 1941.

Jul. 1940–May 1941 Britain withstands nationwide German air attacks.

America Enters the War

In 1941 Japan attacked the U.S. Pacific fleet at Pearl Harbor. The United States declared war on Japan the next day. Germany then declared war on the United States.

★ Although 12 million people eventually joined the armed forces, in 1941 the U.S. military was not prepared for war.

★ Recruits and draftees needed months of intense military training to prepare them for combat in both Europe and the Pacific.

★ Distrusted because of their ancestry, more than 100,000 Japanese Americans were relocated from the West Coast to inland *internment camps*. Most lost their homes.

A Nearly 1,200 men lost their lives on the U.S.S. *Arizona* alone when Japan attacked Pearl Harbor. Many American planes and most large warships stationed at Pearl Harbor were damaged or destroyed.

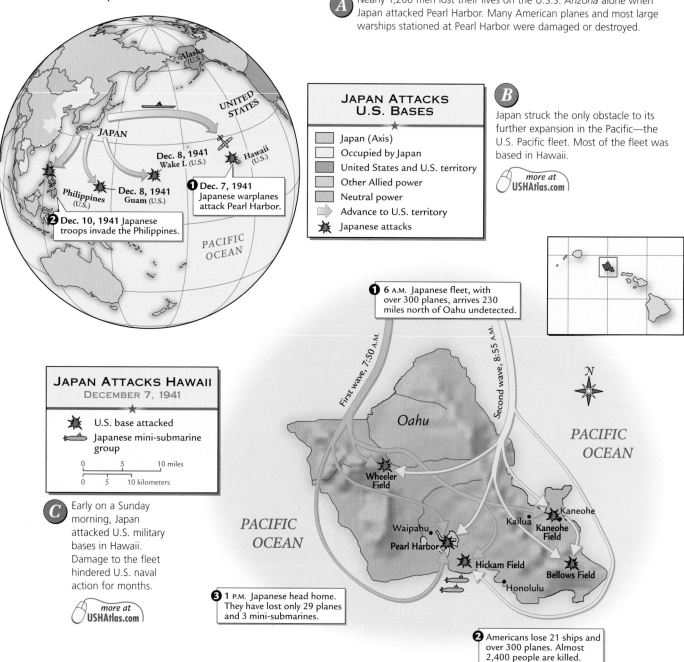

JAPAN ATTACKS U.S. BASES
★

	Japan (Axis)
	Occupied by Japan
	United States and U.S. territory
	Other Allied power
	Neutral power
→	Advance to U.S. territory
✸	Japanese attacks

B Japan struck the only obstacle to its further expansion in the Pacific—the U.S. Pacific fleet. Most of the fleet was based in Hawaii.

more at USHAtlas.com

Dec. 8, 1941 Wake I. (U.S.)

Hawaii (U.S.)

❶ Dec. 7, 1941 Japanese warplanes attack Pearl Harbor.

Dec. 8, 1941 Guam (U.S.)

Philippines (U.S.)

❷ Dec. 10, 1941 Japanese troops invade the Philippines.

JAPAN

UNITED STATES

Alaska (U.S.)

PACIFIC OCEAN

❶ 6 A.M. Japanese fleet, with over 300 planes, arrives 230 miles north of Oahu undetected.

JAPAN ATTACKS HAWAII
DECEMBER 7, 1941
★

✸	U.S. base attacked
🛥	Japanese mini-submarine group

0   5   10 miles
0   5   10 kilometers

C Early on a Sunday morning, Japan attacked U.S. military bases in Hawaii. Damage to the fleet hindered U.S. naval action for months.

more at USHAtlas.com

First wave 7:50 A.M.

Second wave, 8:55 A.M.

Oahu

Wheeler Field

Waipahu

Pearl Harbor

Hickam Field

Honolulu

Kailua

Kaneohe

Kaneohe Field

Bellows Field

PACIFIC OCEAN

PACIFIC OCEAN

N

❸ 1 P.M. Japanese head home. They have lost only 29 planes and 3 mini-submarines.

❷ Americans lose 21 ships and over 300 planes. Almost 2,400 people are killed.

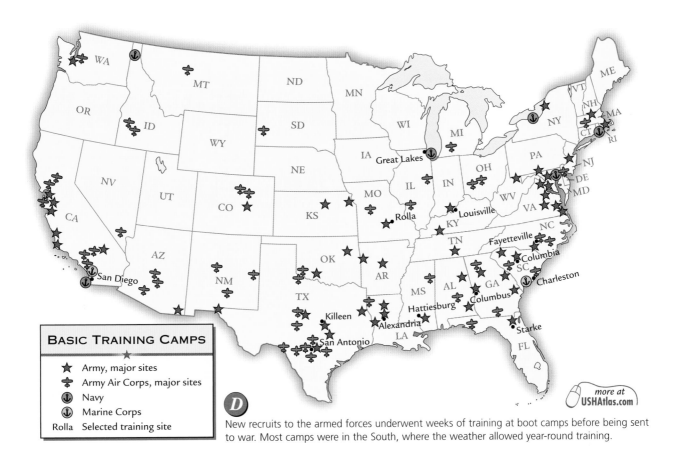

BASIC TRAINING CAMPS

★ Army, major sites
✈ Army Air Corps, major sites
⚓ Navy
⚓ Marine Corps
Rolla Selected training site

D New recruits to the armed forces underwent weeks of training at boot camps before being sent to war. Most camps were in the South, where the weather allowed year-round training.

more at
USHAtlas.com

E All Japanese American families along the West Coast were relocated, even though none had committed acts of spying or sabotage.

F While their families lived in crowded barracks, surrounded by barbed wire and armed guards, many Japanese Americans fought for their country. The 442nd Regiment, all Japanese American, was the most decorated unit in U.S. history.

"I didn't understand what I'd done. I was a native-born American citizen. I'd lived all my life in America."

—SYLVIA KOBAYASHI, JAPANESE AMERICAN
RELOCATED TO MINIDOKA, IDAHO

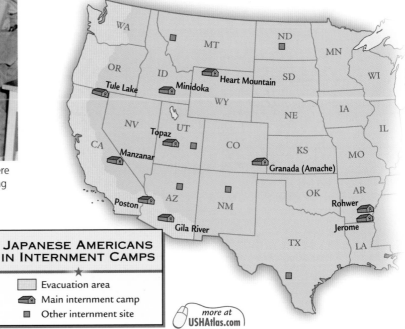

JAPANESE AMERICANS IN INTERNMENT CAMPS

★

▢ Evacuation area
🏠 Main internment camp
▪ Other internment site

more at
USHAtlas.com

Fighting the War in Europe

The Allies halted German advances in 1942, then went on the offensive to reverse earlier Axis gains.

★ Allied advances pushed Axis troops out of France, Italy, and the Soviet Union. Italy surrendered on September 3, 1943.

★ By 1945 the conflict had become a true world war, involving nearly 60 nations from six continents.

★ In 1945 Allied troops fought their way toward Berlin from the east, west, and south. Germany surrendered on May 7.

A Aerial bombings played a key role throughout the war. Both Axis and Allied bombers, such as the B-24s in this painting, attacked transportation routes, military facilities, and factories, many located in crowded cities.

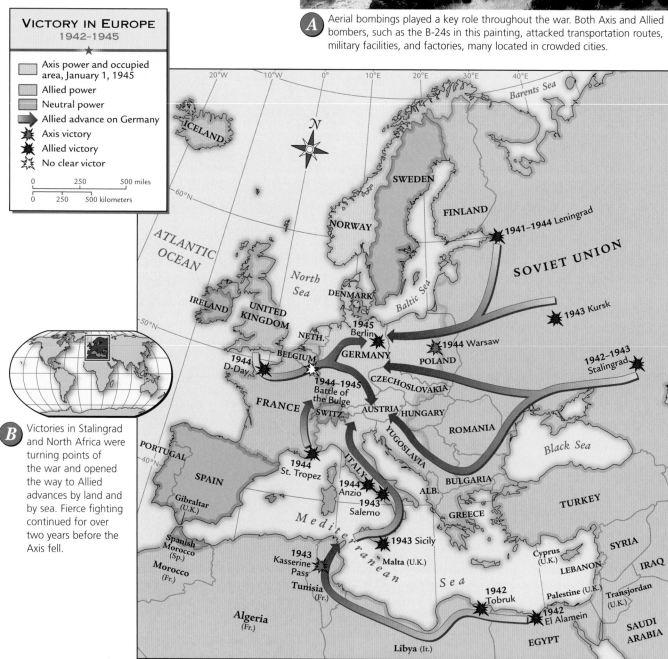

VICTORY IN EUROPE
1942–1945

- Axis power and occupied area, January 1, 1945
- Allied power
- Neutral power
- Allied advance on Germany
- Axis victory
- Allied victory
- No clear victor

0   250   500 miles
0   250   500 kilometers

B Victories in Stalingrad and North Africa were turning points of the war and opened the way to Allied advances by land and by sea. Fierce fighting continued for over two years before the Axis fell.

1941–1944 Leningrad
1943 Kursk
1944 Warsaw
1945 Berlin
1942–1943 Stalingrad
1944 D-Day
1944–1945 Battle of the Bulge
1944 St. Tropez
1944 Anzio
1943 Salerno
1943 Sicily
1943 Kasserine Pass
1942 Tobruk
1942 El Alamein

SWEDEN, FINLAND, NORWAY, SOVIET UNION, DENMARK, IRELAND, UNITED KINGDOM, NETH., BELGIUM, GERMANY, POLAND, CZECHOSLOVAKIA, FRANCE, SWITZ., AUSTRIA, HUNGARY, ROMANIA, YUGOSLAVIA, BULGARIA, ALB., GREECE, TURKEY, PORTUGAL, SPAIN, Gibraltar (U.K.), Spanish Morocco (Sp.), Morocco (Fr.), Tunisia (Fr.), Algeria (Fr.), Libya (It.), Malta (U.K.), Cyprus (U.K.), SYRIA, LEBANON, IRAQ, Palestine (U.K.), Transjordan (U.K.), EGYPT, SAUDI ARABIA, ICELAND, ATLANTIC OCEAN, North Sea, Baltic Sea, Barents Sea, Black Sea, Mediterranean Sea

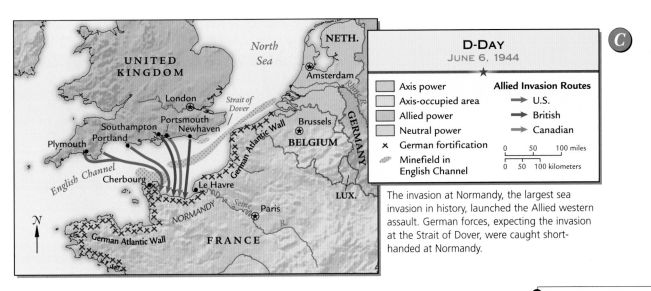

D-DAY
JUNE 6, 1944

Axis power

Axis-occupied area

Allied power

Neutral power

× German fortification

Minefield in English Channel

Allied Invasion Routes

→ U.S.

→ British

→ Canadian

0   50   100 miles

0   50   100 kilometers

C

The invasion at Normandy, the largest sea invasion in history, launched the Allied western assault. German forces, expecting the invasion at the Strait of Dover, were caught short-handed at Normandy.

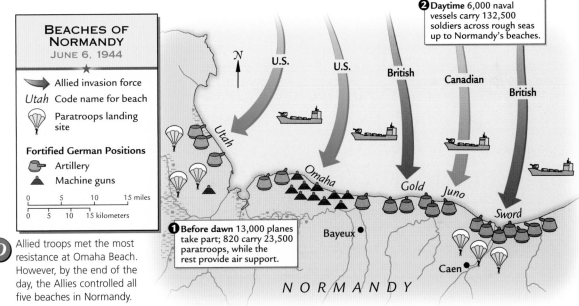

BEACHES OF NORMANDY
JUNE 6, 1944

Allied invasion force

Utah Code name for beach

Paratroops landing site

Fortified German Positions

Artillery

Machine guns

0   5   10   15 miles

0   5   10   15 kilometers

❷ **Daytime** 6,000 naval vessels carry 132,500 soldiers across rough seas up to Normandy's beaches.

❶ **Before dawn** 13,000 planes take part; 820 carry 23,500 paratroops, while the rest provide air support.

D Allied troops met the most resistance at Omaha Beach. However, by the end of the day, the Allies controlled all five beaches in Normandy.

E Allied troops faced deadly fire from German artillery as their landing craft fought through the waves to the beaches of Normandy, as in this hand-painted photo.

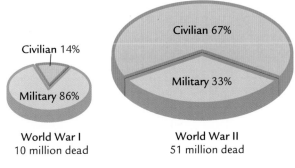

Civilian 14%

Military 86%

World War I
10 million dead

Civilian 67%

Military 33%

World War II
51 million dead

F ## LIVES LOST TO TOTAL WAR

Worldwide, World War II took more lives, mostly civilian, than any other war. Among the civilian dead were up to 13 million targeted by the Nazis as undesirable, about half of them Jews killed during the Holocaust. See the graphs on pages 31, 59, and 77.

Ending the War in the Pacific

As the land war raged in Europe, fighting intensified in the Pacific, and the war effort intensified at home.

★ At home, the entire country aided the war effort, which created jobs and brought the United States out of the Great Depression.

★ Abroad in the Pacific, aircraft carriers and U.S. Marines pushed westward toward Japan.

★ In August 1945, U.S. planes dropped atomic bombs on Hiroshima and Nagasaki. Japan soon surrendered.

★ Its key role in the Allied victory in World War II made the United States a *superpower*.

A Women filled the massive demand for workers in wartime industries. Characters like "Rosie the Riveter" became a symbol for these women.

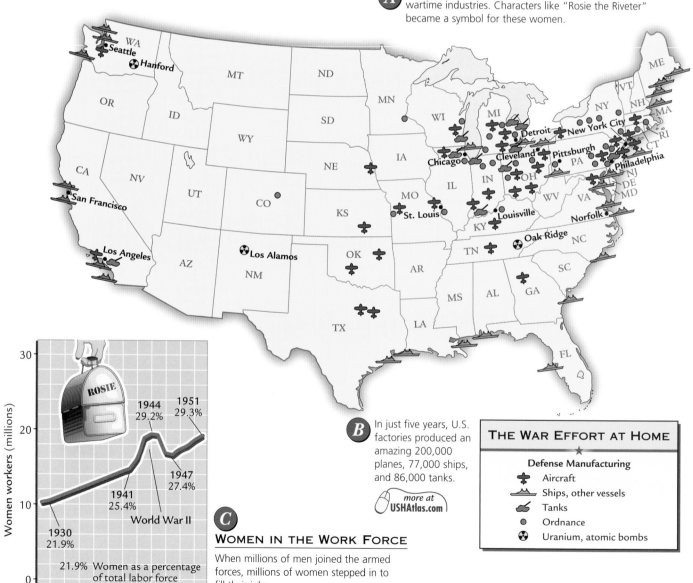

B In just five years, U.S. factories produced an amazing 200,000 planes, 77,000 ships, and 86,000 tanks.

more at USHAtlas.com

C

WOMEN IN THE WORK FORCE

When millions of men joined the armed forces, millions of women stepped in to fill their jobs.

Graph: Women in the Work Force
- Women workers (millions)
- 1930 21.9%
- 1941 25.4%
- World War II
- 1944 29.2%
- 1947 27.4%
- 1951 29.3%
- 21.9% Women as a percentage of total labor force

THE WAR EFFORT AT HOME
★

Defense Manufacturing

✈	Aircraft
🚢	Ships, other vessels
🛡	Tanks
●	Ordnance
☢	Uranium, atomic bombs

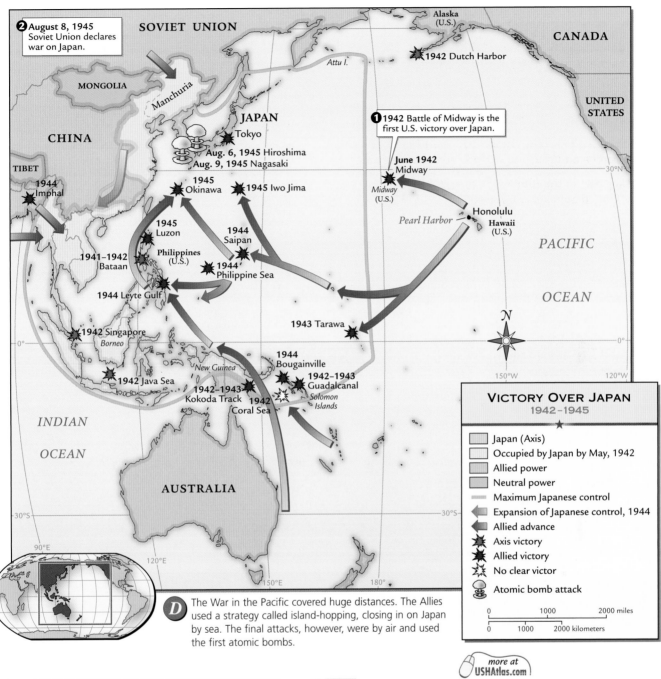

❷ August 8, 1945 Soviet Union declares war on Japan.

SOVIET UNION

MONGOLIA

Manchuria

CHINA

TIBET

1944 Imphal

JAPAN

Tokyo

Aug. 6, 1945 Hiroshima
Aug. 9, 1945 Nagasaki

1945 Okinawa

1945 Iwo Jima

1945 Luzon

1944 Saipan

Philippines (U.S.)

1941–1942 Bataan

1944 Philippine Sea

1944 Leyte Gulf

1942 Singapore

Borneo

1942 Java Sea

New Guinea

1944 Bougainville

1942–1943 Guadalcanal

Solomon Islands

1942–1943 Kokoda Track

1942 Coral Sea

INDIAN OCEAN

AUSTRALIA

Alaska (U.S.)

CANADA

1942 Dutch Harbor

Attu I.

UNITED STATES

❶ 1942 Battle of Midway is the first U.S. victory over Japan.

June 1942 Midway

Midway (U.S.)

Pearl Harbor

Honolulu
Hawaii (U.S.)

PACIFIC

OCEAN

1943 Tarawa

30°N

N

150°W   120°W

0°

90°E

120°E

150°E   180°

30°S

VICTORY OVER JAPAN
1942–1945
★

▢	Japan (Axis)
▢	Occupied by Japan by May, 1942
▢	Allied power
▢	Neutral power
▬	Maximum Japanese control
◀	Expansion of Japanese control, 1944
◀	Allied advance
✴	Axis victory
✴	Allied victory
✴	No clear victor
☁	Atomic bomb attack

0   1000   2000 miles
0   1000   2000 kilometers

D The War in the Pacific covered huge distances. The Allies used a strategy called island-hopping, closing in on Japan by sea. The final attacks, however, were by air and used the first atomic bombs.

more at USHAtlas.com

E U.S. Marines fought Japanese troops on Okinawa for two months. The bloody battle was seen as a preview of far deadlier combat to come if the Allies had to invade Japan. Atomic bombs forced the Japanese to surrender without an invasion.

ERA 9

United States After World War II

1945 TO EARLY 1970s

1949
NATO unites Western nations against the Soviet Union.

1945
World War II ends.
United Nations founded.
Cold War begins.

1950–1953
Korean War fought to a standstill.

1945

1950

1941
Great Migration of blacks resumes, lasts until 1970.

1946
Baby Boom begins, continues to 1964.

American Troops Fight the Korean War

After World War II, Japanese control of Korea ended. U.S. troops occupied the South, Soviet troops the North. In 1948 each side set up its own government.

★ In June 1950, *Communist* North Korea invaded South Korea. The United States led a coalition of United Nations troops against the invaders.

★ An *armistice* ended the war in January 1953. It left Korea divided almost exactly as it had been before the war.

★ The Korean War was the first military fight of the Cold War, a struggle between democratic and communist countries.

A The devastation of war forced many Koreans from their homes. These young *refugees* help their mother as they flee from the danger of a nearby battle.

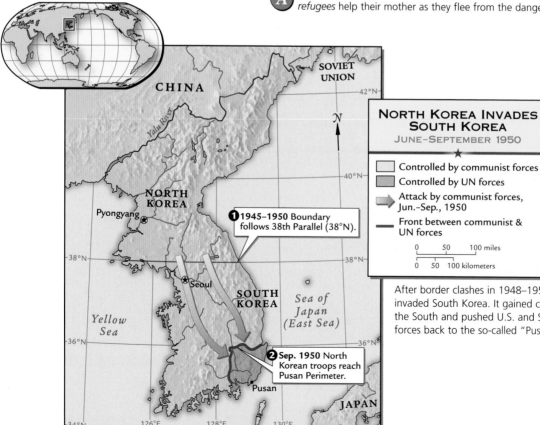

NORTH KOREA INVADES SOUTH KOREA
JUNE–SEPTEMBER 1950
★

- ☐ Controlled by communist forces
- ▧ Controlled by UN forces
- ➡ Attack by communist forces, Jun.–Sep., 1950
- ━ Front between communist & UN forces

0   50   100 miles
0   50   100 kilometers

❶ 1945–1950 Boundary follows 38th Parallel (38°N).

❷ Sep. 1950 North Korean troops reach Pusan Perimeter.

B After border clashes in 1948–1950, North Korea invaded South Korea. It gained control of most of the South and pushed U.S. and South Korean forces back to the so-called "Pusan Perimeter."

1963
President Kennedy assassinated.

1955–1956
Montgomery bus boycott helps launch civil rights movement.

1959
Alaska and Hawaii become states.

1964
Civil Rights Act passed by Congress.

1970
Kent State war protest in Ohio ends in bloody violence.

1957–1964
U.S. military advisers in Vietnam.

1965–1973
Vietnam War fought by U.S. troops.

1975
Communist victory in Vietnam.

1955   1960   1965   1970   1975

1956
Interstate highway system authorized.

1962
Cuban missile crisis leads to U.S.–Soviet showdown.

1968
Martin Luther King, Jr., assassinated in Memphis.

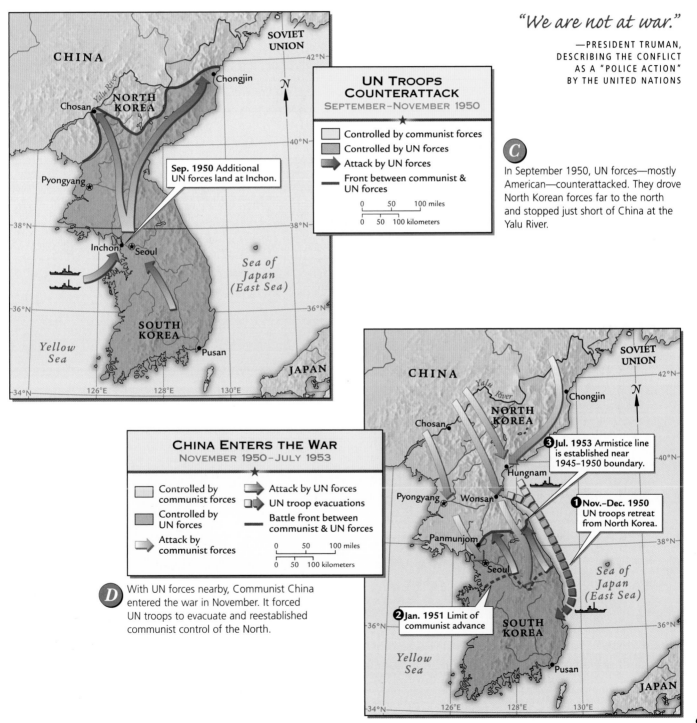

UN TROOPS COUNTERATTACK
SEPTEMBER–NOVEMBER 1950
★

- Controlled by communist forces
- Controlled by UN forces
- Attack by UN forces
- Front between communist & UN forces

0   50   100 miles
0   50   100 kilometers

Sep. 1950 Additional UN forces land at Inchon.

"We are not at war."

—PRESIDENT TRUMAN, DESCRIBING THE CONFLICT AS A "POLICE ACTION" BY THE UNITED NATIONS

C In September 1950, UN forces—mostly American—counterattacked. They drove North Korean forces far to the north and stopped just short of China at the Yalu River.

CHINA ENTERS THE WAR
NOVEMBER 1950–JULY 1953
★

- Controlled by communist forces
- Controlled by UN forces
- Attack by communist forces
- Attack by UN forces
- UN troop evacuations
- Battle front between communist & UN forces

0   50   100 miles
0   50   100 kilometers

D With UN forces nearby, Communist China entered the war in November. It forced UN troops to evacuate and reestablished communist control of the North.

3 **Jul. 1953** Armistice line is established near 1945–1950 boundary.

1 **Nov.–Dec. 1950** UN troops retreat from North Korea.

2 **Jan. 1951** Limit of communist advance

93

Superpowers Face Off in the Cold War

The alliances of the Cold War were led by two superpowers: the democratic United States and the Communist Soviet Union, an outgrowth of Russia.

★ American-led alliances included NATO in Europe and North America and CENTO in Asia.

★ Communist countries in Eastern Europe joined the Warsaw Pact. Other countries became communist as well, including China in 1949 and Cuba in 1959. Most communist countries allied with the Soviet Union.

★ In the most perilous moment of the Cold War, the Cuban Missile Crisis brought the two superpowers to the brink of nuclear war.

A During the 1950s, Americans were so worried about the possibility of nuclear war that schoolchildren regularly practiced atomic bomb drills.

B

Both the United States and the Soviet Union stockpiled nuclear weapons. Each reasoned that fear of retaliation would keep the other from firing the first missile. This policy was known as MAD—Mutual Assured Destruction. *more at* USHAtlas.com

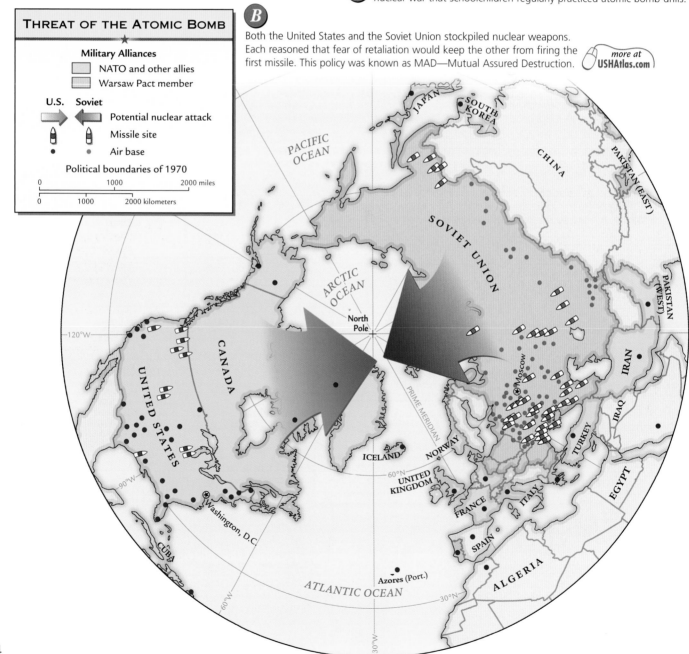

THREAT OF THE ATOMIC BOMB
★
Military Alliances
- NATO and other allies
- Warsaw Pact member

U.S.   Soviet
- → ← Potential nuclear attack
- Missile site
- • • Air base

Political boundaries of 1970

0   1000   2000 miles
0   1000   2000 kilometers

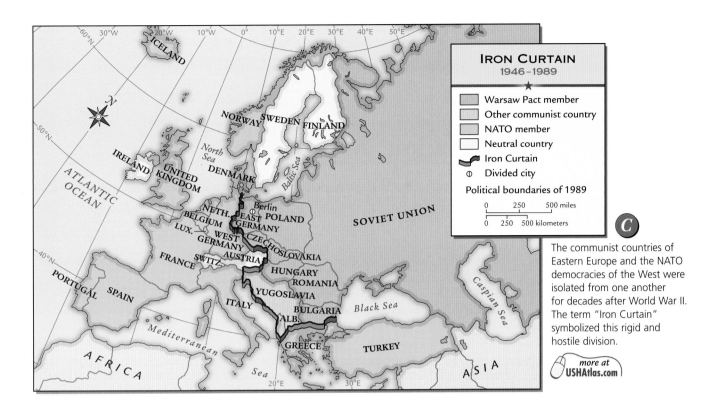

IRON CURTAIN
1946–1989
★

- Warsaw Pact member
- Other communist country
- NATO member
- Neutral country
- Iron Curtain
- Divided city

Political boundaries of 1989

0   250   500 miles
0   250   500 kilometers

C The communist countries of Eastern Europe and the NATO democracies of the West were isolated from one another for decades after World War II. The term "Iron Curtain" symbolized this rigid and hostile division.

more at USHAtlas.com

D When the Soviet Union installed nuclear missiles in Cuba, the United States used a naval *quarantine* (enforced isolation) to force their removal. The world watched, expecting nuclear war. After several tense days, the Soviets finally backed down and removed the missiles.

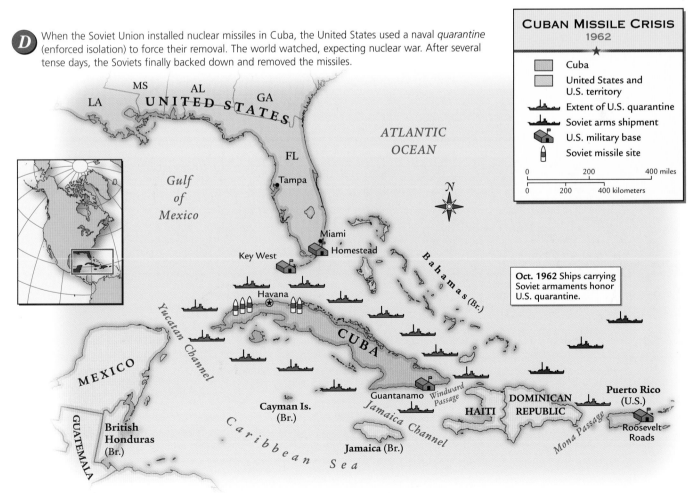

CUBAN MISSILE CRISIS
1962
★

- Cuba
- United States and U.S. territory
- Extent of U.S. quarantine
- Soviet arms shipment
- U.S. military base
- Soviet missile site

0   200   400 miles
0   200   400 kilometers

Oct. 1962 Ships carrying Soviet armaments honor U.S. quarantine.

Baby Boom and Suburban Growth

After World War II, the United States grew in population and admitted its first non-contiguous states.

★ Alaska and Hawaii became states in 1959, the most recent areas to gain statehood.

★ Returning troops by the millions got married and started families, creating a "baby boom."

★ Suburbs boomed too, made accessible by a recovering economy and by federal financing of new highways and low-cost mortgages.

A

BABY BOOM

Americans born during the years 1946–1964 were called the "Baby Boom" generation. Far more babies were born in those years than during the generations before or after.

B Growing families and affordable mortgages created a demand for millions of new *suburban* homes.

C Distant Alaska and Hawaii had grown familiar to Americans during World War II. After the war, Alaska was valued for its forests and minerals, Hawaii as a tourist destination. In 1959 they became the 49th and 50th states.

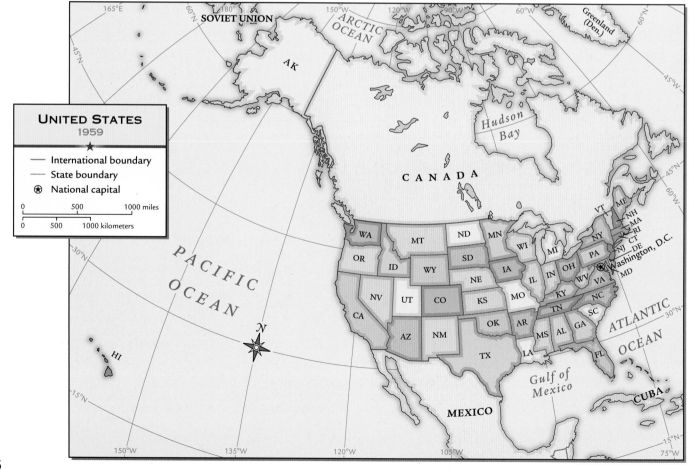

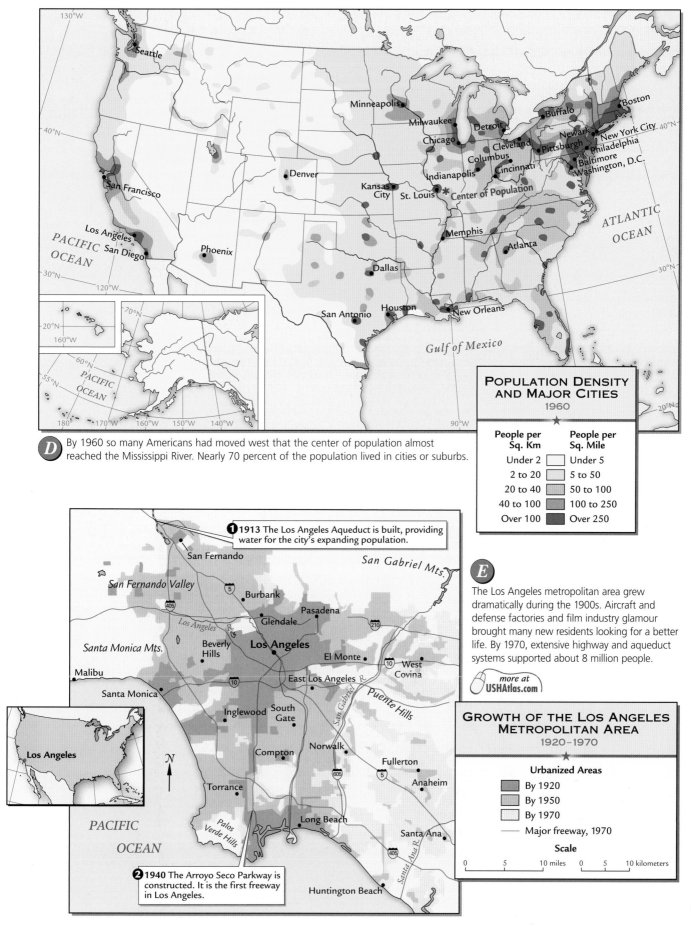

POPULATION DENSITY AND MAJOR CITIES
1960
★

People per Sq. Km	People per Sq. Mile
Under 2	Under 5
2 to 20	5 to 50
20 to 40	50 to 100
40 to 100	100 to 250
Over 100	Over 250

D By 1960 so many Americans had moved west that the center of population almost reached the Mississippi River. Nearly 70 percent of the population lived in cities or suburbs.

1 1913 The Los Angeles Aqueduct is built, providing water for the city's expanding population.

E The Los Angeles metropolitan area grew dramatically during the 1900s. Aircraft and defense factories and film industry glamour brought many new residents looking for a better life. By 1970, extensive highway and aqueduct systems supported about 8 million people.

more at USHAtlas.com

GROWTH OF THE LOS ANGELES METROPOLITAN AREA
1920–1970
★

Urbanized Areas
- By 1920
- By 1950
- By 1970
- — Major freeway, 1970

Scale
0   5   10 miles   0   5   10 kilometers

2 1940 The Arroyo Seco Parkway is constructed. It is the first freeway in Los Angeles.

In Search of the American Dream

After World War II, millions of immigrants and citizens sought better lives in the United States.

★ More and more immigrants came from Latin America and Asia.

★ Between 1940 and 1970, more than 5 million blacks left the South to escape racial discrimination and to seek opportunity elsewhere.

★ The contrast between the fight for freedom during World War II and the lack of freedom at home helped launch the civil rights movement.

B Thousands of refugees fled Cuba after the communist revolution there in 1959. Most eventually gained immigrant status and sought citizenship in the United States.

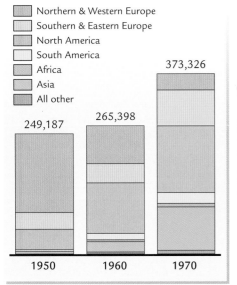

Legend:
- Northern & Western Europe
- Southern & Eastern Europe
- North America
- South America
- Africa
- Asia
- All other

249,187 (1950)
265,398 (1960)
373,326 (1970)

A IMMIGRANT ORIGINS

By 1970 immigrants from the Americas, Africa, and Asia far outnumbered those from Europe.

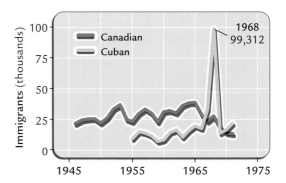

Canadian / Cuban

1968 99,312

Immigrants (thousands): 0, 25, 50, 75, 100
Years: 1945, 1955, 1965, 1975

C CUBAN AND CANADIAN IMMIGRANTS

Cuban refugees surged to the United States in 1959, gaining immigrant status in 1968. In contrast, steady numbers of Canadians moved to the United States until 1965, when immigration laws changed.

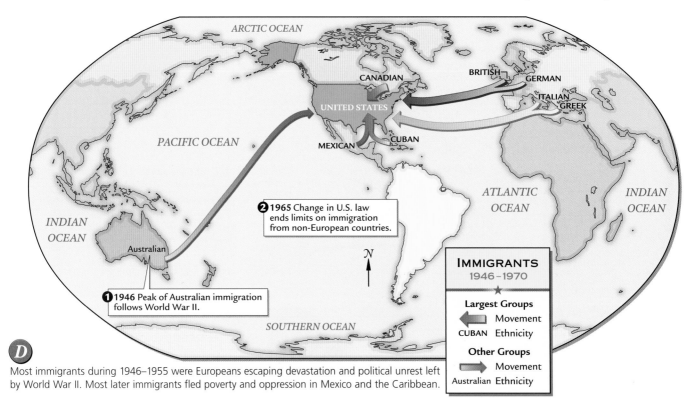

ARCTIC OCEAN

CANADIAN
BRITISH
GERMAN
ITALIAN
GREEK
UNITED STATES
MEXICAN
CUBAN
PACIFIC OCEAN
INDIAN OCEAN
ATLANTIC OCEAN
INDIAN OCEAN
Australian
SOUTHERN OCEAN

2 1965 Change in U.S. law ends limits on immigration from non-European countries.

1 1946 Peak of Australian immigration follows World War II.

N

IMMIGRANTS 1946–1970
★
Largest Groups
← Movement
CUBAN Ethnicity
Other Groups
→ Movement
Australian Ethnicity

D Most immigrants during 1946–1955 were Europeans escaping devastation and political unrest left by World War II. Most later immigrants fled poverty and oppression in Mexico and the Caribbean.

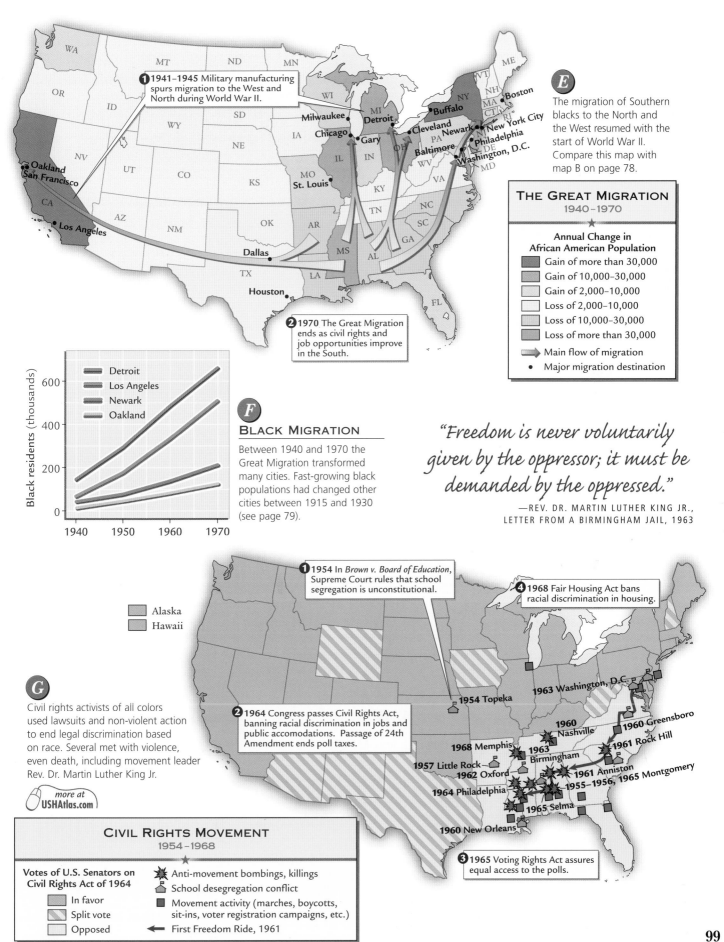

1 1941–1945 Military manufacturing spurs migration to the West and North during World War II.

2 1970 The Great Migration ends as civil rights and job opportunities improve in the South.

E The migration of Southern blacks to the North and the West resumed with the start of World War II. Compare this map with map B on page 78.

THE GREAT MIGRATION
1940–1970
★
Annual Change in African American Population
Gain of more than 30,000
Gain of 10,000–30,000
Gain of 2,000–10,000
Loss of 2,000–10,000
Loss of 10,000–30,000
Loss of more than 30,000
Main flow of migration
• Major migration destination

F
BLACK MIGRATION
Between 1940 and 1970 the Great Migration transformed many cities. Fast-growing black populations had changed other cities between 1915 and 1930 (see page 79).

Black residents (thousands)
Detroit
Los Angeles
Newark
Oakland

"Freedom is never voluntarily given by the oppressor; it must be demanded by the oppressed."
—REV. DR. MARTIN LUTHER KING JR.,
LETTER FROM A BIRMINGHAM JAIL, 1963

1 1954 In *Brown v. Board of Education*, Supreme Court rules that school segregation is unconstitutional.

4 1968 Fair Housing Act bans racial discrimination in housing.

Alaska
Hawaii

G
Civil rights activists of all colors used lawsuits and non-violent action to end legal discrimination based on race. Several met with violence, even death, including movement leader Rev. Dr. Martin Luther King Jr.

more at
USHAtlas.com

2 1964 Congress passes Civil Rights Act, banning racial discrimination in jobs and public accomodations. Passage of 24th Amendment ends poll taxes.

1954 Topeka

1963 Washington, D.C.
1960 Nashville
1960 Greensboro
1968 Memphis
1963 Birmingham
1961 Rock Hill
1957 Little Rock
1962 Oxford
1961 Anniston
1964 Philadelphia
1955–1956, 1965 Montgomery
1965 Selma
1960 New Orleans

3 1965 Voting Rights Act assures equal access to the polls.

CIVIL RIGHTS MOVEMENT
1954–1968
★

Votes of U.S. Senators on Civil Rights Act of 1964
In favor
Split vote
Opposed

✹ Anti-movement bombings, killings
⌂ School desegregation conflict
■ Movement activity (marches, boycotts, sit-ins, voter registration campaigns, etc.)
← First Freedom Ride, 1961

The Vietnam War Ends an Era

In 1957 U.S. military advisers went to assist capitalist South Vietnam, which faced a growing communist rebellion.

★ In 1965 the United States committed troops to fight against both the Viet Cong rebels and Communist North Vietnam, which supported them.

★ As the war went on, Americans at home became dissatisfied. Lack of support for the war eventually led to the withdrawal of U.S. troops in 1973.

★ Without the assistance of American troops, South Vietnam fell to communist forces in 1975.

B Helicopters were the workhorses of the Vietnam War. They were used to spot the enemy, defend ground troops, transport soldiers and supplies, and evacuate the dead and wounded.

❶ May 1954 Vietnamese rebels defeat the French; a divided Vietnam gains independence from France.

❸ Aug. 1964 Naval skirmish prompts Congress to pass resolution letting U.S. troops fight in Vietnam.

❷ Jul. 1959 Two U.S. military advisers become first Americans to die in the Vietnam War.

CHINA

NORTH VIETNAM

Red R.

Dien Bien Phu

Hanoi

Haiphong

Gulf of Tonkin

LAOS

1964 Vinh

1964 Gulf of Tonkin Incident

Vientiane

Mekong R.

Dong Hoi

1954 Demilitarized Zone (DMZ)

THAILAND

Hue

Ho Chi Minh Trail

ANNAMITE MTS.

1960, 1964 Kontum

CAMBODIA

CENTRAL HIGHLANDS

1964 Buon Me Thuot

Nha Trang

Phnom Penh · Trail

SOUTH VIETNAM

1959 Bien Hoa

Sihanouk Trail

Sihanoukville

1963 Ap Bac

1960 Can Tho

Saigon

Mekong Delta

South China Sea

Gulf of Thailand

A
Vietnam had been divided in 1954. North Vietnam sent weapons to the Viet Cong rebels in the South via the Ho Chi Minh Trail. U.S. advisers trained South Vietnamese forces to fight the rebels and cut their supply lines.

peak troop level
543,300

U.S. personnel (thousands)

600
500
400
300
200
100
0

First combat troops arrive in Vietnam

1955   1965   1975

C U.S. MILITARY IN VIETNAM

Millions of Americans served in Vietnam between 1965 and 1973. Before and after that, most Americans in Vietnam were military advisers.

more at USHAtlas.com

U.S. INVOLVEMENT GROWS
1957–1964
★

Areas of Control, 1960

	North Vietnam and Viet Cong
	South Vietnam
	DMZ, 1954
→	Supply route
—	Highway
	U.S. 7th fleet (until 1973)

Battles

✺ U.S. ground, air, naval forces
✺ U.S. advisers or air support
✺ U.S. air strike
✺ No U.S. involvement

(See also maps D and F.)

0   75   150 miles
0   75   150 kilometers

100

U.S. TROOPS CARRY THE LOAD
1965–1968

★

Areas of Control, 1966
North Vietnam and Viet Cong
South Vietnam

Detailed legend on map A.

D In 1965, the U.S. role in Vietnam switched from advising to fighting. U.S. bombers struck targets in the North. Ground troops faced communist forces who used *guerrilla* tactics such as ambushes and mines.

CHINA

NORTH VIETNAM

Red R.

1965–68 Hanoi

1965–68 Haiphong

Gulf of Tonkin

LAOS

Vientiane

1965–68 Vinh

1965–68 Mu Gia Pass

❶ Mar. 1965 First U.S. combat troops arrive in Vietnam.

1966–68 Khe Sanh
DMZ

1968 Hue

Da Nang

THAILAND

Ho Chi Minh Trail

1966–67 Dak To

My Lai

1968 Kontum

Pleiku

1965 Ia Drang Valley

CAMBODIA

CENTRAL HIGHLANDS

❷ Jan. 1968 Tet Offensive by the North fails militarily, but erodes U.S. public support for the war.

1968 Buon Me Thuot

Phnom Penh

Sihanouk Trail

SOUTH VIETNAM

Cam Ranh Bay

Sihanoukville

Gulf of Thailand

1968 Can Tho

Mekong Delta

1968 Saigon

South China Sea

CHINA

NORTH VIETNAM

Red R.

1972 Hanoi

1972 Haiphong

Gulf of Tonkin

LAOS

Vientiane

❸ Jan. 1973 Cease-fire signed, last U.S. troops leave.

DMZ

1972 Quang Tri

Hue

1969 Hamburger Hill

1975 Da Nang

THAILAND

Ho Chi Minh Trail

SOUTH VIETNAM

❷ Jan.–Apr. 1971 South Vietnam invades Laos with U.S. support.

1972 Kontum

❶ May 1970 Secret U.S. invasion of Cambodia sparks opposition by U.S. public and Congress.

CENTRAL HIGHLANDS

1975 Buon Me Thuot

CAMBODIA

Phnom Penh

Sihanouk Trail

Cam Ranh Bay

1972 An Loc

Sihanoukville

1975 Saigon

❹ Apr. 1975 North Vietnamese troops capture Saigon, war ends.

Gulf of Thailand

Mekong Delta

South China Sea

U.S. TROOPS WITHDRAW, THE WAR ENDS
1969–1975

★

Areas of Control, 1973
North Vietnam and Viet Cong
South Vietnam
Major advance
Detailed legend on map A.

F U.S. ground troops played a diminishing role in the war after 1969. More of the fighting fell to the army of South Vietnam. The last U.S. troops left in 1973. Two years later, North Vietnam won the war.

E Many Americans opposed the Vietnam War—some due to its unclear aims and its high cost in money and lives, others to avoid personal harm. Antiwar feelings eventually ended political support for the war.

more at USHAtlas.com

101

Contemporary United States

ERA 10

1969 TO PRESENT

1969
U.S. astronauts land on moon.

1970
Environmental Protection Agency (EPA) founded.

1970

1973
Vietnam War ends for U.S. with pullout.
Oil embargo results in gas shortages.

1978
Love Canal reveals dangers of toxic waste.

1979–81
Iranians hold Americans hostage.

1980
Center of U.S. population moves west of the Mississippi.

1980

1981
AIDS first identified in the United States.

The American Economy Goes Global

America has the world's largest economy and its well-being is closely linked to the rest of the world.

★ However, by the 1970s the United States faced fierce competition in the global economy. Oil prices increased and exports from newly industrializing countries began to outsell U.S.-made products.

★ At the end of the 20th Century, the United States ratified several *free trade* agreements. These agreements provide Americans with cheaper goods but can threaten American jobs.

★ Companies are increasingly selling services from American offices rather than goods from American factories. Services account for two-thirds of the country's *gross domestic product* (GDP).

A Service workers, such as the ones in this call center, account for about 75 percent of jobs in the United States. The fastest growing service industries are financial, legal, and management services.

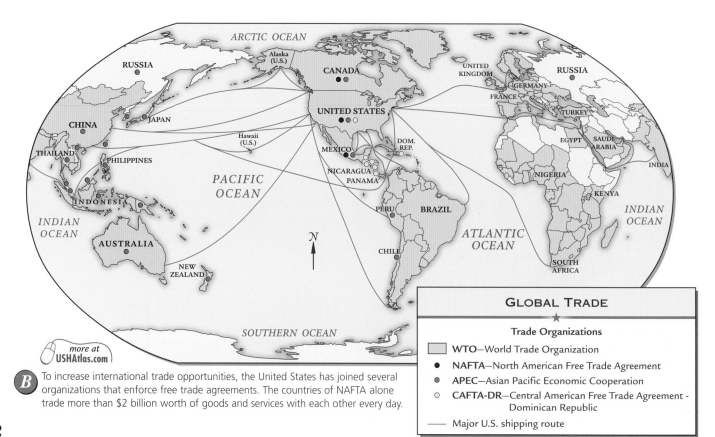

more at USHAtlas.com

B To increase international trade opportunities, the United States has joined several organizations that enforce free trade agreements. The countries of NAFTA alone trade more than $2 billion worth of goods and services with each other every day.

GLOBAL TRADE

★

Trade Organizations

	WTO—World Trade Organization
●	NAFTA—North American Free Trade Agreement
●	APEC—Asian Pacific Economic Cooperation
○	CAFTA-DR—Central American Free Trade Agreement - Dominican Republic
—	Major U.S. shipping route

986 Immigration law lows undocumented iens to stay in U.S.	**1991** **Persian Gulf War** frees Kuwait. **Soviet Union** breaks up, ending Cold War.	**2001** **Terrorists** destroy World Trade Center in New York City.
	1999 **Kosovo genocide** ends by NATO intervention.	**2003** **War in Iraq** begins.
		2009 **Barack Obama** becomes first African-American president.

1990 — **2000**

1994 **North American Free Trade Agreement** goes into effect. **2005** **Hurricane Katrina** devastates the Gulf Coast.

"...the economy of each country is dependent on the economy of all the others."

—RICHARD GRASSO, CHAIRMAN OF THE NEW YORK STOCK EXCHANGE, 1995–2003

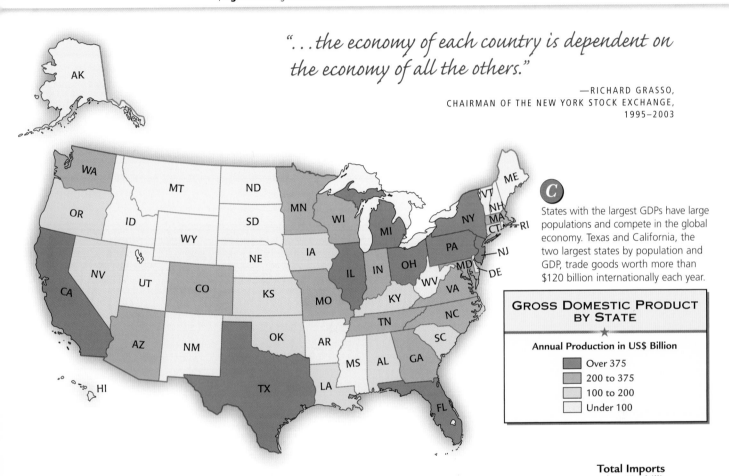

C States with the largest GDPs have large populations and compete in the global economy. Texas and California, the two largest states by population and GDP, trade goods worth more than $120 billion internationally each year.

GROSS DOMESTIC PRODUCT BY STATE

Annual Production in US$ Billion
- Over 375
- 200 to 375
- 100 to 200
- Under 100

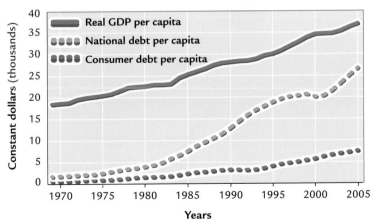

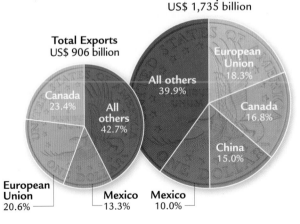

Total Imports US$ 1,735 billion

Total Exports US$ 906 billion

Exports: Canada 23.4%, All others 42.7%, European Union 20.6%, Mexico 13.3%

Imports: All others 39.9%, European Union 18.3%, Canada 16.8%, China 15.0%, Mexico 10.0%

D **U.S. ECONOMY AND U.S. DEBT GROW**

The total U.S. economy (GDP) has increased from about $3 trillion dollars in 1970 to over $13 trillion dollars, more than $35,000 per person, today. Unfortunately, the national debt (owed by the federal government) has been rising even faster. To fund this borrowing, the U.S. government and individual Americans have increasingly needed to turn to foreign lenders.

E **UNITED STATES BALANCE OF TRADE**

Competition from developing countries in Asia and Latin America with lower wages has reduced demand for U.S. goods at home and abroad since the mid-1970s. Today the U.S. *trade deficit* is ten times that of any other country.

103

World Superpower

Despite major international changes since 1970, the United States continues to extend its military powers abroad.

★ The United States continued to oppose the Soviet Union in the Cold War. By 1989, the Warsaw Pact had collapsed, followed by the Soviet Union itself two years later.

★ The United States reduced its armed forces after the Cold War; however, U.S. troops have been involved in more conflicts since 1989 than in 1973–1989.

★ *Terrorists* have repeatedly kidnapped or attacked U.S. citizens since the 1970s, hoping to reduce U.S. influence especially in the Middle East.

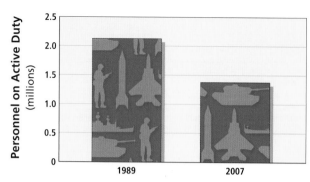

A **U.S. MILITARY STRENGTH**

During the Cold War, the U.S. military was large enough to face another superpower, the Soviet Union. Recent dangers, such as terrorists and regional threats, have needed fewer troops overall.

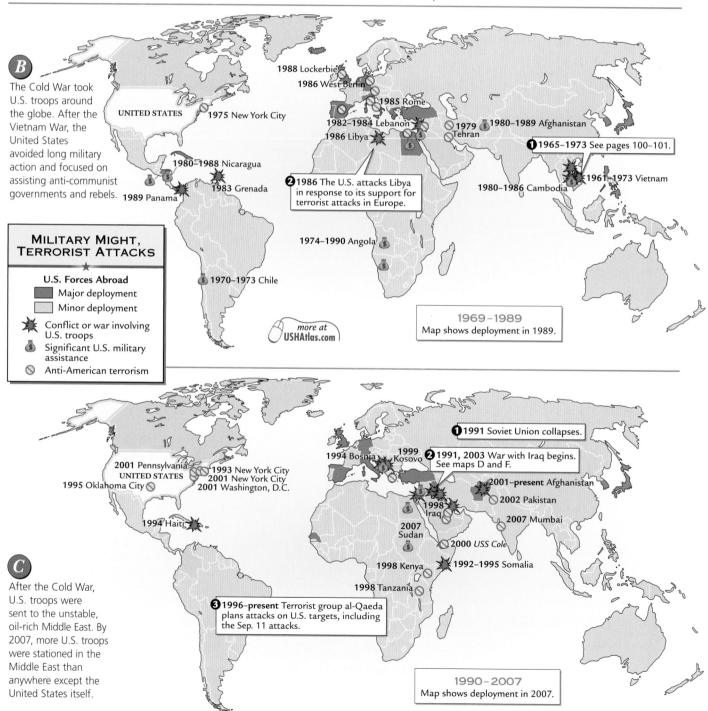

B

The Cold War took U.S. troops around the globe. After the Vietnam War, the United States avoided long military action and focused on assisting anti-communist governments and rebels.

1988 Lockerbie
1986 West Berlin
1985 Rome
1975 New York City
1982–1984 Lebanon
1986 Libya
1979 Tehran
1980–1989 Afghanistan
❶ 1965–1973 See pages 100–101.
1980–1988 Nicaragua
1983 Grenada
1989 Panama
❷ 1986 The U.S. attacks Libya in response to its support for terrorist attacks in Europe.
1980–1986 Cambodia
1961–1973 Vietnam
1974–1990 Angola
1970–1973 Chile

UNITED STATES

more at USHAtlas.com

MILITARY MIGHT, TERRORIST ATTACKS
★
U.S. Forces Abroad
■ Major deployment
■ Minor deployment
✸ Conflict or war involving U.S. troops
💰 Significant U.S. military assistance
⊘ Anti-American terrorism

1969–1989
Map shows deployment in 1989.

C

After the Cold War, U.S. troops were sent to the unstable, oil-rich Middle East. By 2007, more U.S. troops were stationed in the Middle East than anywhere except the United States itself.

❶ 1991 Soviet Union collapses.
1999 Kosovo
1994 Bosnia
❷ 1991, 2003 War with Iraq begins. See maps D and F.
2001 Pennsylvania
UNITED STATES
1993 New York City
2001 New York City
2001 Washington, D.C.
1995 Oklahoma City
2001–present Afghanistan
2002 Pakistan
1998 Iraq
2007 Mumbai
1994 Haiti
2007 Sudan
2000 USS Cole
1998 Kenya
1992–1995 Somalia
1998 Tanzania
❸ 1996–present Terrorist group al-Qaeda plans attacks on U.S. targets, including the Sep. 11 attacks.

1990–2007
Map shows deployment in 2007.

104

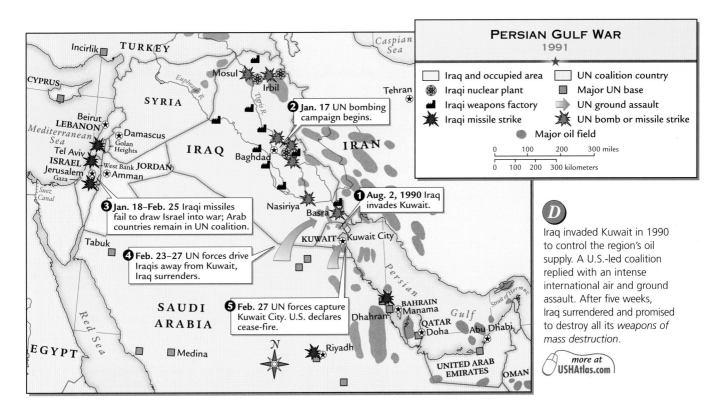

PERSIAN GULF WAR
1991

- ☐ Iraq and occupied area
- ⊛ Iraqi nuclear plant
- ⚒ Iraqi weapons factory
- ✸ Iraqi missile strike
- ☐ UN coalition country
- ◼ Major UN base
- ➡ UN ground assault
- ✸ UN bomb or missile strike
- ⬤ Major oil field

0   100   200   300 miles
0 100 200 300 kilometers

❷ **Jan. 17** UN bombing campaign begins.

❶ **Aug. 2, 1990** Iraq invades Kuwait.

❸ **Jan. 18–Feb. 25** Iraqi missiles fail to draw Israel into war; Arab countries remain in UN coalition.

❹ **Feb. 23–27** UN forces drive Iraqis away from Kuwait, Iraq surrenders.

❺ **Feb. 27** UN forces capture Kuwait City. U.S. declares cease-fire.

(Map labels: Incirlik, TURKEY, CYPRUS, Mosul, Irbil, Caspian Sea, SYRIA, Tehran, Beirut, LEBANON, Damascus, Golan Heights, Mediterranean Sea, Tel Aviv, ISRAEL, Jerusalem, West Bank, JORDAN, Gaza, Amman, IRAQ, Baghdad, Euphrates R., Tigris R., IRAN, Suez Canal, Nasiriya, Basra, Tabuk, KUWAIT, Kuwait City, Persian Gulf, Strait of Hormuz, SAUDI ARABIA, Red Sea, Dhahran, BAHRAIN, Manama, QATAR, Doha, Abu Dhabi, UNITED ARAB EMIRATES, OMAN, EGYPT, Medina, Riyadh)

D Iraq invaded Kuwait in 1990 to control the region's oil supply. A U.S.-led coalition replied with an intense international air and ground assault. After five weeks, Iraq surrendered and promised to destroy all its *weapons of mass destruction.*

more at USHAtlas.com

E On September 11, 2001, the worst terrorist attack in U.S. history occurred when terrorists flew commercial jets into the World Trade Center in New York City, the Pentagon near Washington, D.C., and a field in Pennsylvania, killing thousands of people.

more at USHAtlas.com

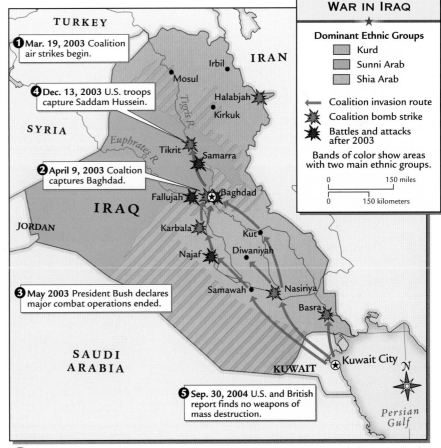

WAR IN IRAQ

Dominant Ethnic Groups
- ☐ Kurd
- ☐ Sunni Arab
- ☐ Shia Arab

- ← Coalition invasion route
- ✸ Coalition bomb strike
- ✸ Battles and attacks after 2003

Bands of color show areas with two main ethnic groups.

0   150 miles
0   150 kilometers

❶ **Mar. 19, 2003** Coalition air strikes begin.

❹ **Dec. 13, 2003** U.S. troops capture Saddam Hussein.

❷ **April 9, 2003** Coalition captures Baghdad.

❸ **May 2003** President Bush declares major combat operations ended.

❺ **Sep. 30, 2004** U.S. and British report finds no weapons of mass destruction.

(Map labels: TURKEY, IRAN, Irbil, Mosul, Halabjah, Kirkuk, SYRIA, Tikrit, Samarra, Euphrates R., Tigris R., Fallujah, Baghdad, IRAQ, JORDAN, Karbala, Kut, Najaf, Diwaniyah, Samawah, Nasiriya, Basra, SAUDI ARABIA, KUWAIT, Kuwait City, Persian Gulf)

F The United States and its coalition partners invaded Iraq in 2003 to search for weapons of mass destruction and unseat Iraqi leader Saddam Hussein. Although the U.S. overthrew the leader quickly, thousands of U.S. troops remained to rebuild and to prevent a civil war between Iraq's ethnic groups.

Health of the Nation

The average American life expectancy has increased by seven years since 1970, but health issues continue to face the country.

★ Half of the U.S. population is over 36, almost four years older than in 1990. America's aging population puts greater burdens on the country's health care resources.

★ New *communicable diseases*, and new strains of older diseases, threaten the public's health. Over a million Americans are now infected with HIV, the virus that causes AIDS, a lethal disease unknown before 1980.

★ Health care costs continue to rise far faster than *inflation*. Health insurance has become too expensive for many people and strains the budgets of individuals, businesses, and governments.

"Instead of helping people...stay healthy, we wait for people to get sick and then we spend billions of dollars every year trying to make them healthy again."

—DR. RICHARD CARMONA,
U.S. SURGEON GENERAL (2002–2006)

A Over the past four decades, exercise has become more popular as increasing numbers of Americans work at jobs that require less physical activity. It is estimated that only 3 in 10 adults exercise enough.

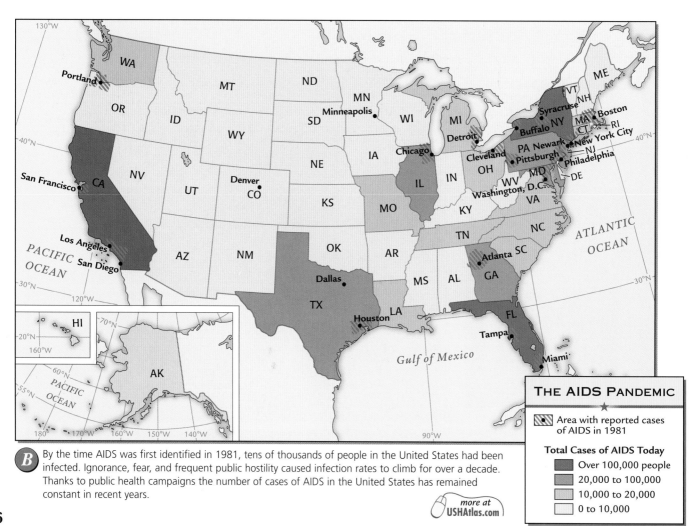

THE AIDS PANDEMIC

Area with reported cases of AIDS in 1981

Total Cases of AIDS Today

- Over 100,000 people
- 20,000 to 100,000
- 10,000 to 20,000
- 0 to 10,000

B By the time AIDS was first identified in 1981, tens of thousands of people in the United States had been infected. Ignorance, fear, and frequent public hostility caused infection rates to climb for over a decade. Thanks to public health campaigns the number of cases of AIDS in the United States has remained constant in recent years.

more at USHAtlas.com

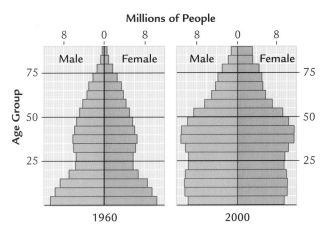

Millions of People

1960

2000

C THE AGING OF AMERICA

The Baby Boom swelled the population in age groups born between 1945 and 1960 (see graph A on page 96). As Baby Boomers age, Medicare and other health programs for senior citizens will become increasingly strained.

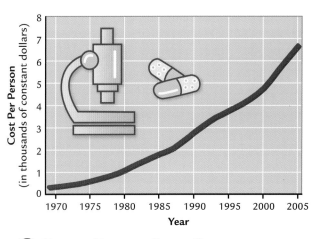

D RISING HEALTH CARE COSTS

Since 1970, expensive new technologies, the threat of malpractice lawsuits, and rising demand from an aging and inactive population have driven up the cost of health care. Attempts to control costs by the health care industry, insurance companies, and the government have been unsuccessful.

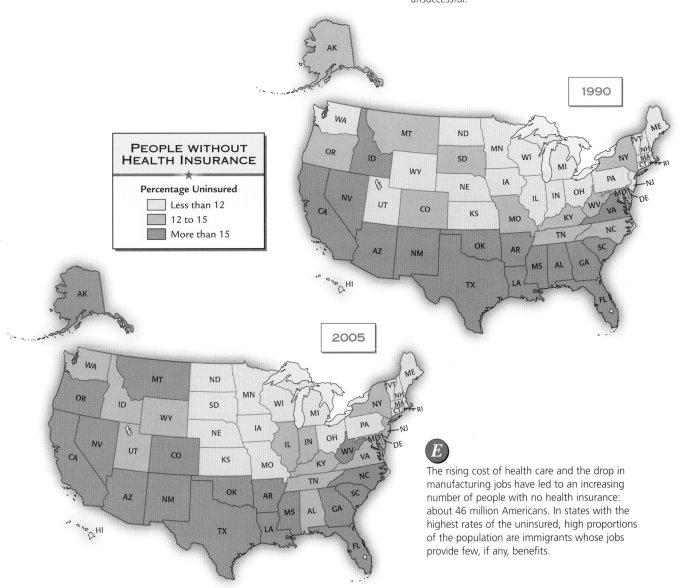

PEOPLE WITHOUT HEALTH INSURANCE

★

Percentage Uninsured

- Less than 12
- 12 to 15
- More than 15

1990

2005

E

The rising cost of health care and the drop in manufacturing jobs have led to an increasing number of people with no health insurance: about 46 million Americans. In states with the highest rates of the uninsured, high proportions of the population are immigrants whose jobs provide few, if any, benefits.

Environmental Challenges

Since the late 1960s, Americans have made considerable progress in protecting the environment, but new challenges continue to emerge.

★ Since 1965, the world's population has nearly doubled to over six billion. Today people are using Earth's land, air, and water resources 20 percent faster than they can be renewed.

★ Farming, logging, and urban sprawl have altered or destroyed grasslands, forests, and wetlands in much of the United States.

★ Carbon dioxide and methane, common in polluted air, are associated with global climate change. Instability during a change in climate makes climate-related disasters more frequent.

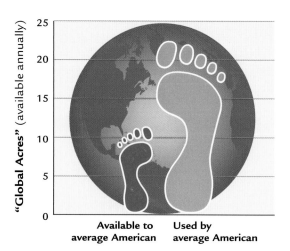

A AN AMERICAN'S ECOLOGICAL FOOTPRINT

Since the late 1960s, Americans have exceeded the sustainable use of the land and water of the United States. As a result, we use the resources of other countries and cause long-term damage to the atmosphere and the oceans.

more at USHAtlas.com

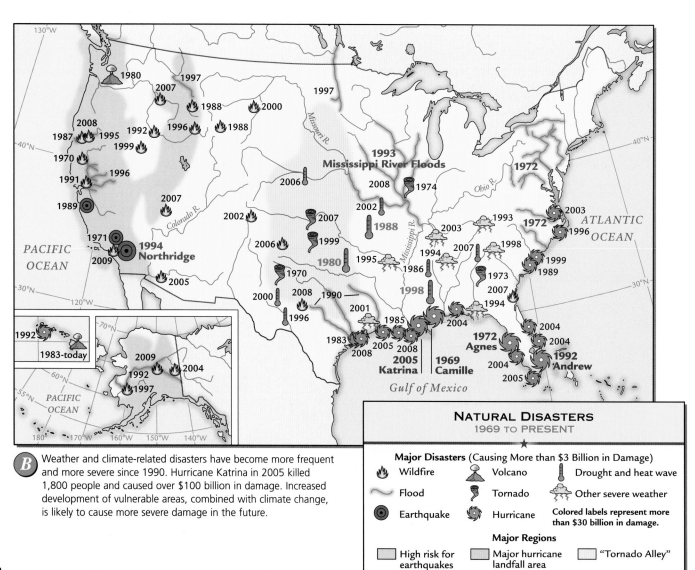

B

Weather and climate-related disasters have become more frequent and more severe since 1990. Hurricane Katrina in 2005 killed 1,800 people and caused over $100 billion in damage. Increased development of vulnerable areas, combined with climate change, is likely to cause more severe damage in the future.

NATURAL DISASTERS
1969 TO PRESENT
★

Major Disasters (Causing More than $3 Billion in Damage)

🔥 Wildfire	🌋 Volcano	Drought and heat wave
〜 Flood	Tornado	Other severe weather
◉ Earthquake	🌀 Hurricane	**Colored labels represent more than $30 billion in damage.**

Major Regions

| High risk for earthquakes | Major hurricane landfall area | "Tornado Alley" |

C Carbon dioxide (CO₂) emissions are the result of burning fossil fuels. The United States, the world's largest emitter of CO_2, causes about 22 percent of the world's total.

more at USHAtlas.com

CARBON DIOXIDE EMISSIONS
★
Million Metric Tons from Fossil Fuels

- Over 300
- 200 to 300
- 100 to 200
- Under 100

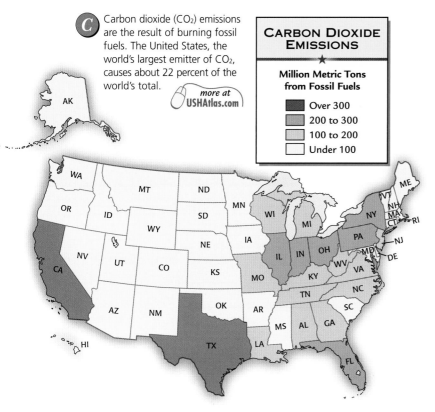

D Los Angeles, above, is the most polluted large city in the United States. The most common sources of air pollution are automobiles and power plants. Air pollution can shorten a person's life.

"We are all part of a family, five billion strong, in fact, 30 million species strong, and we all share the same air, water, and soil—borders and governments will never change that."

—SEVERN CULLIS-SUZUKI,
AGE 12, AT THE 1992 RIO EARTH SUMMIT

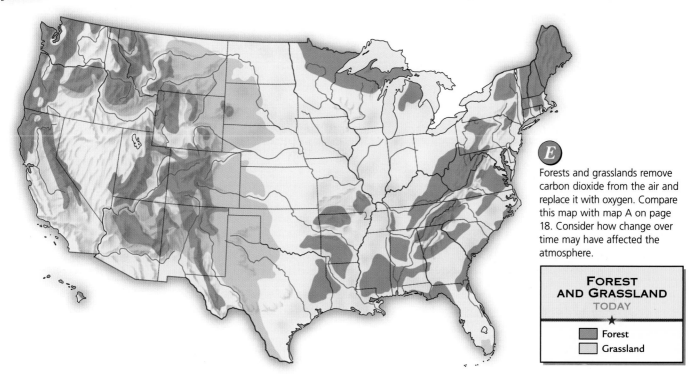

E Forests and grasslands remove carbon dioxide from the air and replace it with oxygen. Compare this map with map A on page 18. Consider how change over time may have affected the atmosphere.

FOREST AND GRASSLAND
TODAY
★

- Forest
- Grassland

The Changing Face of America

Immigration continues to to make the U.S. population more diverse.

★ By 2000 about 12 percent of the U.S. population, over 33 million people, was foreign-born, the highest percentage since 1920.

★ The majority of immigrants to the United States were no longer from Europe but from Asia and Latin America.

★ Immigrants from the Philippines, China, India, Vietnam, and especially Mexico were the most numerous.

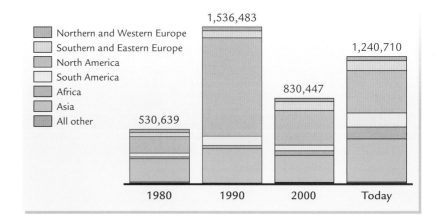

Northern and Western Europe
Southern and Eastern Europe
North America
South America
Africa
Asia
All other

530,639 — 1980
1,536,483 — 1990
830,447 — 2000
1,240,710 — Today

A IMMIGRANT ORIGINS

A 1986 law allowed legal resident status to *undocumented* immigrants who had been in the United States for years. Nearly 3 million foreign-born residents had successfully applied by 1991, when quotas were tightened.

more at USHAtlas.com

B

While most immigrants came from Asia and Latin America, there were also large numbers of voluntary immigrants from Africa—for the first time in history.

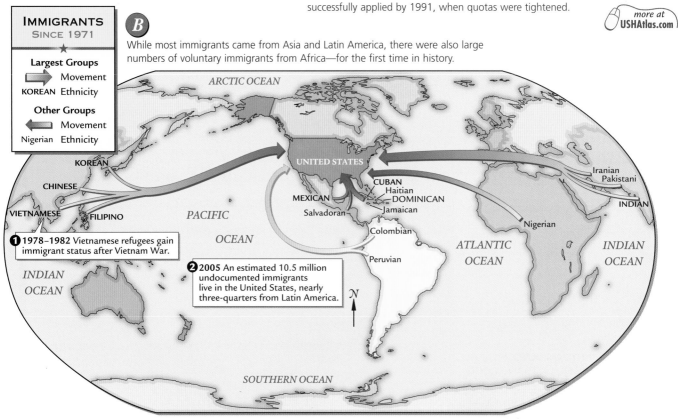

IMMIGRANTS SINCE 1971

Largest Groups
→ Movement
KOREAN Ethnicity

Other Groups
← Movement
Nigerian Ethnicity

ARCTIC OCEAN

UNITED STATES

KOREAN
CHINESE
VIETNAMESE
FILIPINO

PACIFIC OCEAN

MEXICAN
Salvadoran
CUBAN
Haitian
DOMINICAN
Jamaican
Colombian
Peruvian

ATLANTIC OCEAN

Iranian
Pakistani
INDIAN
Nigerian

INDIAN OCEAN

INDIAN OCEAN

SOUTHERN OCEAN

❶ 1978–1982 Vietnamese refugees gain immigrant status after Vietnam War.

❷ 2005 An estimated 10.5 million undocumented immigrants live in the United States, nearly three-quarters from Latin America.

N

C MEXICAN AND FILIPINO IMMIGRANTS

In 1991 nearly 1 million Mexicans, many living in the United States without legal status, gained documentation. *Filipinos* are among the largest groups entering the United States.

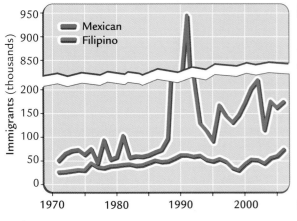

Mexican
Filipino

Immigrants (thousands)

950
900
850
200
150
100
50
0

1970   1980   1990   2000

more at USHAtlas.com

D
Immigrants continue to come to the United States seeking economic opportunity and freedom. At least one-third will become naturalized citizens, as these people are.

110

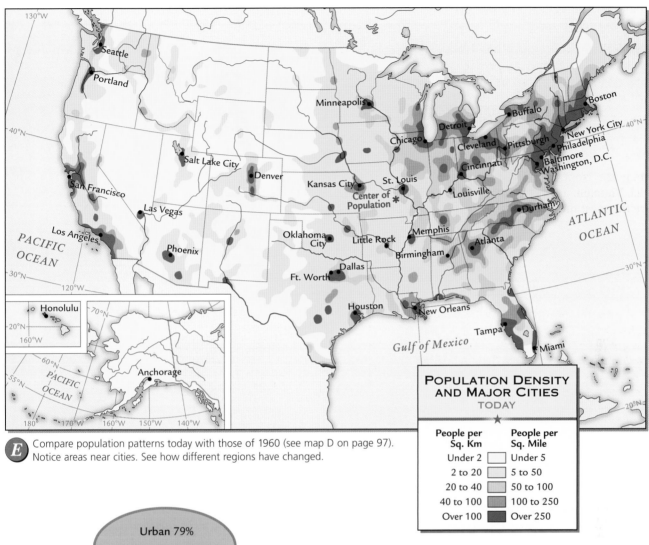

E Compare population patterns today with those of 1960 (see map D on page 97). Notice areas near cities. See how different regions have changed.

POPULATION DENSITY AND MAJOR CITIES
TODAY
★

People per Sq. Km	People per Sq. Mile
Under 2	Under 5
2 to 20	5 to 50
20 to 40	50 to 100
40 to 100	100 to 250
Over 100	Over 250

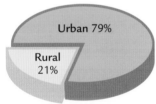

F **URBAN AND RURAL POPULATION, 2000**

During the 1900s, America changed from a rural to an urban—and suburban—nation. Compare this graph with graph A on page 70.

"Everyone is kneaded out of the same dough, but not baked in the same oven."

—FOLK SAYING

G High school students today are part of a population that is different from that of their grandparents. Two generations from now the population of the United States will be even more diverse.

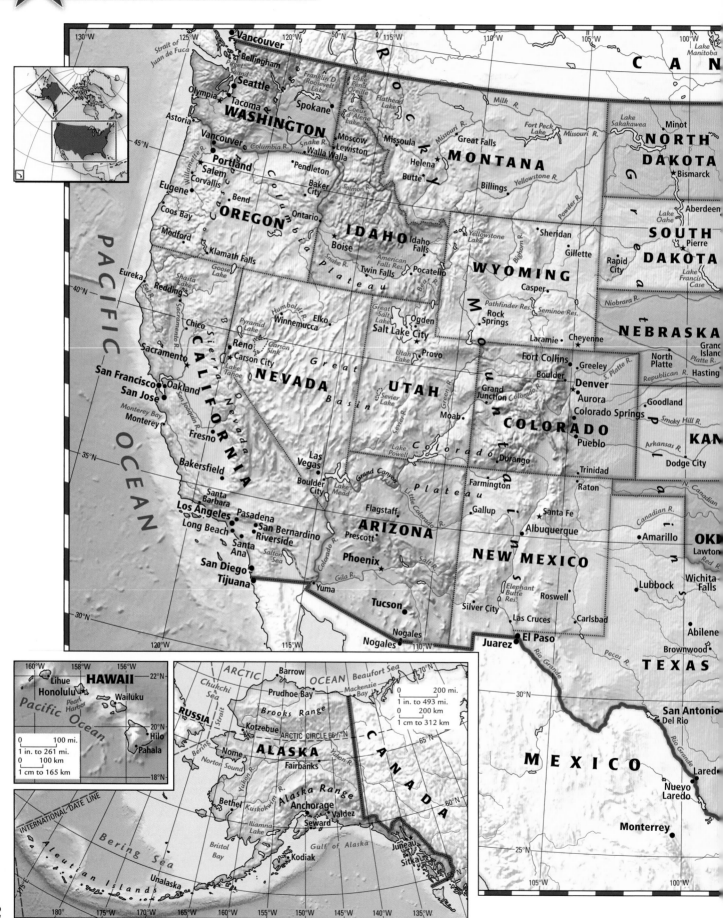

UNITED STATES
POLITICAL MAP

Boundary Symbols
International boundary
State boundary

City Symbols
Los Angeles ● Over 500,000 people
Anchorage • 100,000 to 500,000
Boulder • Under 100,000

Washington, D.C. ⊗ National capital
Honolulu ★ State capital

Scale

0   100   200   300 miles
1 in. to 209 mi.

0 100 200 300 kilometers
1 cm to 133 km

CROSS SECTION
Vertical exaggeration 41 to 1
Scale at 36°N: 1 in. to 256 mi., 1 cm to 162 km

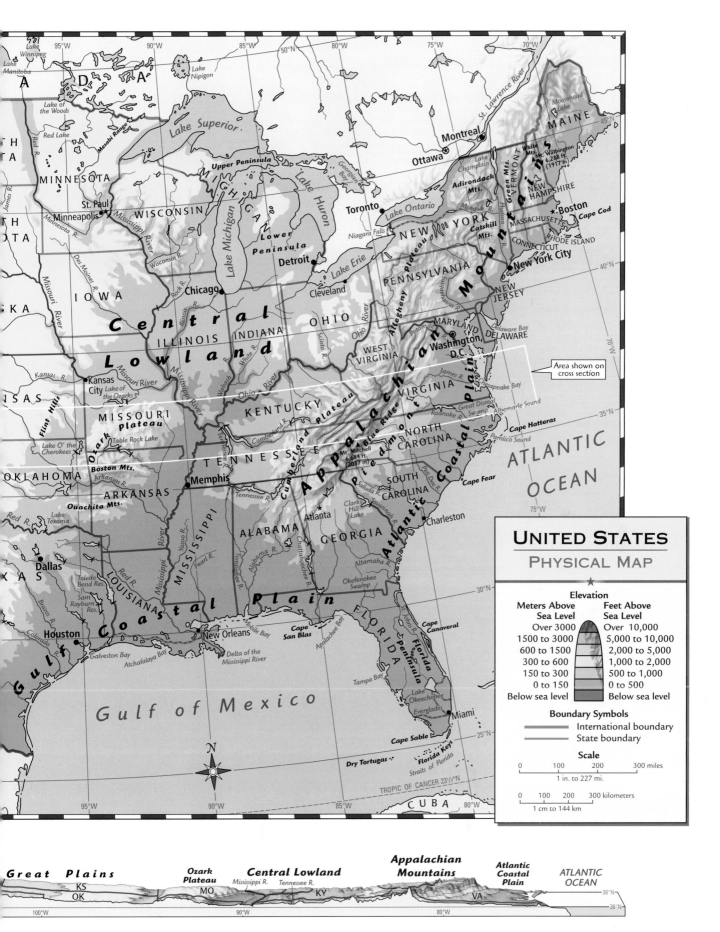

UNITED STATES

PHYSICAL MAP

★

Elevation

Meters Above Sea Level	Feet Above Sea Level
Over 3000	Over 10,000
1500 to 3000	5,000 to 10,000
600 to 1500	2,000 to 5,000
300 to 600	1,000 to 2,000
150 to 300	500 to 1,000
0 to 150	0 to 500
Below sea level	Below sea level

Boundary Symbols

International boundary
State boundary

Scale

0   100   200   300 miles
1 in. to 227 mi.

0   100   200   300 kilometers
1 cm to 144 km

Area shown on cross section

Great Plains   *Ozark Plateau*   *Central Lowland*   *Appalachian Mountains*   *Atlantic Coastal Plain*   ATLANTIC OCEAN

KS   MO   Mississippi R.   Tennessee R.   KY   VA

100°W   90°W   80°W

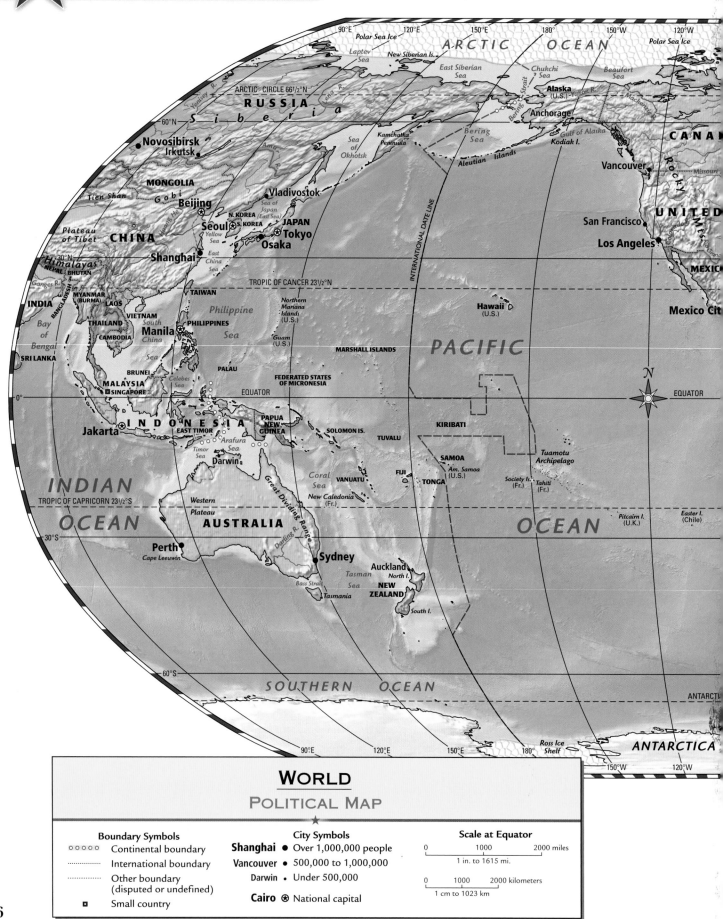

ARCTIC OCEAN

Polar Sea Ice
Laptev Sea
New Siberian Is.
East Siberian Sea
Chukchi Sea
Beaufort Sea
Polar Sea Ice

ARCTIC CIRCLE 66½°N

RUSSIA
Siberia
60°N

Novosibirsk
Irkutsk

MONGOLIA
Gobi
Tien Shan
Beijing
Huang Ho

Vladivostok
Kamchatka Peninsula
Sea of Okhotsk
Bering Sea
Bering Strait

Alaska (U.S.)
Yukon R.
Anchorage
Gulf of Alaska
Kodiak I.
Aleutian Islands

CANAD
Mackenzie R.
Vancouver
Rocky Mts.
Missouri

N. KOREA
Seoul S. KOREA
JAPAN
Tokyo
Osaka
Sea of Japan (East Sea)

San Francisco
Los Angeles
UNITED

Plateau of Tibet
CHINA
30°N
Shanghai
Yellow Sea
East China Sea

MEXICO

Himalayas
NEPAL BHUTAN
Ganges R.
INDIA
BANGLADESH
MYANMAR (BURMA)
LAOS
THAILAND VIETNAM
CAMBODIA
Bay of Bengal
SRI LANKA

TAIWAN
TROPIC OF CANCER 23½°N

Philippine Sea

Northern Mariana Islands (U.S.)

Hawaii (U.S.)

Mexico Cit

South China Sea
Manila
PHILIPPINES
China

Guam (U.S.)

MARSHALL ISLANDS

PACIFIC

PALAU

FEDERATED STATES OF MICRONESIA
EQUATOR

EQUATOR
N

BRUNEI
MALAYSIA
SINGAPORE
Celebes Sea

Jakarta
INDONESIA
EAST TIMOR
PAPUA NEW GUINEA
SOLOMON IS.
TUVALU
KIRIBATI

Arafura Sea
Timor Sea
Darwin
Coral Sea
VANUATU
New Caledonia (Fr.)
FIJI
SAMOA
Am. Samoa (U.S.)
TONGA
Society Is. (Fr.)
Tahiti (Fr.)
Tuamotu Archipelago

INDIAN OCEAN

TROPIC OF CAPRICORN 23½°S
30°S

Western Plateau
AUSTRALIA
Great Dividing Range
Darling R.

OCEAN

Pitcairn I. (U.K.)
Easter I. (Chile)

Perth
Cape Leeuwin

Sydney
Auckland
North I.
NEW ZEALAND
South I.
Tasman Sea
Bass Strait
Tasmania

60°S

SOUTHERN OCEAN

Ross Ice Shelf
ANTARCTI

ANTARCTICA

90°E 120°E 150°E 180° 150°W 120°W

WORLD
POLITICAL MAP

Boundary Symbols
○○○○○ Continental boundary
- - - - International boundary
· · · · · Other boundary (disputed or undefined)
▫ Small country

City Symbols
Shanghai ● Over 1,000,000 people
Vancouver ● 500,000 to 1,000,000
Darwin · Under 500,000
Cairo ⊛ National capital

Scale at Equator
0 1000 2000 miles
1 in. to 1615 mi.

0 1000 2000 kilometers
1 cm to 1023 km

"Frontiers are indeed the razor's edge on which hang suspended the modern issues of war and peace, of life or death of nations."

—LORD CURZON
BRITISH DIPLOMAT, 1907

ARCTIC OCEAN
Polar Sea Ice

Svalbard (Nor.)
Franz Josef Land
Novaya Zemlya
Kara Sea
Barents Sea

Baffin Bay
Greenland (Kalaallit Nunaat) (Denmark)
Jan Mayen (Nor.)
Norwegian Sea
ARCTIC CIRCLE 66½°N
Ob R.

Baffin Island
Davis Strait
Denmark Strait
Reykjavik
ICELAND
Faeroe Is. (Den.)
St. Petersburg
Ural Mts.
Volga R.
RUSSIA
60°N
Moscow

Hudson Bay
Iqaluit
Hudson Str.
NORWAY
SWEDEN
FINLAND
EST.
LAT.
LITH.
BELARUS
KAZAKHSTAN

Great Lakes
St. Lawrence R.
UNITED KINGDOM
IRELAND
DEN.
NETH.
GERMANY
POLAND
UKRAINE
Chicago
Toronto
London
BEL.
LUX.
CZ
SL.
MOL.
Caucasus Mts.
Caspian Sea
UZBEKISTAN
KYR.
Appalachian Mts.
New York City
Paris
FRANCE
SWITZ.
LIECH.
AUS.
HUN.
ROMANIA
GEO.
TURKMENISTAN
TAJ.
STATES
Washington, D.C.
ANDORRA
CRO.
BOS.
SERB.
MON.
BULG.
Black Sea
ARM.
AZER.
Atlanta
Madrid
Rome
KOS.
MAC.
GREECE
TURKEY
Tehran
IRAN
AFGHANISTAN
Mississippi R.
PORTUGAL
SPAIN
ITALY
ALB.
CYPRUS
SYRIA
30°N
Houston
Miami
Str. of Gibraltar
Casablanca
Sicily
Mediterranean Sea
LEBANON
ISRAEL
IRAQ
KUWAIT
PAKISTAN
Karachi
Gulf of Mexico
BAHAMAS
Morocco
Atlas Mts.
TUNISIA
Algiers
Cairo
JORDAN
BAHRAIN
QATAR
U.A.E.
INDIA
CUBA
HAITI
Puerto Rico (U.S.)
Canary Is. (Sp.)
Western Sahara (adm. Morocco)
ALGERIA
LIBYA
EGYPT
Nile R.
SAUDI ARABIA
OMAN
Mumbai (Bombay)
Deccan Plateau
JAMAICA
DOM. REP.
ANTIGUA & BARBUDA
Sahara
Red Sea
Arabian Sea
BELIZE
HONDURAS
DOMINICA
MAURITANIA
MALI
NIGER
CHAD
YEMEN
GUATEMALA
EL SALVADOR
NICARAGUA
BARBADOS
TRINIDAD & TOBAGO
CAPE VERDE
SENEGAL
GAMBIA
SUDAN
ERITREA
DJIBOUTI
MALDIVES
Caribbean Sea
COSTA RICA
PANAMA
Caracas
VENEZUELA
GUYANA
SURINAME
French Guiana (Fr.)
GUINEA-BISSAU
GUINEA
BURKINA FASO
BENIN
NIGERIA
C. AFR. REP.
ETHIOPIA
Central America
Bogota
COLOMBIA
SIERRA LEONE
LIBERIA
COTE D'IVOIRE (IVORY COAST)
GHANA
TOGO
Lagos
CAMEROON
Ethiopian Highlands
SOMALIA
Galapagos Is. (Ecuador)
ECUADOR
Amazon Basin
EQ. GUINEA
SAO TOME & PRINCIPE
GABON
CONGO REP.
Congo Basin
UGANDA
KENYA
EQUATOR
0°
Diego Garcia (U.K.)
PERU
Lima
Andes Mts.
BRAZIL
OCEAN
Congo R.
RWANDA
BURUNDI
L. Victoria
Nairobi
SEYCHELLES
Cabinda (Ang.)
Kinshasa
CONGO
TANZANIA
Dar es Salaam
INDIAN
BOLIVIA
Brazilian Highlands
ANGOLA
ZAMBIA
MALAWI
COMOROS
MAURITIUS
PARAGUAY
Rio de Janeiro
NAMIBIA
ZIMBABWE
MOZAMBIQUE
Reunion (Fr.)
TROPIC OF CAPRICORN 23½°S
Sao Paulo
BOTSWANA
Mozambique Channel
MADAGASCAR
Amsterdam I. (Fr.)
St. Paul I. (Fr.)
Santiago
URUGUAY
SWAZILAND
OCEAN
San Felix (Chile)
San Ambrosio (Chile)
Juan Fernandez Is. (Chile)
CHILE
Buenos Aires
ARGENTINA
SOUTH AFRICA
LESOTHO
30°S
Cape Town
Prince Edward Is. (S. Afr.)
Crozet Is. (Fr.)
Kerguelen I. (Fr.)
PRIME MERIDIAN
Falkland Is. (U.K.)
South Georgia (U.K.)
South Orkney Is. (U.K.)
60°S
CIRCLE 66½°S
South Shetland Is.
SOUTHERN OCEAN
60°E
ARCTIC OCEAN
Antarctic Peninsula
Weddell Sea
Ronne Ice Shelf
90°W
60°W
30°W
0°
30°E
ASIA
NORTH AMERICA
EUROPE
ASIA
PACIFIC OCEAN
AFRICA
INDIAN OCEAN
SOUTH AMERICA
ATLANTIC OCEAN
INDIAN OCEAN
AUSTRALIA
SOUTHERN OCEAN
ANTARCTICA

ATLANTIC

90°W   60°W   30°W   0°   30°E   60°E

117

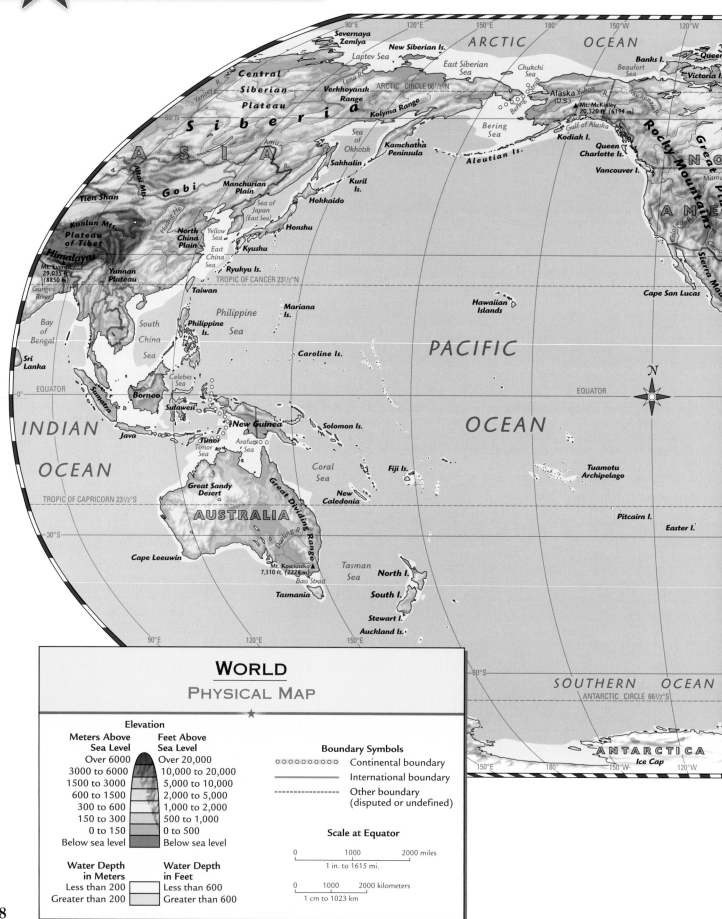

WORLD
PHYSICAL MAP
★

Elevation

Meters Above Sea Level	Feet Above Sea Level
Over 6000	Over 20,000
3000 to 6000	10,000 to 20,000
1500 to 3000	5,000 to 10,000
600 to 1500	2,000 to 5,000
300 to 600	1,000 to 2,000
150 to 300	500 to 1,000
0 to 150	0 to 500
Below sea level	Below sea level

Water Depth in Meters	Water Depth in Feet
Less than 200	Less than 600
Greater than 200	Greater than 600

Boundary Symbols

ooooooooooo Continental boundary

———— International boundary

- - - - - - - Other boundary (disputed or undefined)

Scale at Equator

0   1000   2000 miles
1 in. to 1615 mi.

0   1000   2000 kilometers
1 cm to 1023 km

"There are no boundaries in the real Planet Earth...
Rivers flow unimpeded across the swaths
of continents. The persistent
tides, the pulse of the sea,
do not discriminate."

—JACQUES-YVES COUSTEAU,
FRENCH OCEANOGRAPHER
(1910–1997)

ARCTIC OCEAN

Ellesmere I.
Elizabeth Is.
Baffin Bay
Baffin I.
Hudson Bay
Hudson Str.
Davis Strait
Ice Cap
Greenland
Denmark Strait
Cape Farewell
Iceland
Svalbard
North Cape
Norwegian Sea
Novaya Zemlya
Barents Sea
Kara Sea
ARCTIC CIRCLE 66½°N
Scandinavian Peninsula
Ural Mountains
West Siberian Plain
Volga R.
Aral Sea
L. Balkhash
ASIA
Pamirs

Canadian Shield
NORTH Shield
AMERICA
Great Lakes
St. Lawrence R.
Newfoundland
British Isles
Northern European Plain
EUROPE
Alps
Black Sea
Caspian Sea
Caucasus Mts.
Mt. Elbrus
18,510 ft.
(5642 m)
Plateau of Iran
30°N

Mississippi R.
Appalachian Mts.
ATLANTIC
Azores
Mediterranean Sea
Str. of Gibraltar
Atlas Mts.
Canary Is.
Sicily
Deccan Plateau

Gulf of Mexico
Bahama Is.
TROPIC OF CANCER 23½°N
Cape Verde Is.
Sahara
Ahaggar Mts.
Tibesti Mts.
Arabian Peninsula
Arabian Sea

Cuba
West Indies
Caribbean Sea
Central America
Panama Canal
Cape Verde Is.
Sahel
AFRICA
Niger R.
Red Sea
Ethiopian Highlands

Galapagos Is.
Guiana Highlands
OCEAN
Ascension I.
Congo R.
L. Victoria
Congo Basin
Mt. Kilimanjaro
19,340 ft.
(5895 m)
Zanzibar I.
INDIAN
Maldives
EQUATOR
Seychelles
Chagos Archipelago
0°

Amazon Basin
Andes Mountains
Amazon
SOUTH
AMERICA
Brazilian Highlands
Bie Plateau
Comoros
OCEAN
Mauritius
Madagascar

San Felix I.
San Ambrosio I.
Kalahari Desert
Drakensberg
Mozambique Channel
TROPIC OF CAPRICORN 23½°S

Juan Fernandez Is.
Aconcagua
22,831 ft.
(6959 m)
Pampas
Patagonia
Cape of Good Hope
Amsterdam I.
St. Paul I.
30°S

Falkland Is.
Tierra del Fuego
Cape Horn
South Georgia I.
Kerguelen I.

South Shetland Is.
Antarctic Peninsula
Weddell Sea
SOUTHERN OCEAN
60°S

90°W   60°W   30°W   0°   30°E

ARCTIC OCEAN
ASIA
NORTH AMERICA
EUROPE
ASIA
PACIFIC OCEAN
AFRICA
INDIAN OCEAN
SOUTH AMERICA
ATLANTIC OCEAN
INDIAN OCEAN
AUSTRALIA
SOUTHERN OCEAN
ANTARCTICA

Glossary

abolition Elimination of slavery.

AIDS (Acquired Immunodeficiency Syndrome) Lethal communicable disease that weakens the body's ability to fight infection.

Allies 1. Nations that fought the Central Powers in World War I. Included France, Russia, the United Kingdom, and the United States. 2. Nations that fought the Axis Powers in World War II. Included France, the Soviet Union, the United Kingdom, and the United States.

annex To add territory to a place with established boundaries, such as a city or country.

armistice Temporary agreement between two or more countries to stop fighting. A truce.

Articles of Confederation The first constitution of the United States, ratified in 1777 and replaced in 1788 by the Constitution. It granted fewer powers to the national government and more to the states than the Constitution does.

Axis Powers Nations that fought the Allies in World War II. It included Germany, Italy, and Japan.

balance of trade The difference between the goods bought from another country (imports) and the goods sold to other countries (exports).

blockade Isolation of a place by ships or troops to prevent people and goods from entering or leaving.

boomtown Town that experiences rapid population growth.

boundary Shared border separating places such as states or countries. When two places do not agree on the location of their shared boundary, the boundary is said to be disputed.

boycott Method of expressing political or social disfavor by refusing to buy products, patronize businesses, or use services.

casualty Person killed, wounded, captured, or missing in action after a battle or war.

center of population Place within a country where equal numbers of people live to the north, south, east, and west.

Central Powers Nations that fought the Allies in World War I. Included Germany, Austria-Hungry, and the Ottoman Empire.

cession Territory surrendered by one country to another as a result of a war or treaty.

charter Document issued by a government to create a smaller unit of government or other institution and to define its rights and responsibilities.

civil rights Freedoms guaranteed to U.S. citizens by the Constitution.

civil war War between two groups or regions of the same country.

Cold War Political and military tension between communist and democratic nations following World War II. It stopped short of open warfare between its main adversaries, the United States and the Soviet Union.

colony Settlement or region governed by a distant parent country.

communicable disease Disease that can be transmitted from person to person.

communist Advocate of a system of government ownership and control of the property and equipment used for producing food, goods, and services. Communist countries do not have democratic governments.

compromise Method of settling differences in which both sides agree to give up some of their demands.

Confederate States of America The 11 Southern states that seceded from the United States during the Civil War. Also called the Confederacy.

confederation System of government similar to a federal system, but with greater power to local governments.

constitution Document that sets forth the powers, duties, and structure of a government. The U.S. Constitution was ratified in 1788 and has been amended more than 25 times.

contiguous Connected or touching.

country 1. Land with one government. 2. Large region, such as the "Oregon Country."

Crusade One of eight wars between 1096 and 1270 when Christian armies from Europe tried to win control of Palestine (the "Holy Land") from its Muslim rulers.

culture Ethnic, racial, or religious group.

D-Day Abbreviation for the "designated day" of a military offensive. Usually refers to the Allied invasion of Normandy during World War II.

democracy 1. Government by the people, in which citizens vote in free elections. 2. Country with a democratic system of government.

deployment Location of troops on active military duty.

depression Severe drop in a country's economy that causes rising unemployment and falling prices.

disenfranchisement Prevention from using a right of citizenship, such as voting.

drought Long period of unusually low rainfall.

emigrant Person who leaves one region or country to settle in another.

empire Set of nations or territories sharing a single ruler.

established church Religion or denomination supported by the government.

Fall Line Imaginary line connecting a series of rapids and waterfalls where rivers drop from the Piedmont to the Atlantic Coastal Plain. It marks the farthest point that boats traveling upstream from the Atlantic can reach.

famine Severe and widespread shortage of food.

federal System of government in which a union of states allocates some powers to one central authority.

Filipino Person from the Philippines.

fossil fuel Natural fuel formed from the remains of plants and animals over millions of years. Fossil fuels include petroleum, natural gas, and coal.

free trade Trade between countries without taxes or restrictions.

front Forward line of an army, often where the army faces its opponent.

gap Opening through mountains. A pass.

genocide Intentional extermination of a national, ethnic, racial, cultural, political, or religious group.

glacier Large, slow-moving mass of ice formed from a long-lasting accumulation of snow.

global acre The amount of biological productivity found on an average acre of land or water in one year. Used to measure the sustainability of land and water use.

gross domestic product (GDP) The combined value of all final goods and services produced in a country in one year.

guerrilla Member of a military unit who fights in territory occupied by enemy forces. Guerrilla fighters usually use surprise tactics.

Harlem Renaissance Period of African American cultural expression in the 1920s and early 1930s centered in, but not limited to, the New York neighborhood of Harlem.

Holocaust Attempted genocide of Europe's Jewish population by Nazi Germany, resulting in 6 million killed.

homestead Land claimed by a settler.

Ice Age Period of history when ice sheets cover huge regions of the earth's surface. Ice Ages last thousands of years and cause sea level to drop as large amounts of water are trapped on land as ice.

ice sheet Expanse of ice one to three miles thick that covers a large part of the earth.

immigrant Person who enters a new country to settle there permanently.

Indian Term commonly used to refer to Native Americans. Columbus called the native people he encountered "Indians" because he believed he had reached the Indies.

Indies European term for the islands and mainland of Southeast Asia, India, and coastal China. Today "East Indies" mainly refers to the islands of Southeast Asia and "West Indies" to the islands in and near the Caribbean Sea.

indigo Plant from which blue dye can be made.

inflation An extended rise in the price of goods and services.

internment camp Location where large numbers of people are confined for political or military reasons, usually during wartime.

irrigate To supply dry land with water by artificial means, usually for farming.

Jim Crow laws State and local legislation, found mostly in the South, designed to discriminate against and suppress the rights of African Americans. Most Jim Crow laws were overturned or dropped during the 1950s and 1960s.

labor union Organization created to protect the rights and safety of workers in their workplace, and to negotiate employment contracts on their behalf.

literacy test Assessment of a person's ability to read and write.

Manifest Destiny The 19th-century belief that the United States had the right and the duty to expand westward to the Pacific.

migration Mass movement of people from one region to another.

military adviser Person who instructs foreign armed forces on military strategy, tactics, and procedure, and who may participate in battle.

mission Religious facility used as a base for promoting the spread of Christianity.

Mormon Believer in the Bible and the Book of Mormon. Member of the Church of Jesus Christ of Latter Day Saints.

nation Large group of people bound together by shared culture, history, or geography; often but not always the citizens of a country.

national debt Debt owed by the federal government.

naturalized citizen Foreign-born person who becomes a citizen of the United States.

New World Continents west of the Atlantic Ocean; North and South America.

North Atlantic Treaty Organization (NATO) Military alliance established in 1949 to discourage attacks by the Soviet Union and Soviet-occupied Eastern Europe. Early members included Canada, the United States and 10 countries in Europe.

Old World Continents east of the Atlantic Ocean. Europe, Asia, and Africa.

ordnance Combat equipment such as ammunition, weapons, and vehicles.

Panama Canal Zone Strip of land crossing the Isthmus of Panama from which the United States administered and operated the Panama Canal; U.S. territory from 1903 to 1979.

per capita Per person. Calculated by dividing a figure by the population.

piedmont 1. Gently sloping land along the foot of a mountain or mountain range. 2. **Piedmont** Region between the Appalachian Mountains and the Atlantic Coastal Plain

plain Broad area of land that is gently rolling or almost flat.

plateau Elevated plain, usually with at least one steeply dropping or rising side. Some plateaus are heavily eroded.

poll tax Fee that must be paid before a person can vote. Designed to prevent Southern blacks from voting.

population density Number of people per square mile or square kilometer.

quota Limit or maximum number.

racism Political and/or social system of racial discrimination.

rainfall Rain or the equivalent amount of water from snow, sleet, and hail. Annual rainfall is the total for a typical year.

range 1. Connected line of mountains. 2. Open land where cattle, buffalo, or other livestock wander and graze.

ratify To formally approve.

Reconstruction Period from 1865 to 1877 when former Confederate states were readmitted to the Union and subject to federal control following the Civil War.

reform Action intended to solve a country's social problems and improve the conditions of its citizens.

refugee Person who flees a country due to war, political oppression, or religious persecution.

relief Financial or other assistance provided by the government to those in need.

Renaissance 1. Revival of classical art and culture in Europe from 1300 to 1600. 2. A period of intense artistic and cultural creativity.

republic Country whose leader is elected by the citizens or their chosen representatives.

reservation Land set aside by a government, especially land set aside for Native Americans.

revolution Overthrow of a country's government by citizens of that country.

rural Belonging to the countryside, as opposed to towns and cities.

sea ice Ice floating on the sea. Some sea ice forms a permanent cover near the North Pole, while other sea ice is seasonal.

secede To formally leave a union.

segregate To separate from others.

settlement 1. Community or colony especially if newly established. 2. The act of establishing homes in a new place.

sharecropper Person who farms the land of another and pays rent with an agreed share of the harvested crops.

siege Period when an army surrounds a city or other place to force it to surrender.

sit-in Method of protest by demonstrators who seat themselves in a public place and refuse to move.

slave Person who is owned by another and is forced to work without pay.

slavery Condition of being owned as a slave; practice of owning slaves.

state Part of a country with laws and leaders of its own. The United States consists of 50 states.

suburban Relating to the ring of smaller towns that make up the outer part of an urban area.

superpower Influential nation with internationally dominant military power. Usually used to describe the United States and the Soviet Union during the Cold War.

tactics Maneuvers used to achieve a military goal.

territory 1. Part of a country that does not have the full rights of a state or province. 2. Any large region, often with poorly defined boundaries.

terrorist Individual or organized group that uses violence or intimidation against civilians to advance social or political objectives.

textile Cloth, usually knitted or woven.

topsoil Surface layer of earth that includes organic matter necessary to nourish plants.

Tornado Alley Region of the United States in which tornados strike most frequently.

trade Business of selling and buying products.

trade deficit Negative balance of trade occurring when imports exceed exports.

transcontinental Crossing a continent.

treaty Formal agreement between two or more countries, usually dealing with peace or trade.

Underground Railroad Not a true railroad, but an escape route and series of hiding places to help runaway slaves reach the free states or Canada.

undocumented Lacking the legal documents required for living or working in a country.

Union 1. A short name for the United States of America. 2. The Northern and Western states that remained part of the United States during the Civil War. 3. See labor union.

United Nations International organization that includes most countries of the world. Created in 1945 to resolve world problems peacefully.

urban Consisting of towns or cities. The opposite of rural.

viceroyalty Province governed by a viceroy (governor).

Warsaw Pact Military alliance established in 1955 to discourage attacks by NATO; treaty that created the alliance. Original members included the Soviet Union and seven Eastern European countries under its control.

weapons of mass destruction Nuclear, biological, or chemical weapons capable of causing immense destruction to people and property.

State Facts

State	Capital	Largest City	Admitted to Union (order)	U.S. House Members	Population	Rank in Population	% Urban	Area in Sq. Mi. Sq. Km	Rank in Area	Postal Abbrev.
ALABAMA	Montgomery	Birmingham	1819 (22)	7	4,599,030	23	55	51,718 133 950	29	AL
ALASKA	Juneau	Anchorage	1959 (49)	1	670,053	47	66	591,004 1 530 693	1	AK
ARIZONA	Phoenix	Phoenix	1912 (48)	8	6,166,318	16	88	114,007 295 276	6	AZ
ARKANSAS	Little Rock	Little Rock	1836 (25)	4	2,810,872	32	53	53,183 137 742	27	AR
CALIFORNIA	Sacramento	Los Angeles	1850 (31)	53	36,457,549	1	94	158,648 410 896	3	CA
COLORADO	Denver	Denver	1876 (38)	7	4,753,377	22	84	104,100 269 618	8	CO
CONNECTICUT	Hartford	Bridgeport	1788 (5)	5	3,504,809	29	88	5,006 12 966	48	CT
DELAWARE	Dover	Wilmington	1787 (1)	1	853,476	45	80	2,026 5 246	49	DE
FLORIDA	Tallahassee	Jacksonville	1845 (27)	25	18,089,888	4	89	58,681 151 982	22	FL
GEORGIA	Atlanta	Atlanta	1788 (4)	13	9,363,941	9	72	58,930 152 627	21	GA
HAWAII	Honolulu	Honolulu	1959 (50)	2	1,285,498	42	91	6,459 16 729	47	HI
IDAHO	Boise	Boise	1890 (43)	2	1,466,465	39	66	83,574 216 456	13	ID
ILLINOIS	Springfield	Chicago	1818 (21)	19	12,831,970	5	88	56,343 145 928	24	IL
INDIANA	Indianapolis	Indianapolis	1816 (19)	9	6,313,520	15	71	36,185 93 720	38	IN
IOWA	Des Moines	Des Moines	1846 (29)	5	2,982,085	30	61	56,276 145 754	25	IA
KANSAS	Topeka	Wichita	1861 (34)	4	2,764,075	33	71	82,282 213 110	14	KS
KENTUCKY	Frankfort	Louisville	1792 (15)	6	4,206,074	26	56	40,411 104 665	37	KY
LOUISIANA	Baton Rouge	New Orleans	1812 (18)	7	4,287,768	25	73	47,720 123 593	31	LA
MAINE	Augusta	Portland	1820 (23)	2	1,321,574	40	40	33,128 85 801	39	ME
MARYLAND	Annapolis	Baltimore	1788 (7)	8	5,615,727	19	86	10,455 27 077	42	MD
MASSACHUSETTS	Boston	Boston	1788 (6)	10	6,437,193	13	91	8,262 21 398	45	MA
MICHIGAN	Lansing	Detroit	1837 (26)	15	10,095,643	8	75	58,513 151 548	23	MI
MINNESOTA	St. Paul	Minneapolis	1858 (32)	8	5,167,101	21	71	84,397 218 587	12	MN
MISSISSIPPI	Jackson	Jackson	1817 (20)	4	2,910,540	31	49	47,695 123 530	32	MS
MISSOURI	Jefferson City	Kansas City	1821 (24)	9	5,842,713	18	69	69,709 180 546	19	MO

State	Capital	Largest City	Admitted to Union (order)	U.S. House Members	Population	Rank in Population	% Urban	Area in Sq. Mi. Sq. Km	Rank in Area	Postal Abbrev.
MONTANA	Helena	Billings	1889 (41)	1	944,632	44	54	147,047 380 849	4	MT
NEBRASKA	Lincoln	Omaha	1867 (37)	3	1,768,331	38	70	77,359 200 358	15	NE
NEVADA	Carson City	Las Vegas	1864 (36)	3	2,495,529	35	92	110,567 286 367	7	NV
NEW HAMPSHIRE	Concord	Manchester	1788 (9)	2	1,314,895	41	59	9,283 24 044	44	NH
NEW JERSEY	Trenton	Newark	1787 (3)	13	8,724,560	11	94	7,790 20 175	46	NJ
NEW MEXICO	Santa Fe	Albuquerque	1912 (47)	3	1,954,599	36	75	121,599 314 939	5	NM
NEW YORK	Albany	New York City	1788 (11)	29	19,306,183	3	87	49,112 127 200	30	NY
NORTH CAROLINA	Raleigh	Charlotte	1789 (12)	13	8,856,505	10	60	52,672 136 421	28	NC
NORTH DAKOTA	Bismarck	Fargo	1889 (39)	1	635,867	48	56	70,704 183 123	17	ND
OHIO	Columbus	Columbus	1803 (17)	18	11,478,006	7	77	41,328 107 040	35	OH
OKLAHOMA	Oklahoma City	Oklahoma City	1907 (46)	5	3,579,212	28	65	69,903 181 048	18	OK
OREGON	Salem	Portland	1859 (33)	5	3,700,758	27	79	97,052 251 365	10	OR
PENNSYLVANIA	Harrisburg	Philadelphia	1787 (2)	19	12,440,621	6	77	45,310 117 351	33	PA
RHODE ISLAND	Providence	Providence	1790 (13)	2	1,067,610	43	91	1,213 3 142	50	RI
SOUTH CAROLINA	Columbia	Columbia	1788 (8)	6	4,321,249	24	60	31,117 80 593	40	SC
SOUTH DAKOTA	Pierre	Sioux Falls	1889 (40)	1	781,919	46	52	77,122 199 744	16	SD
TENNESSEE	Nashville	Memphis	1796 (16)	9	6,038,803	17	64	42,146 109 158	34	TN
TEXAS	Austin	Houston	1845 (28)	32	23,507,783	2	83	266,874 691 201	2	TX
UTAH	Salt Lake City	Salt Lake City	1896 (45)	3	2,550,063	34	88	84,905 219 902	11	UT
VERMONT	Montpelier	Burlington	1791 (14)	1	623,908	49	38	9,615 24 903	43	VT
VIRGINIA	Richmond	Virginia Beach	1788 (10)	11	7,642,884	12	73	40,598 105 149	36	VA
WASHINGTON	Olympia	Seattle	1889 (42)	9	6,395,798	14	82	68,126 176 446	20	WA
WEST VIRGINIA	Charleston	Charleston	1863 (35)	3	1,818,470	37	46	24,231 62 759	41	WV
WISCONSIN	Madison	Milwaukee	1848 (30)	8	5,556,506	20	68	56,145 145 414	26	WI
WYOMING	Cheyenne	Cheyenne	1890 (44)	1	515,004	50	65	97,818 253 349	9	WY

Index

San Diego, city in California, 36, 46, 87, 97, 112
San Felipe de Austin. *See* Austin
San Fernando, city in California, 97
San Fernando Valley, California, 97
San Francisco, city in California, 36, 42–43, 46, 48–49, 64–65, 71, 75, 90, 97, 106, 111, 112
San Gabriel Mountains, California, 97
San Jacinto, Texas, battle of, 46
San Joaquin River, California, 49, 114
San Jose, city in California, 36, 49, 112
San Juan, capital of Puerto Rico, 20
San Juan Hill, battle in Cuba, 72–73
San Salvador, island in Caribbean Sea, 13
Sand Creek, massacre in Colorado Territory, 66
Santa Ana, city in California, 97
Santa Barbara, city in California, 36, 112
Santa Fe, capital of New Mexico, 18, 20–22, 36, 42, 43, 46, 48, 82, 112, 123
Santa Monica Mountains, California, 97
Saratoga, Revolutionary War battle in New York, 30
Saudi Arabia, country in Middle East, 102, 105, 117
Sauk, Indian nation, 40–41
Savannah, city in Georgia, 24, 27, 30, 44–45, 59–60, 113
Scandinavia, region of Europe, 14, 62
Scots-Irish, European immigrant group, 25, 33, 50, 62
Seattle, city in Washington, 49, 90, 97, 111, 112
Sedalia Trail, cattle trail, 62, 64
Selma, city in Alabama, 99
Seminole, Indian nation, 41
Seneca, Indian nation, 41
Senegal River, western Africa, 16
Seoul, capital of South Korea, 92–93, 116
Serbia, country in Europe, 76–77
Seven Days, Civil War battles in Virginia, 57
Sevier River, Utah, 49, 114
Seward's Folly, name for Alaska Purchase, 69
Sharpsburg. *See* Antietam
Shawnee, Indian nation, 18, 30, 40–41
Sherman, William T., Union general, 59
Shia, religious faith, 105
Shiloh, Civil War battle in Tennessee, 57
Shoshone, Indian nation, 18, 39, 42
Sicily, island region of Italy, 11, 88, 119
Sierra Nevada, mountains in United States, 42, 49, 67–68, 114
Silk Road, past network of trade routes in Asia, 12
Silver City, city in New Mexico, 68, 112
Singapore, World War II battle, 91, 116
Sioux, Indian nation, 18, 39, 41–42
Skagway, city in Alaska, 69
Skeleton Canyon, battle in Arizona, 66
slavery, 16–18, 20, 25–27, 33, 50–53, 54, 58, 60
Snake River, United States, 39, 42, 48, 114
Somalia, country in Africa, 84, 104, 117
Somme, World War I battle in France, 77
Songhai, past empire in Africa, 7, 9
South Africa, country in Africa, 102, 117
South America, 8, 15, 19–20, 27, 37, 119
   immigrants from, 50, 98, 110
South Carolina, U.S. state and British colony, 24–25, 32–33, 52, 61, 113, 123
South China Sea, Pacific Ocean, 72, 100–101, 118
South Dakota, U.S. state, 71, 112–113, 123
South Gate, city in California, 97
South Korea, country in Asia, 92–93, 94, 110, 116
South Pass, Wyoming, 48
South Vietnam, past country in Asia, 100–101
Southern Colonies, colonial region, 24, 26, 30
Soviet Union, past country in Europe and Asia, 85, 88, 91, 92–96. *See also* Russia
Spain, country in Europe, 30, 36, 72, 94, 95, 117
   exploration and colonization, 10–13, 15–16, 20–22, 26, 28–29, 32, 36–38
Spanish-American War, 72–73
Spice Islands, island region of Asia, 13
Springfield, capital of Illinois, 51, 113, 122

Sri Lanka, island country in Indian Ocean, 10, 13, 116
Stalingrad, World War II battle in Soviet Union, 88
Stamp Act, British tax, 29
Stowe, Harriet Beecher, U.S. author, 51
Sudan, country in Africa, 104, 117
Sugar Act, British tax, 29
Sunni, religious faith, 105
Supreme Court, U.S. high court, 52–53, 78, 81, 99
Susquehanna River, Pennsylvania, 44, 115
Sutter's Fort, U.S. settlement in California, 42, 48–49
Sweden, country in Europe, 11, 22–24, 33, 74, 95, 117
Syracuse, city in New York, 106, 113
Syria, country in Middle East, 105, 117

T

Taino, early Native American culture, 17, 26
Tallahassee, capital of Florida, 113, 122
Tampa, city in Florida, 72, 95, 106, 111, 113
Tangier, city in Africa, 9, 11
Tanzania, country in Africa, 104, 117
Taos, Pueblo settlement in New Mexico, 22
Tea Act, British law, 29
Tecumseh, Shawnee leader of Indian confederation, 40
Tehran, capital of Iran, 104, 105, 117
Tennessee, U.S. state and terr., 33–34, 43, 61, 113, 123
Tenochtitlan, Aztec capital, 8, 17
Texas, U.S. state and past republic, 46, 52–55, 112–113, 123
Texas Annexation, territorial acquisition, 47
Thailand, country in Asia, 100–101, 102, 116
13th Amendment, U.S. Constitution, 60
Tikal, Mayan city, 8
Tikrit, city in Iraq, 105
Timbuktu, city in Africa, 9
Tippecanoe, War of 1812 battle in Indiana, 40
Tobruk, World War II battle in Libya, 88
Tokyo, capital of Japan, 85, 91, 116
Toledo, city in Ohio, 44, 113
Tonkin Incident, Gulf of, North Vietnam, 100
Topeka, capital of Kansas, 99, 113, 122
Toronto, city in Canada, 40, 51, 117
Torrance, city in California, 97
Townshend Act, British tax, 29
Trenton, capital of New Jersey, 24, 30, 113, 123
Tubman, Harriet, U.S. abolitionist, 51
Tucson, city in Arizona, 36, 48, 68, 112
Tulsa, city in Oklahoma, 82, 113
Turkey, country in Middle East, 74, 94, 95, 105, 117
21st Amendment, U.S. Constitution, 81

U

Uncle Sam, character symbolizing the United States, 76
Uncle Tom's Cabin, novel by H.B. Stowe, 51
Underground Railroad, 50–51
Union, United States during Civil War, 56–60
Union Pacific Railroad, United States, 62, 64–65
United Arab Emirates, country in Middle East, 105
United Kingdom, country in Europe. *See* Britain
United Nations, organization of countries, 92–93, 105
United States, country in North America, 32–33, 43, 55–56, 71, 73, 96–97, 111, 112–113
Ushant, naval battle near Britain, 31
Utah, U.S. state and terr., 48–49, 52, 55, 71, 96, 112, 123
Ute, Indian nation, 18, 42, 46, 49

V

vaquero, Mexican rancher, 47
Venezuela, country in South America, 117

Venice, past country in Europe, 9, 11–12
Veracruz, city in Mexico, 22, 46
Verdun, World War I battle in France, 77
Vermont, U.S. state and terr., 33, 43, 113, 123
Verrazano, Giovanni da, explorer for France, 14
Vespucci, Amerigo, explorer for Spain, 15
Vicksburg, city in Mississippi, 45, 58, 113
Vietnam, country in Asia, 100–101, 104, 110, 116
Vietnam War, 59, 100–101
Vikings, Scandinavian adventurers, 7, 14
Vinland, region of North America, 14
Virgin Islands, island terr. in Caribbean Sea, 26, 73
Virginia, U.S. state and British colony, 17, 24–25, 32–33, 59, 113, 123
Voting Rights Act (1965), 99

W

wagon trails, 48–49
Wake Island, U.S. terr. in Pacific Ocean, 73, 86
Walker, Joseph R., U.S. explorer, 42
Walla Walla, city in Washington, 49, 112
Wampanoag, Indian nation, 18, 21
War of 1812, 29, 40
War with Mexico, 46, 59
Warsaw, World War II battle site in Poland, 85, 88
Warsaw Pact, Communist alliance, 94–95, 104
Wasatch Range, Utah, 49, 114
Washington, D. C., capital of the United States, 35, 40, 43, 56–60, 75, 96–97, 99, 104–106, 111, 113
Washington, U.S. state and terr., 48–49, 53, 55, 71, 112, 113
Washoe, Indian nation, 42
Webster-Ashburton Treaty, 1842 pact, 47
Wendat, Indian nation, 18, 28
West Covina, city in California, 97
West Germany, past country of Europe, 95
West Indies, island region of North America, 17–18, 20, 26–27, 31, 119
West Virginia, U.S. state, 56, 71, 113, 123
Western Front, World War I battle zone, 77
Westport, Civil War battle in Missouri, 59
Wheeler Field, site of World War II attack, 86
Whitehaven, naval battle near Britain, 31
Wilderness, Civil War battle in Virginia, 59
Wilderness Road, route across Appalachian Mts., 34
Willamette River, Oregon, 49, 114
Williamsburg, British settlement in Virginia, 24
Wilmington, city in Delaware, 24, 113
Wilmington, city in North Carolina, 24, 45, 79, 113
Wilson's Creek, Civil War battle in Missouri, 56
Winchester, Civil War battles in Virginia, 57, 59
Winnebago, Indian nation, 40
Wisconsin, U.S. state and terr., 52, 55, 113, 123
World Trade Organization (WTO), trade organization, 102
World War I, 59, 76–78, 84
World War II, 59, 84–91
Wounded Knee Massacre, South Dakota, 63, 66
Wyandot, Indian nation, 28, 40–41
Wyoming, U.S. state and terr., 71, 112, 123

X–Y–Z

Yalu River, China and North Korea, 93
Yellow Sea, Pacific Ocean, 85, 93, 118
Yellowstone River, United States, 39 ,114
York. *See* Toronto
Yorktown, Revolutionary War battle in Virginia, 30
Ypres, World War I battle in Belgium, 77
Yugoslavia, past country in Europe, 84–85, 88, 95
Yukon River, North America, 69, 114
Yukon Territory, Canada, 68–69
Zuni, early Native American settlement, 17